Ship's Colours: White and Scarlet
Motto: "We fight as one"
Pennant Number: G07

Battle Honours
Bay of Biscay—1943
Arctic—1943-44
English Channel—1944

Unlucky Lady

ATHABASKAN

*Dedicated to the men and women of Canada's armed forces
who made the supreme sacrifice in the Second World War.*

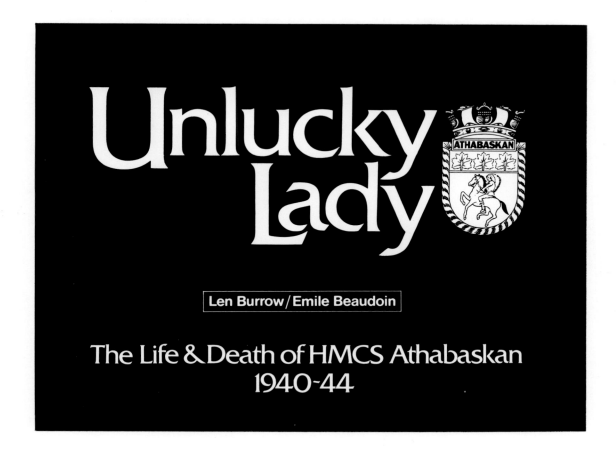

Unlucky Lady

ATHABASKAN

Len Burrow / Emile Beaudoin

The Life & Death of HMCS Athabaskan 1940-44

McClelland and Stewart

THIS BOOK WAS WRITTEN about a ship and the men who served in her. It does not pretend to be a naval historical document nor a novel. It is really a memorial, which at the same time tells a story about Canadians who served at sea some forty years ago.

Athabaskan's story has been recorded here by two men, one of whom served in her as a Leading Telegraphist and the other an ex-member of the RCAF whose brother was lost in the ship. Their sources of information are many and varied—diaries of men who were lost, official Allied and enemy records, and personal interviews with surviving members of *Athabaskan's* company.

The opinions and sometimes criticisms expressed herein are solely those of the authors and may be influenced by the passage of time. In no way can they be attributed to Canadian government official viewpoints or statements.

The authors would have liked to mention and thank all those who assisted them, but the majority wish to remain anonymous. The authors wrote this story—the others "also served".

Canadian Cataloguing in Publication Data

Burrow, Len, 1915-
Unlucky lady - the life and death of HMCS
Athabaskan

Includes index.
ISBN 0-7710-1812-6

1. Athabaskan (Ship). 2. World War, 1939-1945–
Naval operations, Canadian. I. Beaudoin, Emile,
1919- II. Title.

VA400.B87   940.54'5971   C82-090086-9

First Published
Canada's Wings, Inc. 1982

Reprinted 1987 by
The Canadian Publishers
McClelland and Stewart
481 University Avenue
Toronto, Ontario
M5G 2E9

Cover design and graphics by
Edward A. Stewart Limited.

Printed and bound in Hong Kong.

TABLE OF CONTENTS

Vice-Admiral Harry George DeWolf, CBE (1946), DSO (1944), DSC; RCN retired; b. Bedford, NS, 26 June 1903; s. Harry George and Kate A. (Fitzmaurice) D.; e. Roy. Naval Coll. of Can., grad. 1921; Roy. Naval Staff Coll., Greenwich, Eng., grad. 1937; m. Gwendolen Fowle, d. Thomas St. George Gilbert, Bermuda, 5 May 1931; children: Suzette, James; joined RCN, 1918; Commdr. HMCS St. Laurent, *1939-40,* Haida, *1943-44,* Warrior, *1947,* Magnificent, *1948; Rear Adm., Flag Offr. Pacific Coast, 1948-50; Vice Chief of Naval Staff, 1950-52; Chrmn., Candn. Jt. Staff, Wash., DC, 1952-55; promoted Vice-Adm., 1956; Chief of Naval Staff, 1956-60, retired 1961; Offr., Legion of Merit (USA) 1946; Legion of Hon. (France) 1947; King Haakon Cross of Liberation, 1948.*

L. to R.
Huron's Lt. Cdr. H.S. Rayner
Haida's Cdr. H.G. DeWolf
Athabaskan's Lt. Cdr. J.H. Stubbs
early in 1944.

I AM HONOURED TO have been invited to write a foreword to the story of the *Athabaskan*. For a brief period at the end of her career, she was one of my ships. In the organization of the 10th Flotilla, *Haida* and *Athabaskan* formed a sub-division. We worked together and fought together as a team of two. I knew and had a high regard for both her Captains; the first, a close and long-time friend, the second, a much younger friend already distinguished for gallant action in the Battle of the Atlantic.

This is a story of a ship and her crew—a very special ship—the second of the Canadian Tribals, big, powerful, and beautiful. Every man who served in one of these magnificent ships in World War II swells with pride at the memory. There is a story for every ship faithfully recorded in the log, day after day, and in the end, almost invariably, it is buried in the archives and forgotten. *Athabaskan's* story is one that needed to be told. The same need urged her survivors to keep in touch after the war; to muster in reunion after twenty years, and after thirty years to return across the ocean in organized pilgrimage to the graves of their old ship and their old shipmates. To keep the faith with those who died.

The story of all the Tribals is told elsewhere. When the Canadian ships came into service in 1943, only four of an original sixteen British Tribals remained afloat. *Athabaskan's* career, unhappily, was to follow the pattern of so many of her illustrious sisters. In a short life of fifteen months, of which three were spent licking her wounds, she was pounded by the sea and battered by bombs, gunfire, and torpedoes. Her finest hours and her final hours were spent fighting alongside her sisters in the 10th Flotilla. Early in the spring of 1944, four Canadian and two British Tribals and two Polish ships were assembled at Plymouth for the purpose of clearing the English Channel of German destroyers prior to the invasion. At this stage of the war, enemy ships ventured out only at night and it was necessary therefore to intercept them as they moved from port to port under cover of darkness. In night actions, there is always an element of chance. Here, in addition to the normal hazards of navigating in strong tides on a strange and unlighted coast, there were considerations of enemy mine fields and shore batteries. The success of the 10th Flotilla is a matter of history. The price paid was the loss of *Athabaskan* in her second encounter in three days. Before the summer ended, her loss had been avenged again and again.

There is now a third *Athabaskan*, also big and powerful—very sophisticated—but not, in the eyes of one old sailor, nearly so beautiful. The name lives on, and with it, the spirit of GO7, and her gallant crew.

Vice-Admiral H.G. De Wolf
CBE, DSO, DSC, CD, RCN (Retired)
The Old Post Office
Somerset, Bermuda

Chapter One

Birth of a
Tribal Class Destroyer

H.M.C.S. "ATHABASKAN."

LAUNCH

TUESDAY, 18ᵀᴴ NOVEMBER, 1941.

Lady Susan Tweedsmuir
Frederick Hudd
Vice-Admiral Baldwin Wake
Commander Taylor, RCN
Lord Tweedsmuir
Helwood Maxwell
Kay Caldwell
J.B. Caldwell, RCN
H.S. Rayner, RCNVR
W.P. Marshall, RCNVR
J. MacGillivray

ON 18 NOVEMBER 1941 the graceful hull of a fighting ship slid down the ways at Vickers-Armstrong's High Walker yard into the grimy waters of the River Tyne. Less than fifteen months later, on 3 February 1943, this same vessel, now a fully-equipped fighting ship, was commissioned as a warship of the Royal Canadian Navy. She was Canada's second Tribal class destroyer, His Majesty's Canadian Ship GO7 *Athabaskan*. Her career was destined to be a short one, even by wartime standards. On 29 April 1944, her hull shattered by two explosions, *Athabaskan* disappeared beneath the sea off the north-west coast of France. During her fifteen months of active life she had faced the enemy in many forms, from U-boats and robot bombs to destroyers. She was to be the only Canadian warship sunk in the course of a surface action. Above all, she was to weld her ship's company into a team second to none, and together they were to bring such honour to their name that there was to be a second and then a third *Athabaskan* among Canada's fighting ships.

The presence of Canadian destroyers in the force that fought the Royal Navy's last major surface actions in European waters in the spring of 1944 was the product of a very long gestation period. With the exception of an abortive attempt to form a naval reserve in the late 1880s, there was no Canadian naval force for the first forty years of the country's existence. In the early years of the twentieth century, through a growing sense of nationhood and increasing awareness of the German menace, Canada was torn by a controversy as to the best means of naval defence—the establishment of a Canadian navy or financial contributions to the Royal Navy. Not much of either was done. Two ancient cruisers were purchased in 1910 for use as training ships and a naval college was established that same year, but this embryo naval service then languished for lack of support until the start of the First World War. Even during this conflict the Royal Canadian Navy did not rise much above the stature of a local patrol force. Between the two world wars the RCN went through various vicissitudes. It was very much the Cinderella of the three services and, in the early part of the Depression, narrowly avoided being disbanded entirely. Yet during this period it did have one advantage never possessed

before: the Chiefs of Naval Staff had a reasonably clear idea of the type of naval force they were trying to create—a destroyer navy. Unlike the Australians, who opted for a cruiser force to cover their long trade routes, the Canadian senior naval officers believed that a force of modern destroyers, with their high speed and combined gun and torpedo armament, would provide the best value for the limited money available in defending Canada's long and irregular coastline. Between 1930 and 1939 the RCN acquired seven destroyers. These ships, named after Canadian rivers, whether built specifically for Canada or purchased from the Royal Navy, were identical to the British vessels in the "A" to "I" classes which made up the bulk of the RN's destroyer flotillas. In these vessels the officers and men of the pre-war RCN, who were to be the backbone of the enormously expanded wartime navy, learned their trades. Most of their war service might be in minesweepers, corvettes, or frigates, but they never forgot that, originally, they were destroyer men.

It was during the Second World War that the RCN really came of age, expanding from thirteen vessels and less than 3000 regular and reserve personnel to five hundred vessels and nearly 100,000 officers and men. After the fall of France in 1940, almost the entire strength of this growing force was devoted to maintaining the vital sea route to Britain—the Battle of the Atlantic. New escort vessels from Canadian shipyards and destroyers acquired from Britain or the United States were hurriedly manned and thrown into the grim battle against the unrelenting U-boats. In 1943, as a result of pre-war planning, the RCN found it possessed, in addition to its hardbitten escort forces, four powerful fleet destroyers. They were the fighting Tribals *Iroquois*, *Athabaskan*, *Haida*, and *Huron*.

The Tribal class destroyers of the Royal Navy were the high point of British destroyer design in the last years before the war. Between 1929 and 1937 the RN took delivery of a total of seventy-nine destroyers and leaders of the "A" to "I" classes. These basically similar vessels plus some First World War survivors formed most of the RN's pre-war destroyer force. They were sturdy and extremely seaworthy craft of approximately 1350 tons and with a gun armament of four 4.7-inch weapons. Successful and economical as these ships were, the Royal Navy grew increasingly apprehensive during the 1930s because of a tendency in other navies, both potential allies and enemies, to construct destroyers that were considerably larger than the British standard and with a heavier armament. The existence of these superior (at least on paper) rivals was cause for concern, particularly in view of the budgetary restrictions which hampered the RN. In 1934 the RN issued a requirement for the design of a ship that would provide a counterpart to the large foreign destroyers, and sixteen examples of the resulting design were ordered under the 1935 and 1936 building programmes. Most were launched in 1937 and commissioned in 1938.

The new vessels, originally intended to weigh 1850 tons, ended up at approximately 2000. Initial plans had called for a main armament of ten 4.7-inch guns, but the final design featured only eight. The new destroyers were striking in appearance, with a forward-raked bow and rearward-raked funnels and masts. The overall impression was one of power and aggressiveness.

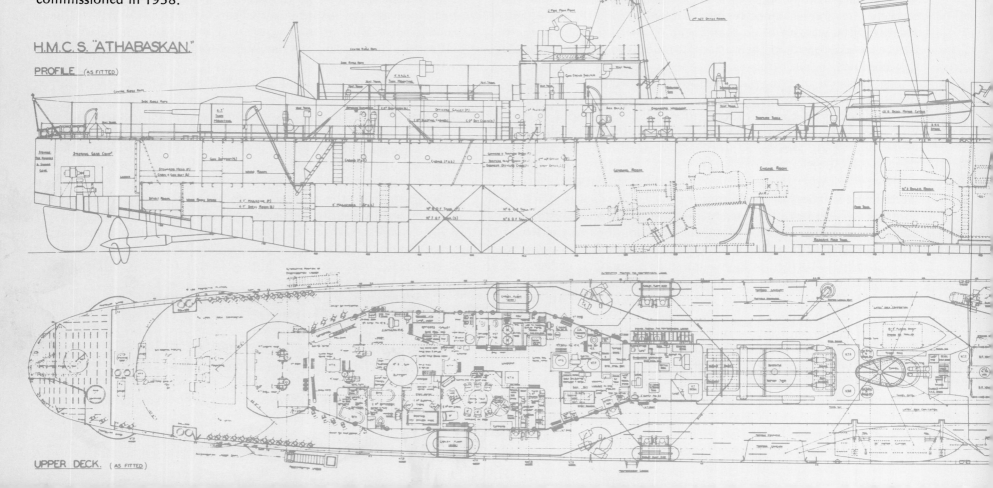

H.M.C.S. "ATHABASKAN."

PROFILE (AS FITTED)

UPPER DECK. (AS FITTED)

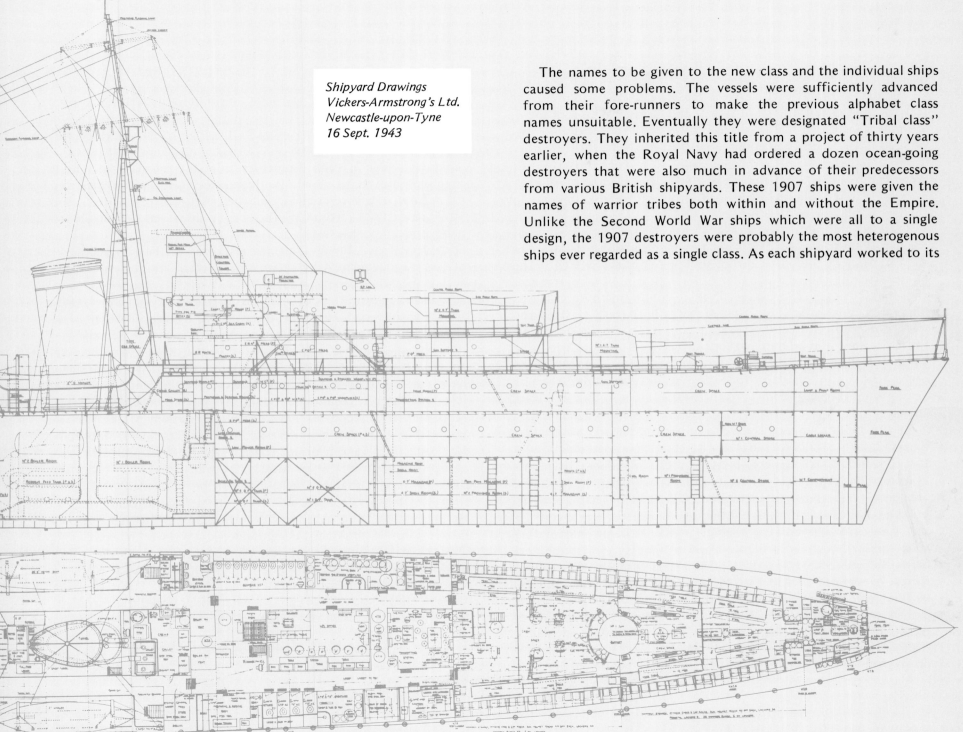

*Shipyard Drawings
Vickers-Armstrong's Ltd.
Newcastle-upon-Tyne
16 Sept. 1943*

The names to be given to the new class and the individual ships caused some problems. The vessels were sufficiently advanced from their fore-runners to make the previous alphabet class names unsuitable. Eventually they were designated "Tribal class" destroyers. They inherited this title from a project of thirty years earlier, when the Royal Navy had ordered a dozen ocean-going destroyers that were also much in advance of their predecessors from various British shipyards. These 1907 ships were given the names of warrior tribes both within and without the Empire. Unlike the Second World War ships which were all to a single design, the 1907 destroyers were probably the most heterogenous ships ever regarded as a single class. As each shipyard worked to its own concept and design, most of the first Tribal class were examples of unbridled individualism. Indeed, one, HMS *Viking,* was the only six-funnelled ship ever to serve in the Royal Navy. Despite their lack of consistency, the stern test of the Great War proved them, without exception, highly successful ships. The sixteen Tribals ordered in 1935 and 1936 adopted most of the names of the earlier Tribal class, with some additions. Two were named after North American races—HMS *Mohawk* and HMS *Eskimo*—the latter rather inappropriately named after probably the least warlike people on the face of the earth.

At the start of the Second World War the Tribals were the elite of the British destroyer flotillas. They retained this status and were in the forefront of the battle throughout the conflict, serving in the North Atlantic, home waters, the North Sea, the Mediterranean, and the Far East. The degree of their commitment to battle is illustrated by the fact that only four of the sixteen survived the war. From the beginning they proved to be excellent fighting ships. Initially, their anti-aircraft armament was woefully inadequate, a common defect in all British warships of the period, but the Tribals underwent a continuous process of modification during the war years which markedly improved their capabilities in this and other areas.

In the months immediately preceding the Second World War Canada and Australia each decided to supplement their destroyer forces by a flotilla of seven Tribals, the most formidable destroyers available. The Australians chose to build their Tribals in Australia, and only three were ever completed. Canada, too, had hoped to build her Tribals at home, but at the start of the war it was realized that Canadian shipyards were simply not capable of constructing such complex, high-performance warships. The necessary technical expertise and advice that had been expected from the United Kingdom was not available with the British shipbuilding industry working at maximum capacity. It was obvious by late 1939 that if Tribals were to join the RCN in the near future they would have to be ordered from Britain. There was considerable difficulty making the necessary arrangements, as British orders were monopolizing the shipyards. Protracted negotiations involving the construction of escort vessels for the Royal Navy in Canada were undertaken, and eventually orders were placed in 1940 for four Canadian Tribals to be constructed in Britain. The remaining three (later increased to four to replace the first *Athabaskan*) were to be built in the Halifax shipyard. Of the first group, *Iroquois* and *Athabaskan* were launched in 1941 and *Haida* and *Huron* slid down the ways in 1942. Construction of the four Canadian-built examples proceeded slowly, with *Micmac, Nootka, Cayuga,* and the second *Athabaskan* being launched in 1943, 1944, 1945, and 1946 respectively. None of these four ships was commissioned before the end of the war.

Each of these ships was named after one of the native peoples of Canada. The name *Athabaskan* is particularly interesting because it does not represent a modern tribe. Once a widespread North American aggregation of peoples, including the Navaho and Apache tribes of the south-western United States and about twenty-five tribal groups distributed throughout north-western Canada, the Athapaskans, as they were originally called, have long since disappeared as an entity. The name now refers to their still-surviving language, a sing-song dialect indicative of an Oriental influence, having a distinct, euphonious sound. Its melodious characteristics are easily understood by the Chipewyan, Beaver, Slave, Yellowknife, Dogrib, Hare, Sekani, Kaska, Kutchin, Tutchone, Mountain, Han, and Bear Lake tribes of Canada's North-West and serve as a recognized means of communication between them.

It is thought that the Athapaskan tribe originated in Siberia, migrating tens of thousands of years ago across the land bridge at Bering Strait. In company with other tribes, the Athapaskans moved into North America and fanned out all over the continent. This huge migration lasted for many centuries, and the tribes gradually settled in the particular regions of their choice. Many of the Athapaskans, being a hardy breed of peoples, chose to make their home in North-West Canada, where they pitted their strength and endurance against the cruel and uncomprising forces of the elements.

This was a heritage of which the men of the Tribal class destroyer GO7 *Athabaskan* were to prove themselves worthy followers.

THE DECISION TO HAVE the first four Canadian Tribal class destroyers built in Britain was both prudent and wise. Canadian shipyards at the time lacked the proper facilities and skilled workmen to produce these complicated ships of war, so it was natural to call upon Britain's expertise. Furthermore, construction of the Tribals abroad enabled Canada to press on with her busy program of building the minesweepers, corvettes, and, eventually, frigates which were desperately needed for escort duties in both the North Atlantic and Canadian coastal waters. *Iroquois* and *Athabaskan*, the first Tribals for the Royal Canadian Navy, were ordered on 5 April 1940.

As the first rivets were driven into the keel-plates of *Iroquois* and *Athabaskan* at Vickers-Armstrong, High Walker Yard, Newcastle-on-Tyne, on 19 September 1940, the international situation was particularly grim. Most of Western Europe lay prostrate beneath the enemy's heel. Hitler and his cohorts were riding high on a wave of popularity at home as victory after victory was added to his laurels. His rising tide of ruthless conquests only whetted his appetite for more. Britain, with her Commonwealth family, was standing alone at this hour, tired but resolute. Invasion seemed imminent, and the rest of the free world believed that it was only a matter of time before the gallant island bastion fell. They were perilous days filled with danger and uncertainty, but shining too with hope and determination through the words of the great leader who had nothing to offer but "blood, sweat, and tears".

While construction of *Iroquois* and *Athabaskan* had begun on the same day, *Iroquois* was destined to be Canada's first Tribal, and scores of Canadian eyes were watching her progress with pride and admiration. The Royal Canadian Navy had a number of River class destroyers and seven of the ancient ex-American four-stackers, but nothing to compare with the size, speed, and offensive power of the Tribals. They were to be the spearhead of Canada's naval thrust, and many young officers and ratings hoped and dreamed that they would have the chance to join one of these ships.

Toward the latter part of the year, the fortunes of war began to change. It was a grim but significant time for Britain and the free world. The Battle of Britain had drawn to a successful conclusion,

To commemorate the country's war effort, a set of postage stamps depicting various aspects of the campaign was produced for issue in 1942. The one dollar denomination showed *Iroquois* at speed—a significant tribute to Canada's first Tribal and her sisters.

won by the indomitable spirit of her people and the heroic "few" of the Royal Air Force. It was her finest hour indeed as the vanquished enemy paused to lick his wounds before releasing the deadly onslaught of night bombing. London became the prime target of this campaign, intended to bring Britain to her knees.

Despite tremendous damage to industry and housing and the great loss of life, the net result was to strengthen the desire to resist and the will to win of British civilians and services alike. The blitz soon spread to other major cities and industrial areas, which lay well-nigh helpless beneath the incessant rain of bombs.

Construction continued steadily on the twin Tribal ships throughout the dark winter of 1940/41, but so did the night bombing of Britain's cities and towns. Thousands of killed, maimed, and homeless citizens were the victims of Hitler's anger. Some targets might have been called legitimate, but many were not—and during a raid which must be admitted to fall into the former category, a strange stroke of fortune interchanged the destinies of Canada's first two Tribals.

In April 1941 the *Luftwaffe* started to bomb the east coast towns of Britain. It was on one of these raids that *Iroquois* was hit, and a hurried inspection soon revealed that the damage was severe. Her steel stringers and plates had been buckled and distorted by the enemy's bombs. New construction would be delayed by several months and the contemplated launching date postponed indefinitely. What could be done? Canada's first Tribal had been stricken, long before her hull plates had felt the caress of salt water. It was a sickening blow and a bitter disappointment to all who had been looking forward to the excitement of launching.

Athabaskan *slides down the ways.*

Beside her, *Athabaskan* had progressed by leaps and bounds. Canada's second Tribal was unscathed, and her form was quickly taking shape. At the yard's regular rate of construction, she would be riding in the river long before her twin sister. At a conference of naval and ship builder's representatives, it was decided that *Athabaskan* should be renamed *Iroquois* and the bomb-damaged *Iroquois* would become *Athabaskan.* It was a natural decision, and would allow *Iroquois* to be launched according to the scheduled date. Thus, *Athabaskan* first felt the slings and arrows of outrageous fortune long before she was ready to do battle with the foe. Nevertheless, the twisted plates were repaired or replaced, construction progressed at a steady rate, and eventually the great day arrived.

The launching of a ship is always a memorable and exciting affair, and so it was with *Athabaskan.* Despite wartime secrecy and restrictions, the news about her launching travelled quickly up and down Tyneside. At the appointed time a jubilant and high-spirited group of maties, sailors, authorities, and guests had assembled to witness the ceremony.

There was a cloudy, overcast sky and a light, chill breeze blowing on 18 November 1941. A special stand for the dignitaries had been erected facing *Athabaskan,* her forepeak rising high above the crowd. As everyone waited, the voices of the "Geordie" workmen could be heard in jovial banter:

'Aye, she's a rum one.'

'I'll be working on't boilers soon.'

'I say, Fred, did you ever find a wrench in't Number 2 oil tank?'

'Well blimey, look 'ose up there. It's old Nobby the blacksmith. 'Ow'd he manage it?'

Then a hush came over the crowd as a tall, regal-looking woman approached the stand, assisted by an officer in military uniform. They were followed by naval officers and officials from the Admiralty, the RCN, and the builder. As they took their places, a swell of hand-clapping provided a welcome greeting from the spectators.

The ceremony was brief and simple—no bands nor bunting to brighten the scene. It was wartime, and Hitler's star was still in the ascendant. By this time his armies had driven deep into Russia and

Lady Tweedsmuir with her son and Vickers-Armstrong representatives on the launching platform, 18 November 1941.

were just beginning to feel the first raw winds of winter.

After the usual speeches, Lady Tweedsmuir, the widow of Canada's first wartime Governor-General, stepped forward, the bottle of champagne burst on the ship's stem, drenching her bow, and the sponsor's voice rang out firm and clear: 'I christen thee *Athabaskan.*' Her son, the second Lord Tweedsmuir, on special leave from the Canadian Army, beamed with pride as he watched his mother perform the important ritual. Almost immediately *Athabaskan* was sliding down the ways, to become water-borne for the first time in her life. The onlookers cheered and waved as Canada's second Tribal floated out into the River Tyne to be taken in tow by waiting, impatient tugs.

The ceremony was over. The dignitaries left for an official luncheon and the crowd dispersed. *Athabaskan* was taken to the fitting-out basin where engines, reduction gear, boilers, internal fittings, and equipment were to be installed.

Vice-Admiral Percy W. Nelles, RCN, Canada's Chief of Naval Staff, said in the official announcement of *Athabaskan's* launching:

> The addition of this ship marks another step in the growth of Canada's navy as a formidable fighting force. These most up-to-date, efficient combat units will bring welcome strength to our naval arm in the work it has undertaken. Sponsorship of H.M.C.S. *Athabaskan* by Lady Tweedsmuir was a most happy circumstance, for the regard in which she is held by Canadians, and the tremendous interest she holds in all things Canadian, make connection with our new destroyer more than a merely formal one. The Naval Service is most gratified that Lady Tweedsmuir, whose husband was formerly our Commander-in-Chief, was able to act as sponsor.

The need for destroyers was urgent, and there were never enough of them. These sleek greyhounds of the sea were required for escort, screening, and patrol duties, attacks on enemy shipping, and other tasks including destruction of the dreaded U-boats. It was a familiar cry. Nelson had needed frigates badly in the pursuit and search that led to Trafalgar. Chasing Villeneuve across countless miles of the Atlantic, he complained bitterly, 'When I die you will find this want of frigates graven upon my heart.' And in the approaching Pacific war, the United States Navy would find itself handicapped severely by its lack of destroyers.

These complicated modern warships could not simply be churned out like sausages. *Athabaskan* was to remain in the fitting-out basin for more than a year. As well as the normal installations, there were numerous additions and modifications to be made in the light of the wartime experiences of her British sister ships.

The British Tribals had revealed weaknesses in construction and armament in the course of their Herculean tasks during the first two years of war. These deficiencies, which had to be remedied piecemeal in the British ships when the opportunity presented itself, were rectified in the Canadian vessels during their construction. They were therefore known as the Improved Canadian Tribals.

Work on *Athabaskan* continued without interruption throughout 1942. It was a year of relentless pressure on the Allies, who were gradually gaining strength despite the enemy's onslaught. Hitler's armies had reached the limit of their eastern advance into Russia and were just beginning to feel the sharp sting of defeat on all fronts. The Japanese tide of conquest was at its height. The Aleutian Islands had been occupied and the enemy was approaching the continent of Australia. But United States' offensive power was gaining strength, and the long island-hopping campaign to victory had commenced with the savage struggle for Guadalcanal. In North Africa, Rommel and his army had advanced to within seventy miles of Alexandria. They were destined to go no further, as later that year, following the second battle of El Alamein, the Axis armies began a retreat that was to end only when the last of their forces in North Africa ultimately laid down their arms. 1942 was a year of decision for the free world, and the close of it saw *Athabaskan* reaching completion.

The second of the Canadian Tribals had taken her shape as a warship while she lay in the fitting-out basin. Her funnels, masts, and guns were in place to form a familiar profile. Below decks, boilers, propulsion gear, and a host of other machinery and equipment had been installed. Many workmen were moving about the ship, testing, checking, and making final adjustments to a maze of piping, wiring, and machinery—all necessary for the efficient functioning and handling of a modern, complicated ship of war. And scattered throughout *Athabaskan* were a few

Canadian sailors who formed the skeleton advance party. Their job was to get acquainted with the ship and make all necessary preparations for the arrival of their shipmates who were gathering at HMCS *Niobe*, the RCN Shore Establishment at Greenock, Scotland.

The commissioning ceremony itself on 3 February 1943 was brief but impressive. The officers and ratings who had been "standing by" the ship during her completion had fallen in on the high-angle gun platform. The silence that had so far accompanied the ceremony was broken by the First Lieutenant's order: 'Ship's company, 'shun.' This signalled the arrival of the Bishop of Newcastle, who was to dedicate the ship and commend her, with all who were to serve in her, to the care and keeping of God. The Bishop, wearing order and medal ribbons which indicated his services with the armed forces in the First World War, was received by Commander George R. Miles, OBE, RCN, *Athabaskan's* first Commanding Officer, on the quarter-deck.

The First Lieutenant's next command—'Ship's company, off caps'—was the cue for the Bishop to step forward and commence the service. He led the gathering in several short prayers—prayers for protection in storms and in dangers, for safe departures and returns. Perhaps one like this, taken from *The Book of Common Prayer* was said:

> O God, our heavenly Father, who art present in thy power in every place: Preserve, we beseech thee, all who travel by sea or land or air; *especially those who sail in this ship;* surround them with thy loving care; protect them from every danger; and bring them in safety to their journey's end; through Jesus Christ our Lord. *Amen.*

There was the Lord's Prayer, in which they all joined, and then the simple dedication. At the end of the service the officers and ratings, at the First Lieutenant's order, replaced their caps and turned so that they looked aft, facing the ensign staff, on which the White Ensign of the Senior Service was to be hoisted for the first time.

The shrill notes of the boatswain's call heralded the hoisting of the ensign. It was a proud moment for the ship's company when they came to the salute. On the dockside, a number of officials and maties, who had done their part in the building of the ship stiffened to attention. The Commissioning Pennant and White Ensign whipped in the breeze at the staff's head, as a lonely seagull hovered over it with noisy unconcern. The boatswain's call shrilled once more, this time signalling 'Carry on'. The ship was commissioned—HMCS *Athabaskan* of the Royal Canadian Navy.

One small ceremony yet remained before the ship, Captain, and ship's company could be regarded as a complete fighting team. According to long-standing naval tradition the Captain had to give his new company a commissioning speech. The officers and men were mustered in the waist of the ship, and Commander Miles delivered a short but significant challenge:

> We have a brand new ship with a brand new name. The ship and the name are what we make them. I'm a believer in the old sailing ship motto, "One hand for the ship and one for yourself." But lads, remember—the hand for the ship comes first.
>
> We have a job to do. We have, I'm sure, no illusions about it. Let us all, then, work together to do that job.

A few minutes later *Athabaskan* received her first visitor. A ginger-coloured cat, sleek and smart, stalked up the gangway. It was immediately adopted by the ship's company as mascot.

Almost before the commissioning party had left, the work of getting the destroyer ready for the sea was under way. There are no minutes wasted in preparing a fighting ship for her duties of seeking out and engaging the enemy. The commissioning of *Athabaskan* was but a prelude to this preparation. Ammunition, fuel, stores, and victuals were taken aboard as fresh young seamen continued to arrive from *Niobe*. Personal baggage was hoisted aboard and hammocks were stowed below decks in the various messes. When the remainder of the men arrived they found everything in readiness. At long last *Athabaskan* had become a live ship, and "home" to more than 250 young, eager, and energetic Canadian sailors, as well as a few older hands.

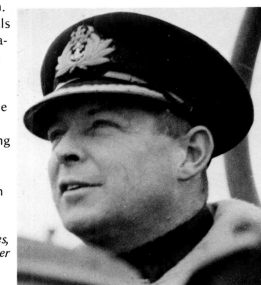

Commander George R. Miles,
Athabaskan's *first Commanding Officer*

Chapter Two

A Fine Company of Men

*The Clock Tower at Halifax,
a familiar landmark to Canadian seamen,
both in war and peace, since 1803.*

ATHABASKAN WAS THE LATEST word in destroyer design and workmanship, representing an investment by Canada of two million dollars. As such, she was going to require tender, loving care by an expert ship's company to keep her in fighting trim. She would need to be shown the utmost respect if her seaworthiness and offensive capability were to be maintained at all times. To meet these demands, *Athabaskan* needed a wartime complement of ten seaman specialist officers, one of whom was the captain, two engineer officers, one paymaster officer, one medical officer, one gunnery officer, 110 seaman, thirty stokers, fifteen engineer artificers and mechanics, nine telegraphists, nine signalmen, three coders, four cooks, four stewards, and more than fifty other men from several specialist branches. In each category there was a proportion of senior ratings of the leading, chief, and petty officer rates. They were all to be packed into every conceivable space available, living and working as a tightly-knit group.

Athabaskan's company did not arrive in one large draft. Some men were early birds who had seen their ship grow from the keel-

laying operation. They had watched as she slowly but steadily took shape, and were proud and elated when the completion date was finally reached. It had been a long, slow, monotonous wait, and they had sometimes wondered if she would be finished before the war ended.

When the full complement was reached, it was a mixed bag of Canadians, all young, healthy, and eager to show their stuff. This motley conglomeration of novice sailors hooted and hollered as they hurried to get aboard. Some of them were seasoned tars who knew the ropes, but the majority had never set foot on the steel deck of a destroyer. It was a totally new experience for them; the beginning of exciting new lives as members of the Tribal family. They were certainly proud to be called Athabaskans.

The ship's company came from every province in Canada. As each new draft arrived, a certain cry became familiar: 'Anyone here from the West?' And in salty sailors' language, a voice would answer and tell them how they could dispose of the West. A similar query would be raised about the East, and again a strong voice would yell out what they could do with the East. They argued the

The newly commissioned HMCS Athabaskan

merits of Eastern and Western Canada in a good-natured spirit of rivalry, and the air buzzed with typical seaman's banter, as friend recognized friend and home towns became the topic of the hour.

It did not take long for the Athabaskans to settle down to the tasks at hand. From bow to stern and bridge down, the men quickly busied themselves getting acquainted and familiarizing themselves with an expensive shipload of equipment and gear. Those who had never lived on a ship before had to learn a whole new vocabulary. Underfoot was the "deck", not the floor, and overhead was not the ceiling, but the "deck-head". The seaman did not speak of the morning, afternoon, evening, and night, but of the morning, forenoon, afternoon, dog, first, and middle watches.

Leading Telegraphist Herbert Attwood was a member of the first draft of fifteen men which came aboard the ship in January 1943:

> Our group lived on board helping to set up wireless equipment. We worked regular watches, four hours on and four hours off till four o'clock in the afternoon. Then the dog-watch would commence from four to six, and six to eight, after which regular watches resumed. It was a busy time, but I found it very enjoyable. Two watches could go ashore while one stayed on duty. There was no liberty boat because the ship was tied up to the dock and we just walked down the gangplank. The people of Newcastle and the Tyneside were very friendly.

The ranks among the Athabaskans included a commander, lieutenant-commander, surgeon-lieutenant, lieutenants, sub-lieutenants, warrant engineer, chief petty officers, petty officers, chief yeoman of signals, leading seamen, able bodied seamen, and ordinary seamen. Each rank carried its own special degree of responsibility for the dispensing of proper naval order, both in the care and maintenance of the ship and discipline amongst the ship's company. Normal progression was based on the Royal Canadian Navy's system of advancement and all Athabaskans were assured of promotion, if they worked for it.

During her fitting-out period *Athabaskan* was crammed with a vast quantity of equipment to be installed, much of it still in boxes, packing-cases, and crates. The builder's workmen were also busy all over the ship, so it was inevitable that living space was at a premium. Consequently, groups of Athabaskans were billeted in private homes where they ate and slept, travelling back and forth to their ship for daily duties. 'It was a nine to five job while it lasted,' recalled Stoker Harry Handy. 'Mr. and Mrs. J. Hunter of Newcastle treated us like members of their own family and we thoroughly enjoyed our stay.' Stoker Handy was one of the seasoned Canadian sailors who had come to grips with the sea. He had been a stoker serving on the British Tribal HMS *Somali* when she was torpedoed south of Iceland 20 September 1942:

> It was a Sunday evening, and the torpedo went clean through the engine-room. Naturally, we began to take on a lot of water and the situation looked serious. Somali was taken in tow by H.M.S. Ashanti and only a skeleton crew was left aboard our ship. The first night I stayed on a U.S.N. trawler where I had my initial taste of corned beef fried in batter. The next night I was transferred to H.M.S. Eskimo and stayed with her till we arrived in port. Sometime during the fifth night, Somali suddenly buckled and sank, taking with her most of the skeleton crew, including one Canadian Leading Stoker.

As sailors and the dockyard maties, also known as Geordies, rubbed shoulders and bumped elbows in the confines of the ship, it was natural for a spirit of fellowship to develop between them. The Tynesiders came to like the Canadians and constantly plied them with good-natured questions, usually about relatives in Canada:

'Aye, I've got a brother in Manitoba. Would yer know 'im?'

'My sister married a Canadian after First War and went out to Vancouver. Could yer look 'em up sometime?'

'Aye, I was thinkin' of going to Canader in '39 but the blinkin' war came along and spoiled the lot.'

On and on rolled the conversation, and the Athabaskans gradually came to understand the maties' accents and queries. Food parcels, ration cards, cigarettes, and other such valuable items were shared with the workmen, who by this stage of the war were finding life on the home front a rather drab affair. The hospitality of many of their homes was extended to the Canadians in return, and lasting friendships developed during this period of *Athabaskan's* construction.

There was a dry canteen aboard *Athabaskan* which was open three times a day for the sale of basic luxuries. It was a popular place where items such as cigarettes, chocolate bars, peanuts, soft drinks, postage stamps, stationery, and sewing materials were sold at rock-bottom prices. The canteen was open during the morning, afternoon, and evening so that all Athabaskans had an opportunity to satisfy their needs. From there, they usually drifted back to their respective mess decks to relax in a variety of ways, depending on the ship's state of readiness. Some played cards, wrote letters, slept, or pursued personal hobbies, while others sat in groups to talk over everything from home and family to the duties that lay ahead.

Beer and liquor were not available at the canteen, but each day between 1100 and 1200 the men received their daily issue of rum. This long-standing naval tradition was normally dispensed in the Supply Assistant's office by a Chief Gunner's Mate with the Officer-of-the-Day in attendance. With a hand dipper, the Chief Gunner's Mate would carefully dole out each man's tot into a measure and then pour it into his cup. The ratings drank the liquor immediately. A few more senior hands, despite orders to the contrary, carefully stored their ration in a bottle for future use. Sailors under the age of twenty-one were not allowed to share in this naval ritual, but, in lieu of it, a daily sum of six cents was credited to their pay records.

Altogether, 546 men climbed *Athabaskan's* gangplank to tread her decks and come under her protective guardianship for a time. Some of the company were there from the early days of construction, watching every rivet driven into place, and stayed with her to the bitter end. Others came along at commissioning and likewise remained for the finale. Drafts of seamen and officers arrived or departed at various intervals, each one of them making his contribution to *Athabaskan's* story. Some men came aboard just a few days before her final patrol, and the new supply officer is known to have arrived just a scant couple of hours prior to her last departure. He hadn't even had time to stow his gear properly before the final action.

With such a great number of men it would be impossible to describe each individual, but the following personal vignettes may help to illustrate the varied backgrounds of the Athabaskans.

The position of Commanding Officer of Canada's second Tribal was an appointment highly coveted by every RCN officer. *Athabaskan's* first Captain, Commander G.R. Miles, was one of the most experienced Canadian naval officers on shipboard, with an impressive pre-war background both ashore and afloat and a distinguished wartime record.

George Ralph Miles was born on 26 February 1902 in Saint John, New Brunswick, where he spent his early years and received his elementary education. He entered Rothesay Collegiate Institute at the age of nine as a boarder, and quickly accumulated many scholastic credits. It was probably here that he became interested in his favourite hobbies, shooting and fishing. In 1916, at the age of fourteen, he passed into the Naval College at Halifax. The aspiring young Midshipman had scarcely commenced his career when he was injured by flying glass during the Halifax explosion of December 1917. The Naval College was wrecked, so young Miles and his colleagues were transferred to the Royal Military College in Kingston to continue their studies. Following graduation, Midshipman Miles was transferred to England, where he was attached to the Royal Navy. This was a common practice in the RCN between the two world wars, designed to give its officers a greater variety of experience than they would find in the small Canadian service. In the spring of 1919, Miles went to sea in the battleship HMS *Malaya*.

Promoted to Sub-Lieutenant in 1921, he took technical courses in England and was sent to sea again in the sloop HMS *Clematis*. In 1922 he became a Lieutenant, and in 1924 returned to Canada where he held shore appointments at Halifax for the next two years.

Lieutenant Miles returned to the Royal Navy again in 1926, this time serving in the battlecruiser HMS *Repulse* under the famous "Evans of the *Broke*".* In 1928 the Canadian government added two destroyers to the RCN, *Champlain* and *Vancouver*, and Lieutenant Miles then came back to Canada as First Lieutenant of the former vessel. He served in *Champlain* until 1930, when he was once again sent to England for a tour of duty aboard the battleship HMS *Royal Oak*.

*Daring Captain of HM destroyer *Broke* who distinguished himself in service with the Dover Patrol during the First World War.

Commander Miles on Athabaskan's *bridge. Lieutenant F.B. Caldwell is using the telecom.*

Miles returned to Halifax in 1932 as a reserve training officer, and in 1934 was appointed Assistant Director of Naval Reserves at RCN Headquarters in Ottawa. After two years of desk duty, he was named First Lieutenant of the destroyer HMCS *Saguenay*. His service with this ship was interrupted by a shore appointment at Halifax for the first six months of 1939, but in July he returned to *Saguenay*—this time as Commanding Officer.

Saguenay formed part of the escort for the first convoy HX-1 to sail from Halifax to Britain, shortly after the Second World War broke out. It was the beginning of her wartime service and a fresh challenge to her Captain, who was promoted to the rank of Commander the following January.

During the evening of 1 December 1940, while escorting a convoy to Britain, *Saguenay* was torpedoed by the Italian submarine *Argo*. The Canadian destroyer's bow was wrecked and fire broke out in her forward lower mess deck, but she remained afloat. For a nerve-wracking length of time the fire appeared to be getting out of control, and Commander Miles was forced to leave the bridge to take up a position at the after steering post on the searchlight platform. It was daylight before the flames were finally quenched and the forward watertight bulkhead shored up and strengthened. Most of the ship's company were then transferred to a British rescue vessel. They wanted to stay with *Saguenay*, but the Captain ordered them away with the parting remark: 'We may stop another of those things, and every extra man means another bunch of flowers, and you know how expensive they are!'

With his brave and resourceful skeleton crew, Commander Miles set his course for the nearest British port. For four anxious days the crippled *Saguenay* struggled painfully across the North Atlantic, finally reaching the Isle of Man under her own power. A naval board of inquiry later found that the incident represented 'a considerable feat of seamanship and endurance and is one that reflects great credit on her Captain, officers, and ship's company.' Commander Miles was decorated with the Order of the British Empire for his conduct during this epic voyage.* Miles' pride in receiving the award was marred by the sad loss of twenty-one ratings in the action.

*Captain Crepas, .commander of the Italian submarine *Argo*, was decorated with an important German naval award, the Oak Leaves, for "sinking" HMCS *Saguenay*!

Commander Miles left *Saguenay* in the spring of 1941 and occupied several shore appointments for the next two years. One of these, which he held for most of 1941, was that of Captain (Destroyers, or D) Halifax, in which capacity he was in charge of escort vessels leaving the Atlantic port. But desk duty was not his cup of tea, and he was appointed Commanding Officer designate for the *Athabaskan*.

Athabaskan's officers were a well-chosen group of men. Earning increasing respect amongst them was Lieutenant J.A. "Dunn" Lantier of Montreal. A graduate of the Royal Military College, Lantier served as *aide-de-camp* to two of Canada's popular Governors-General, Lord Tweedsmuir and the Earl of Athlone, when he first joined the RCN. It is interesting to note that Lantier first served as a midshipman under Commander Miles in *Saguenay* in 1936. He later was given sea duties, and was aboard the Canadian destroyer *Ottawa* in September 1942 when she was torpedoed in the North Atlantic while escorting a westbound convoy. Although Lieutenant Lantier was fortunate enough to be rescued, five officers and 109 ratings perished. The young Montrealer's career with *Athabaskan* would prove colourful and exciting. He was to stay with her from commissioning to her grievous end, experiencing the ravages of prison camp and the ignominious rituals of interrogation and solitary confinement.*

*When one of the other Canadian Tribals, HMCS *Haida*, was recommissioned on 15 March 1952, Commander Lantier became her skipper and remained on her till 28 October 1953. In Korea, Lantier became a successful train hunter, enabling *Haida* to qualify for membership in the Trainbuster's Club.

Two of *Athabaskan's* officers were brothers, who had watched their ship grow and develop from the initial keel-laying stage. They were Lieutenant F. Caldwell, RCN, Executive Officer, and Lieutenant (E) J.B. Caldwell, RCN, Engineer Officer, both born and raised in Amherst, Nova Scotia. They had served as shipmates under Commander G.R. Miles once before, aboard *Saguenay*. F. Caldwell had also done tours of duty with HMC destroyers *St. Laurent* and *Ottawa*. True to service tradition, the brothers addressed each other respectively as "Number One" and "Chief" while aboard ship, such designations always being applied to the First Lieutenant and Chief Engineer.

When Lieutenant Robin Hayward joined *Athabaskan* just before commissioning at Newcastle, he was twenty-two, single, and keenly looking forward to his assignment as her Navigating Officer. Born in Duncan, British Columbia, of English parents, young Hayward entered the training ship *Conway* as a Merchant Navy cadet-in-training after his formal education. In 1939 he was one of twelve *Conway* cadets selected to attend the Royal Naval College in Dartmouth, England. After several months at Dartmouth, Midshipman Hayward joined the battleship HMS *Nelson*. One year later he was drafted to the destroyer HMS *Kipling*, one of the ships in Lord Louis Mountbatten's famous Fifth Destroyer Flotilla. Shortly after this campaign, *Kipling* was involved in the *Bismarck* episode and was within twenty minutes of the final action. Hayward later returned to *Nelson* and was aboard her when she was damaged by torpedoes during convoy escort duty in the Mediterranean Sea. After several months at gunnery and navigation schools, Sub-Lieutenant Hayward returned to Canada for a well-earned leave in the summer of 1942. When he stepped aboard *Athabaskan* for the first time, Hayward was a seasoned young Lieutenant with a fine service record.

Jim Evans, the chief boatswain's mate (Buffer), was one of the most experienced sea-dogs on the lower deck when he joined *Athabaskan* at commissioning. He was thirty-six years of age and had accumulated a fine record of naval service. Jim was born in Halifax, and the pulse of the sea was in his veins from a very early age. His parents came from the Codroy Valley region of Newfound-

Lieutenant F. Caldwell and his brother Lieutenant (E) J.B. Caldwell

Lieutenant Robin B. Hayward Athabaskan's *Navigating Officer*

Chief Petty Officer James E. Evans, the chief boatswain's mate (the Buffer)

Leading Seaman Francis J. "Doc" Savage

land, and were rugged, healthy fisherfolk. It was natural for Jim to follow in his father's footsteps as a fisherman as he grew older. During the days of the United States prohibition he indulged in a little rum-running with his brother-in-law, adding excitement to his life and augmenting his meager income. In 1929 the Buffer joined the RCN in Halifax. He was a young, energetic recruit at the time, as far as the Navy was concerned, but he also had a life-time of experience as a mariner behind him. His total service career was to span twenty-six years, ending in an honorable discharge and several decorations. Evans' record at shore-based establishments and in warships reads like a Who's Who of the RN and RCN. His travels carried him to many corners of the world, including two voyages with *Athabaskan* beyond the Arctic Circle, thus qualifying him to become a member of the Bluenose Club.

Many of *Athabaskan's* more seasoned seamen had first donned uniforms, not through some patriotic impulse, but as a direct response to economic conditions. One such was Frank "Doc" Savage. In 1935 his father, a hard-working railwayman in the city of Edmonton, was worried about the state of the economy and the nation. It was a low period in the country's economic life, often called the "Dirty" or "Hungry Thirties", and Savage was particularly concerned about his eldest lad, Frank.

'Frank,' he said, 'I'm at my wit's end. Here you are, fifteen, and still in grade eight. What's the matter with you? You've been playing hookey and your report card is disgraceful. I just don't know what to do with you. The only thing I can suggest is to join the Royal Navy—they'll make a man out of you. I'll pay your passage to England, and from there you're on your own.'

Young Savage seized the offer and eventually landed in London, heading straight for the nearest Royal Navy recruiting office. In the ensuing years the eager young Canadian cruised all over the world, visiting famous ports in every hemisphere. He served on HM Ships *Revenge, Nelson, Berwick, Orion,* and *Blencathra,* acquiring substantial skill in gunnery and seamanship in the course of his duties. His service also included training at the famous Royal Navy Gunnery School at Whale Island, Portsmouth. By the time Leading Seaman Savage joined *Athabaskan* in the summer of 1943, he was

*The pre-war RCNVR was composed of part-time sailors, but in wartime the name encompassed all but the permanent members of the RCN. Most of them had never been to sea before. They joined for the duration of hostilities only, though some stayed in after the war and made happy careers.

an experienced killick and a valuable addition to her company. He had come a long way from the dull days in Edmonton, and though he may not have been the greatest scholar in the Navy, any shortcomings in this area were far outweighed by his natural abilities to counsel and instill confidence in the men with whom he served.

Another member of *Athabaskan's* company with pre-war experience was Albert Jean Germain Dion, always called Jean by his family and friends. He was born in Quebec City, the second of nine children. His father worked in a shoe factory where wages were low and the hours long. Money was always in short supply, and fulfilling the needs of a large family was a never-ending problem. Jean managed to reach Grade Ten before he was forced to find work to aid his family. The Hungry Thirties were lean years indeed for this typical Quebec brood. Finally, in 1938, Jean joined the Royal Canadian Naval Volunteer Reserve* as an ordinary seaman. In the latter part of 1939 he was transferred to Halifax where he became a bandsman. Shore duty was not his style, so he took a stoker's course to qualify for sea-going duties. He served on a boom defence vessel for about a year and then took a commando course in time to join the invasion force of Sicily and Italy. Young Dion was wounded during this campaign when his landing-craft was hit and sunk. He was taken to *Niobe* and hospitalized till he was fit and able to join *Athabaskan.*

Like thousands of his contemporaries from Quebec who served in Canada's armed forces, Jean was a dedicated serviceman. With his warm, happy disposition, he was always the life of the party, and was both loved and admired by his friends and large family. Jean had a girlfriend, the apple of his eye and they were fortunate enough to enjoy some precious, fleeting hours together during his few periods at home. This gallant young French-Canadian was twenty-four years of age when he sailed with *Athabaskan* on her last voyage.

Leading Stoker Albert J.G. Dion

Raymond Moar was born in Chatham, New Brunswick, the youngest of a family of eighteen—a sizable family even by pre-war standards. By the time young Moar completed Grade Eight he had had enough of schooling and so abandoned further education. Despite the efforts of a concerned priest, the young drop-out said goodbye to school and took a job in a sawmill. Here he received his first taste of hard manual labour, working a ten-hour day at the rate of eight cents per hour. It was a boring, dead-end job, so Moar soon quit and became a trucker, hauling freight from the railway station to stores and other businesses in town. He was now making eighteen dollars a week, and was sitting pretty until the guns of war thundered around the world, impelling him to join the RCNVR. Able Seaman Moar was eventually drafted to *Athabaskan* and stayed with her till the end.

Most Athabaskans were young men who had joined the RCNVR after Canada entered the war. In many cases this meant the abandoning of a promising career. One such was William George Stewart, the oldest boy in a family of one daughter and five sons. During his education in Hamilton, Ontario, he exhibited an encouraging artistic talent. As a member of the YMCA he won a bronze medallion for a charcoal sketch of a bust sculptured by the late Emmanuel Hahn, and later was apprenticed to a leading engraving firm as a retoucher. After moving to Toronto to work for a prominent Canadian engraving house, Stewart joined the RCNVR in 1940. He entered the Signal School at St. Hyacinthe, graduating as top signalman in his class Following several tours of duty he was drafted to *Athabaskan* on commissioning. Stewart's talents as an artist were used to advantage on many occasions during his service. He designed *Athabaskan's* first ship's crest, which eventually received Royal approval.* If this brave young Canadian had survived, there is little doubt that his talents and enterprising spirit would have carried him far in the graphic arts field.

*The ship's badge depicts a Plains Indian astride a pinto pony.

Leonard Mumford was the younger son of the distinguished Reverend Dr. W. J. Mumford of the Methodist and United Churches of Canada. Born in Little Current, Ontario, Leonard was raised to share warmly with his brother and parents in the family life of Christian service. He was educated in Toronto, eventually graduating from Central Technical School. Mechanically minded, he worked in a machine-shop after leaving school, and later in an aircraft plant. When Leonard joined the RCNVR in 1942, he took an Engine-Room Artificer's course and passed with high marks as an ERA, Grade 4. He joined *Athabaskan* early in 1943 and stayed with her throughout her whole career. This promising young engineer would celebrate his twenty-fifth birthday just before *Athabaskan* sailed on her last patrol.

The Navy had not been the first choice of all Athabaskans.

Herman Sulkers grew up in the Winnipeg area. His education came to a halt at Grade Ten, but if he fell somewhat short as a scholar, he made up for it with his athletic prowess. Football, hockey, bicycle riding, swimming, skiing, bowling—name the sport and Herman had a hand in it or fell on his face trying. After leaving school, this

active young man started work with a chain grocery store (which went by the rather unusual name of "Piggly-Wiggly") at the rate of six dollars for a seventy-hour week. After three months he received eight dollars, and when the union organized the employees he moved up to fifteen dollars for a forty-eight hour week. Young Sulkers had arrived. One of his burning ambitions was to fly, and he became a member of the Junior Airmen of America Club so that he could learn the basic requirements of this exciting sport. At the outbreak of the Second World War it was quite natural for Herman to try to join the air force as a pilot, but all that was offered him was a position as air gunner because of his limited formal education. This wasn't good enough, and in unmistakable language Sulkers told the recruiting team just what they could do with their air force—and promptly joined the RCNVR. It was the Navy's gain, because Herman was an active young man who was destined to become an efficient Leading Seaman aboard *Athabaskan*. Little did he realize at the time that his physical fitness and stamina would help him survive the loss of his ship, and the long, frustrating, debilitating months in prison camp.

John Laidler was born in Saskatoon, a prairie metropolis surrounded by massive farms stretching out to the horizon on every side. Unaffected by the land around him, Laidler was always to consider himself a city boy. He received his education locally, graduating from secondary school in the middle of the Great Depression, when there was little money, no work, and barely enough food on the table. They were grim days, and young Laidler, like so many of his contemporaries, had little hope of finding employment. There were days when he would pick an acre of potatoes and receive a bushel of them as his only payment. Fortunately, he became apprenticed to a printer, receiving a salary of fifty cents every week, half of which went to his mother to help meet the family needs. Later, John moved to another printing company and was paid at the unbelievable rate of twenty-five cents per hour. John was certainly on his way. But events in Europe suddenly altered the comfortable course of the young printer. John was a member of the Saskatoon Light Infantry (Machine-Gun) Militia at the outbreak of the Second World War, and he lost no time in going active with his unit. Yet the call of the sea must have been strong, for he applied for remuster to the RCNVR, and was transferred in 1941. After initial induction and service at various shore establishments, John was drafted to *Athabaskan*. He joined her at commissioning, and was twenty-four when he sailed with her on her final patrol.

Athabaskan also took aboard some Royal Navy sailors, who were drafted for boiler cleaning duties, engine and machinery checks, and other routine maintenance tasks. These were essential procedures, and bringing extra men in to do these jobs enabled other divisions to proceed on leave or courses as circumstances arose. At least three RN sailors were aboard at the final journey's end. One of these, Mechanic Norman Rutherford, was a radar technician, the only person with any idea how to keep *Athabaskan's* primitive radar functioning. Unfortunately, he was among the missing.

These few examples illustrate the types of men who were to shake down together to form *Athabaskan's* company. Their bonds of association became firmly cemented as they worked in close proximity with one another on active duty. At close quarters, a man's sincerity shone through, and shirkers were not suffered gladly. Everyone realized that the safety of their ship and her company depended upon each man's sense of responsibility and his obedience to orders. This personal challenge created a strong fellowship of men who would live up to the spirit of their ship's motto: "We Fight as One".

Comradeship was important, and it went a long way toward molding a happy ship, but there was something else which was significant to the Canadians. They were all volunteers, and they felt proud of this. It was an invisible ingredient which closed their ranks even more tightly in the bitter confrontation with the enemy. As volunteers, they had no one to blame but themselves for the problems they encountered, and by the same token, were prepared to meet their fate head-on, with neither doubt nor recrimination.

Regardless of age, rank, or service history, all these men were entitled to be called Athabaskans and Tribals. It was an honour they were proud to acknowledge both aboard ship and on shore.

George (Buck) Parsons
with Chris Palmer shortly before
their marriage, November 21, 1940.

Ruth Moore marries Lieutenant John Stubbs,
Victoria, B.C., February 28, 1940.

The parade square at HMC Dockyard, Halifax, N.S., 1942.

Chapter Three   *First Voyage to the Arctic*

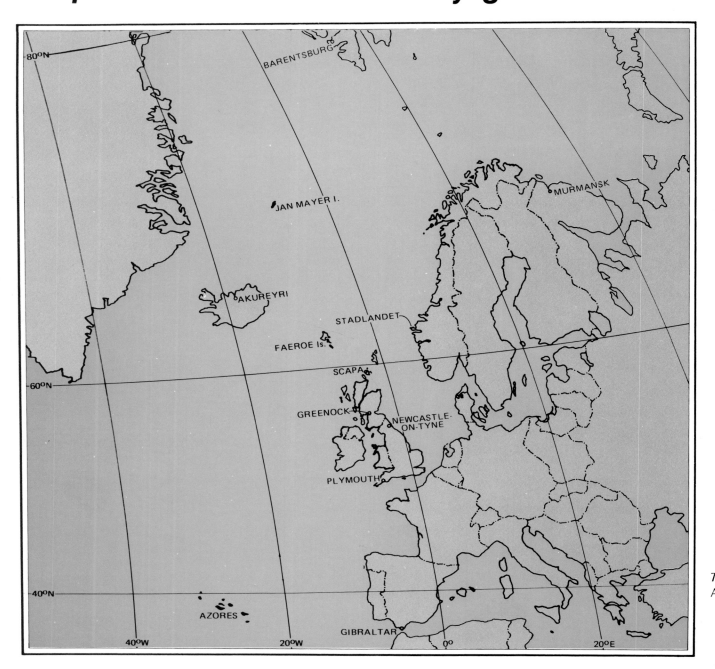

Theatre in which
Athabaskan *was to operate.*

ALTHOUGH *ATHABASKAN* WAS NOW a fully commissioned Tribal class destroyer, two important steps remained to be taken before she could be classed as an effective fighting ship. These were her trials and her working-up period, both extremely important tests of a new warship's efficiency. After *Athabaskan* was commissioned on Wednesday, 3 February 1943, she was given a final inspection and ordered to undergo trials for active service. The first part of the month was devoted to a series of daily checks and examinations which would prepare her for a full-power and acceptance trial by the 15th.

First on the list was fire-fighting drill. The ship's company was mustered for the purpose of getting acquainted with the proper handling and maintenance of *Athabaskan's* fire-fighting equipment. This all-important procedure was high on the list of priorities, because a ship's company that was alert and proficient in fire-fighting could spell the difference between safety and disaster for their ship. Commander Miles recognized this vital fact all the more after his experience with *Saguenay*. He gave *Saguenay's* company full credit for their heroic efforts in making it possible for him to bring her safely to port after damage from enemy action in 1940.

Fire-fighting drill was followed by the next order, 'Ammunition ship'. This back-bending, tiresome job was not greeted with enthusiasm, but it was an essential task which would provide *Athabaskan* with the necessary clout when meeting the enemy. Over 2000 4.7-inch and 4-inch shells were hoisted aboard and stored in *Athabaskan's* magazines, including low-angle, high-angle, and star shells. 14,000 rounds of 2-pounder ammunition and 10,000 rounds of ammunition for the six 20-millimetre Oerlikons were also hoisted aboard and made ready. Forty depth charges were brought aboard to complete the procedure. It took the better part of the day to finish, and loud hails of relief sounded when the last piece of this impressive arsenal was safely stowed away.

The following day *Athabaskan* was moved to the ship-turning basin for machinery trials. Scores of maties and Athabaskans worked throughout the ship, checking and testing equipment. The list seemed endless; there were turbines, reduction gears, pumps, motors, steering gear, gun mountings, and ammunition hoists to be put through their paces. Switchboards, electrical controls and circuits, steam pipes, air and fuel lines, boiler firing equipment, fire-control apparatus, and the torpedo mounting had to be checked. There was auxiliary equipment to be inspected, too, as a back-up for regular installations in the event of damage or destruction. *Athabaskan* was a storehouse of the best equipment that contemporary engineering technology could devise, and she would need every ounce of it.

It was a busy day for maties and sailors alike, and a significant step forward on the way to active service. *Athabaskan* returned to the naval yard and for the next two days went through deperming, a process which decreased the strength of the magnetic field of the ship through special electric wiring as a protection against magnetic mines.

The 9th and 10th of February were taken up with more exciting duties and tests. The quickly developing warship proceeded to the depth charge range and commenced practice. The depth charge throwers and chutes functioned perfectly, giving the less experienced members their first encounter with the sounds and sights of underwater explosions. There were gun trials too, contributing additional noises and cordite smell to the activity. All divisions responded to commands with energy and enthusiasm.

Anchor trials provided an opportunity for the ordinary and able seamen to strain their muscles as they handled lines, cables, and anchors. The busy two days included magnetic compass trials and adjustments, voice-pipe and range-finder vibration tests, and other equipment tests. Altogether, the trials program was a demanding ordeal, and by this time the Athabaskans were becoming impatient.

'When the hell are we going to get moving?'

'The war will be over before we get cracking.'

'We're tired of horsing around.'

'Not another test!'

Despite these natural reactions from a group of red-blooded, healthy, Canadian sailors, eager to do their part in winning the war, a few days still remained before the program was completed.

On 11 February, *Athabaskan* sailed for preliminary full-power trials. For over an hour she responded to a string of orders from the bridge: 'Full speed ahead . . . Stop . . . Full speed astern . . . Stop . . . Full speed ahead . . . Hard a port . . . Hard a starboard . . . Stop.' These and other signals kept the engine-room staff on their toes as the twin Parsons turbines whined and hummed in the hot atmosphere of the engine-room. In the gearing room abaft the twin turbines, the reduction gears purred smoothly as shaft bearings and their housings heated to normal operating temperatures.

Forward, in the three boiler rooms, busy stokers were going about their duties, checking, adjusting, and watching numerous gauges and instruments. The three Admiralty 3-drum, water-tube boilers, working at pressures of 300 pounds per square inch and temperatures of $620^{\circ}F$, throbbed and pulsed as they strained to provide adequate steam to the voracious turbines.

Elsewhere in the ship there were similar scenes of activity. The Chernikeef Log was adjusted, there were final echo-sounding trials and Radio Direction Finding (RDF) tests, and a host of other procedures took place. The cooks, too, worked incessantly, providing food when needed and seeing that plenty of hot tea was always brewing, a blessing for the band of thirsty mariners.

Athabaskan returned to the yard at the end of the day. She had had a good trial and there was a feeling of general satisfaction amongst her company and builder's representatives. She had handled well and had responded quickly to commands, although her speed trial of thirty knots was disappointing in view of her contract speed of thirty-six.

For the next three days Athabaskan lay quietly at the naval dockyard while final examinations of her machinery and equipment were carried out. Defects were inspected, remedied, and double-checked by a dedicated group of naval trouble-shooters. Last minute stores were hoisted aboard and fuel-oil tanks were topped. Canada's second Tribal class destroyer was finally ready for a full-power and acceptance trial.

At 0900 on Monday, 15 February, Athabaskan slipped her lines from the naval dockyard and headed downstream. Watchers on the quay waved in farewell and uttered words of fellowship and affection:

'She's a fine ship.'

'There goes a rum lot.'

'She'll give jolly good 'count o' erself.'

''Ow about a cheer for the Canadians, maties?'

The onlookers, many of them workers who had helped to build Athabaskan from her earliest stages, gazed for the last time on this impressive ship as she quickly gathered way. Down the Tyne she proceeded, past mile after mile of shipyards, eager to feel the waves of the North Sea against her bow plates. Toots, whistles, and signals of recognition could be heard along the shore as she rapidly made headway to her rendezvous.

It was a repetition of her preliminary trial and all went well. Athabaskan had on board thirty-two maties and other members of the trial party who put her through her paces again to everyone's satisfaction. A few adjustments here, some regulating there, and soon she was complete. Commander Miles signed the acceptance papers in his day cabin and Athabaskan became an official unit of the RCN. The long, frustrating months of building and fitting-out had been a trying time for all concerned, but at last she was ready to face the enemy. With a fighter escort provided by the Royal Air Force, Athabaskan made haste for Methil, Scotland, where she disembarked the trial crew. The RCN's new destroyer then continued northward to Scapa Flow, arriving at 0930 on the 16th.

16 February 1943 was a dull and dreary day with a cold wind driving from the north-west. For most of the Athabaskans, it was their first sight of the famous anchorage of Scapa Flow. The bleak, treeless, rolling hills coming down to the water's edge did not impress the young seamen as they made ready for mooring. Occasional snow squalls enveloped the ship as the men went about their tasks, reminding them vividly of similar weather at home. The typical shipboard rumours about Athabaskan's future circulated throughout the mess-decks:

'We're on our way to Russia.'

'I heard it's the Med.'

'Someone said we're going home.'

'How about Liverpool for starters?'

'Anywhere but here.'

These and many other unconfirmed reports buzzed throughout

the ship from time to time, adding tension and excitement to the atmosphere. But at other times the talk centered on the Royal Navy's strategic refuge there in Scapa as older hands recalled tales from the First World War passed on to them over the years. Admiral Jellicoe's Grand Fleet had sheltered in these very waters, later sailing out to meet the enemy at Jutland in 1916. The battleship HMS *Vanguard* had blown up suddenly at Scapa in 1917 with heavy loss of life—magazine temperatures had not been considered important at that time. Scapa had also witnessed the surrender of the German High Seas Fleet and its ignominious end. And moving closer to their own time, the young Athabaskans recalled the daring exploit of *Leutnant* Gunther Prien in U-47; during the early months of the war he penetrated the defences of Kirk Sound, to go on and successfully torpedo HMS *Royal Oak*. From Scapa, the Royal Navy's pride and joy, HMS *Hood*, had sailed on her last voyage to engage the enemy. The eager Athabaskans were also told about the convoys from Scapa Flow to Russia, especially PQ17 and PQ18, both of which went to their doom in 1942.

Against this historical and dramatic background the Canadian seamen began to feel that they were part of a massive force which would not rest till the Nazis were sunk, scuttled, or confined to whatever shelter they could find. They realized that they too would help to make history, as they gazed and marvelled at the vast array of Allied warships moving in and out of the renowned anchorage.

On 17 February *Athabaskan* became engaged in a spirited working-up program arranged by Rear-Admiral (D) Home Fleet for the purpose of bringing ships and those who served in them up to a fine pitch of efficiency. Service as a fleet destroyer required the highest standard of discipline and co-operation by all ranks, and *Athabaskan* continued the training routine till the end of the month. A welcome break interrupted the program on 22 February when she was senior ship screening HMS *Malaya* to Greenock on the Clyde River, later returning to Scapa Flow on the 24th.

Training exercises continued throughout the month of March. Ship and company gradually blended into one fighting entity as they practised and rehearsed the rigorous demands of naval service. During this period *Athabaskan* sustained hull damage when berthing on the oiler *Danmark*. Plates were cracked and rivets sheared, so *Athabaskan* was forced to temporarily break off her training and proceed to Greenock for repairs. Upon their completion, she returned to Scapa Flow and resumed training till the 29th of the month.

On that day *Athabaskan* commenced her first mission. In company with the cruiser HMS *Bermuda*, she was sent to patrol the Faeroe Islands-Iceland passage to intercept enemy blockade runners attempting to reach Germany. These ships, trapped in foreign ports at the start of the war, had become particularly active during the early part of 1943 as the German need for vital raw materials became more desperate. Precautions to prevent these ships from slipping through were increased. *Athabaskan* and *Bermuda* had been ordered to rendezvous with the escort destroyer HMS *Brecon* before commencing the patrol in force, however a violent storm broke on the 30th before *Brecon* could be contacted. The other two ships resumed the patrol against high seas and strong winds which sometimes reached a force of forty knots. *Athabaskan* signalled *Bermuda* to ask if she could reduce speed as the Canadian destroyer was taking a tremendous beating from the high seas. *Bermuda* replied, 'Increase speed to 25 knots.' Because of the increased speed *Athabaskan* was subjected to even more serious damage. Her hull was severely stressed, and bottom plates at the break of the forecastle began to separate. The ship was not in any danger, but crews had to work hard and fast to shift victualling stores and drive in wedges to shore up the separated plates. *Bermuda* lost an officer overboard when he tried to lead a party forward to secure gear on her forecastle. But the two ships were able to remain on station to carry out their duties. The patrol ended on 2 April and the ships returned to Scapa Flow. It was a rugged beginning for the Athabaskans, their first taste of the violent weather for which that part of the world was notorious. No enemy ships had been sighted, but despite the weather and its attendant discomforts, the Royal Navy's operation to stop the blockade runners had been a success. HMS *Glasgow* reported the interception of a blockade runner in northern waters on 30 March, the very day *Athabaskan* was undergoing her ordeal.

After receiving temporary repairs, *Athabaskan* sailed alone for South Shields, Durham, where she underwent hull repairs and strengthening. Stores and ammunition were landed upon arrival and the injured Tribal was placed in drydock, where the necessary work was taken in hand by Middle Docks Engineering Company Limited.

It was a welcome break for the weary seamen. They had experienced a difficult time together and nerves were beginning to wear thin. Seasickness had been a problem, there had been no mail from home, and general shipboard discomforts had been annoying. Except for a skeleton crew, all hands went on seven days leave to relax and recuperate in various spots around Britain.

Cruiser HMS Glasgow, *seen from* Athabaskan *during gale.*

Chapter Four   Flexing Her Muscles

Force "R"

ATHABASKAN'S REFIT WAS COMPLETED on 17 May 1943 and she was ready to put to sea again. Her company, fresh from leave and filled with the excitement of their reunion, were ready and anxious to depart. Re-ammunitioning, storing, and revictualling were put in hand as quickly as possible, and the big destroyer slipped her lines on the 19th and made her way toward Scapa Flow.

She arrived the next day to find a multitude of Allied ships already sheltering in the famous British anchorage. There were ships of all sizes, shapes, and colours. The Athabaskans surveyed the crowded waters, and many exclamations of recognition went up as familiar vessels were sighted:

'Well, I'll be damned; there's good old Ashcan [*Assiniboine*].'

'That's *Bittersweet* over there, I was on her in '41.'

'How about that one over there? It sure looks like Rustyguts [*Restigouche*].'

'Hey, Mac! There's your old friend *Camrose*.'

Athabaskan resumed the work-up that had been interrupted by her storm-tossed patrol for blockade runners and consequent refit, and the following days were busy with activity as all parts of ship bent to the task of getting into shape. On 26 May *Athabaskan* was senior ship of a screen for the battleship HMS *Valiant,* which was exercising a full-calibre shoot, a practice with all *Valiant's* major armament. Three days later *Athabaskan* was officially assigned to the 3rd Destroyer Flotilla, and on 30 May she sailed with the cruiser HMS *Scylla* to take part in a secret operation somewhere in the far North. The Athabaskans suspected something unusual was in the wind, but never dreamed that they were on the way to their first voyage to the Arctic—the land of the midnight sun.

The Norwegian-owned islands of Spitsbergen, located about 400 miles North/North-East of Norway between Greenland and the Barents Sea, were discovered by the Norsemen in 1194 and had been awarded to Norway in 1919. This archipelago near the top of the world was a strategic outpost that could be valuable to either side in the Second World War. Coal mines had been developed there between the wars along with the electric power facilities and other utilities necessary to service a small community. Germany had established a meteorological station on one of the islands early in 1940, but did not attempt to provide a large garrison for its protection.

Later that year, Admiral Philip Vian, famous for his interception of the German prison ship *Altmark* in early 1940, sailed with a force to make a reconnaissance of Spitsbergen. He was to consider it as an alternate advanced base on the route to Murmansk, Russia. Unable to close the coastline due to enemy activity in the area, Vian returned to base. The Admiralty abandoned the idea shortly thereafter as Spitsbergen's fjords were not ice-free in winter and the weather was unpredictable. In keeping with this decision, Admiral Vian led another expedition to the archipelago in August 1941 to make it untenable for enemy occupation. Coal-mining machinery, electric power facilities, and other equipment were destroyed, and about 1000 Norwegian miners were evacuated, as were some Russian and French prisoners-of-war.

Spitsbergen then lay undisturbed until July 1942, when a force of Norwegian troops were landed in an operation known as *Gearbox I. Gearbox II* followed in September to replenish the force with supplies for its winter occupation, and finally in June 1943 *Gearbox III* was planned to relieve the Spitsbergen garrison. *Athabaskan* and *Scylla* were to participate with other ships in this unique operation, which would draw them deep into one of the remotest regions of King Neptune's domain.

Athabaskan, escorting *Scylla,* arrived at Greenock on the Clyde on 31 May to join Force "R", consisting of the British cruisers *Cumberland* and *Bermuda* and the destroyer HMS *Eclipse.* While the larger ships were busy embarking passengers and stores for the secret expedition, rumours about the ultimate destination were rife, and mess decks buzzed with a thousand and one reports. Special precautions had been taken to keep the operation under wraps to prevent leakage of information, but these merely added fuel to the fire of curiosity now infecting all ranks.

'We're off to the Med.'

'I heard it's Iceland.'

'Someone told me we're going to Halifax.'

'This tub won't see Canada; she's just been commissioned.'

'It's Norway for sure.'

These and many other unconfirmed reports continued to circulate throughout the several watches. It was an exciting time and all hands were in high spirits as the buzz continued. There was one individual, however, who was totally unconcerned about the whole affair; Ginger, the ship's cat, lay comfortably sprawled atop one of the lockers in the Chief Petty Officers' mess, purring quietly and enjoying the warmth from a nearby steam pipe.

Force "R", to which had been added the aircraft carrier HMS *Furious* and the British destroyers *Echo* and *Middleton,* sailed from Greenock late on 31 May. While they were on passage the weather was favourable for flying, so aircraft from *Furious* took advantage of the opportunity to fly many training sorties. Enthusiasm for this chance to get in air time was tempered by the rapidly dwindling supply of high-octane gasoline, so the force commander issued an order to all units to 'Close on Iceland'. *Furious, Scylla, Echo, Middleton,* and *Athabaskan* detached and steered for Hvalfjordhur, where the carrier could take on aviation fuel, while the remaining ships veered north to anchor at Akureyri.

On 3 June, *Athabaskan, Eclipse,* and the destroyer HMS *Orwell* weighed anchor and sailed for Akureyri to join Force "R", now awaiting favourable weather. In the comparatively safe haven of Eyjafjordur the ships' companies rested before the next stage of their journey. Sudden storms continually disturbed their peace. Cold winds descending from the mountains to the warmer regions below screamed and shrieked through the fjords. They could agitate calm waters very quickly, causing ships to drag their anchors.

Finally, on 7 June, Force "R" departed Akureyri steering a course North/North-East toward a destination unknown to all but a handful of officers and ratings. The Athabaskans soon realized that the expedition was moving into an Arctic region, particularly when sudden squalls more and more frequently obliterated the view and occasional fog patches added to the difficulties of the Force. The wind blew with searing ferocity, kicking up a rough sea. Able Seaman Andre Audet huddled in the lee of the port bridge sponson and cursed the weather. 'I'll bet they're getting sun-burned back home,' he said. 'What I wouldn't give to be soaking up some of that sunshine.' He might have been pleased to know that the temperature in Eastern Canada was unseasonably cold on that day, and its residents were not much more comfortable than Audet.

Force "R" pressed on, with *Athabaskan* and *Eclipse* labouring to maintain their screening stations on the bows of the leading cruiser. Despite the weather, the passage continued to be uneventful as duty watches strained for sights and sounds of the enemy. Three capital ships with a destroyer screen were sighted heading toward Force "R". After recognition signals were exchanged the battleships proved to be HMS *Duke of York* and US ships *Alabama* and *South Dakota.* At 1930 on the 8th, Jan Mayen Island was sighted on *Athabaskan's* port bow. The snow-covered cone of Beeren Berg, rising 7470 feet above sea level, shone brightly in the evening light, and like a friendly beacon it seemed to say, 'Welcome to the North. My waters are safe and deep. Carry on and good luck.' The lonely sentinel disappeared astern and shortly afterward all hands in *Athabaskan* and *Eclipse* went to action stations to investigate an unproductive asdic contact. Later in the night another contact was made, but this hunt, too, came to nothing.

The expedition pressed on, now well inside the Arctic Circle and still continuing northward. In these high latitudes the sun does not set from the middle of May until the end of July, nor does it rise above the horizon from about 20 November to 24 January. For most of the Athabaskans it was their first journey into this remote region, a journey which automatically qualified them for membership in the Bluenose Club. At last the destination and purpose of the expedition were circulated throughout the mess decks. They were headed for Barentsburg, Spitsbergen to relieve a homesick garrison and replenish dwindling stores. Force "R" had to proceed cautiously, because it was extremely important that the enemy not be alerted of its presence. It was no mean task to avoid detection in the perpetual daylight. Enemy reconnaissance aircraft regularly appeared over Spitsbergen between 0340 and 0840 daily, so it was crucial that Force "R" be at Barentsburg only during the afternoon and evening of 10 June, the projected arrival date. The entire ship's company was warned about the limited time available and all resolved to act accordingly.

Force "R" continued its stealthy approach on a North/North-

East course to its destination. Snow squalls, fog, and high winds persisted in their ferocity against the intrepid task force, and rough, blue-green coloured waves rolled over the ships' bows as they pressed on through the unceasing day.

Suddenly, the rough weather abated and the sun began to shine brightly for the first time in several days—a most welcome sight. Then a cry went up from *Athabaskan's* lookout: 'Land, starboard bow! Land, starboard bow!. Anxious eyes scanned the scene. There, in the distance, was snow-covered Hornsund thrusting 4695 feet above sea level, its summit gleaming in the sun, where Sorkappoya juts out into the sea. In a short while Force "R" was steaming off Isfjorden—the Navy had arrived! It was 1300 on 10 June and *Gearbox III* was proceeding according to plan. *Bermuda* and *Cumberland* closed on Barentsburg and anchored near the jetty; the depth of water was sixty-five fathoms! The disembarkation of

passengers and unloading of stores commenced almost immediately. *Bermuda* lowered her boats for the transfer from *Cumberland* to the jetty, and despite a high wind and rough sea which threatened landing operations, the movement of passengers and stores progressed well.

While this phase of the operation was forging ahead, *Bermuda's* catapult aircraft flew a patrol from nearby Grunfjord. Constant communication was maintained between the aircraft and its mother ship, providing one more safeguard toward the success of the expedition. Fortunately, no enemy ships or aircraft were sighted. *Athabaskan* and *Eclipse* maintained an anti-aircraft and anti-submarine patrol off the entrances to the fjords while the unloading continued at Barentsburg. They, too, could find no trace of the enemy. So far, so good. Morale was high, and thoughts were beginning to turn to the return passage home.

Hornsund from Athabaskan

Cumberland had completed unloading by the last dog-watch, far earlier than the initial estimate of the force commander. This exceptionally rapid work enabled *Cumberland* to leave Barentsburg promptly to join Force "R", which cleared Isfjorden on the 11th at 0115, well before the expected arrival of enemy reconnaissance aircraft. It had been a touch-and-go situation all through the day for everyone concerned, a day filled with excitement and tension.

A total of 116 Norwegian troops had been landed and 101 relieved troops embarked; 180 tons of stores had also been successfully landed. Another minor milestone for *Athabaskan* took place that day as well. For the first time, without previous training, she had **managed to oil from *Cumberland*. This was accomplished by** means of alongside towing and a 180° turn. It was a very primitive method, rarely used, but when necessary, it succeeded admirably.

Athabaskan about to oil from HMS *Cumberland*

Athabaskan *at anchor in Eyjafjordur, Iceland*

The good work of Force "R" was undone three months later when a strong enemy force led by the battleship *Admiral Von Tirpitz*, on the only sortie she was able to make unchallenged, raided Spitsbergen. The Norwegian garrison fought bravely against overwhelming odds and suffered heavy casualties. Significantly, Italy capitulated on 8 September, and it has been suggested that the Spitsbergen raid was an attempt to distract world attention from this Axis disaster.

The homeward passage of *Cumberland, Bermuda, Athabaskan*, and *Eclipse* was uneventful, and they made landfall on Langanes, Iceland by 13 June. Limited visibility due to thick fog convinced the force commander to stay clear of Iceland and carry on to Scapa Flow, where the force arrived the next day. It had been a successful operation which had surpassed the planners' original calculations. Unpredictable weather and the presence of the enemy had failed to prevent the expedition from achieving its goal. The combined efforts of all the ships' companies had been exemplary, and the opportunity for team work would prove of inestimable value to them in the months ahead.

For the Athabaskans, it had been an adventure which knit them more closely together. The majority had never crossed the Arctic Circle before, and this venture into unknown waters had hastened them toward maturity. In a Canadian geographical comparison, the young ship's company journeyed as far north as Ellesmere Island—within twelve degrees of the North Pole!

On 18 June *Athabaskan* engaged in a torpedo-firing exercise in the North Sea with the cruiser HMS *Dido*, an invaluable experience as it was the first opportunity to exercise the torpedo crews on a live target. The capricious finger of Fate suddenly pointed again to Canada's second Tribal. With the torpedo exercises completed, *Athabaskan* was returning alone to Scapa Flow when she collided with the boom defence ship HMS *Bargate,* the western gate vessel at Switha Gate. Apparently *Athabaskan* was easing slowly toward the gate in the boom when the order 'Full Astern' was signalled to the engine-room. The duty Chief Petty Officer responded quickly to the order but the ship kept moving on her forward course. She hit the gate cables with a shudder and her stern swung to port, striking *Bargate;* the tough steel cables meanwhile sliced several feet into *Athabaskan's* bow, bringing her to a halt. Able Seaman Ray Moar was standing on the forecastle at the time and had a grandstand view of the incident:

> The boom was supposed to be open, but the wire cable was still across and it cut into our bow like a hot knife into cheese. It was funny to see the look on the face of *Bargate's* Captain as he opened the door to the bridge. He stared in amazement when he saw us coming and quickly hopped back inside and slammed the door shut. One of the gate vessel's men dived overboard smoking a pipe, and when he surfaced, the pipe was still gripped between his teeth.

Commander Miles ordered the Chief Engineer to the engine-room to investigate the situation, and the engineer was calmly told by the Chief Petty Officer that the steam controls had jammed. It was another one of those unique accidents that can befall any ship in her journeys, one that caused some damage, but greater embarrassment to all concerned. Examination showed that *Athabaskan's* stem bar was distorted and some bow plates would have to be replaced. Temporary repairs were carried out at Scapa Flow, and soon afterward a signal came through: 'Proceed to Devonport Dock, Plymouth for refit.' *Athabaskan* slipped from her buoy on 22 June, a cold, windy day, when the waters of Scapa were very rough. And the mess decks buzzed again with stories and rumours about their destination:

'Plymouth, eh? They say it's a real banana belt compared to this place.'

'I once knew a girl in Plymouth. Her name was Rose. I wonder if she's still there?'

'My dad came from Plymouth. He said to be sure to look up his brother Joe's family.'

'Plymouth my eyeballs! We're just as likely to be shipped back to the Arctic.'

'Someone told me to try out the Devon cream. They say it's pretty good stuff.'

Athabaskan arrived at Plymouth Sound on the 24th, eased her way past Drake's Island, veered to starboard, and entered Devonport Dock, where she received a warm welcome. Ships at anchor and ships in transit whistled a hearty welcome to the Canadian ship and her company. It was *Athabaskan's* first visit to this ancient port, and her company relished the new experience with excitement and anticipation. Drake, Hawkins, Raleigh, and their fellow captains had all sailed from here on explorations to the New World. It had been Drake's departure point when he sailed out to disperse the trespassing Spanish Armada in the English Channel. In 1620 the Pilgrim Fathers left Plymouth to found the first permanent settlement in New England. These formed only part of the historic panorama; the whole area was steeped in naval lore and tradition, and it would open up a new chapter of activity and interest for the Canadian sailors.

If the crew had held any doubts about the reason they were at war, all uncertainties were quickly dispelled when the first party went ashore, for the scene that met their eyes was appalling. Everywhere they looked was another picture of awesome destruction. Churches, schools, houses, office buildings, and shops had all felt the force of the enemy's anger. The main business centre was simply a flat heap of raked rubble. Senior Athabaskans who had touched on Plymouth in earlier days tried vainly to visualize names and places. The year 1941 would never be forgotten by the people of Plymouth, for it was the year that Plymouth was reborn after her terrible ordeal by fire and blast. British and Canadian sailors would also remember, for many of their shipmates had died in the wreckage of the Plymouth naval depots HMS *Drake* and HMCS *Niobe.*

Yard for yard and mile for mile, Plymouth had suffered more

than any other city in Britain during the blitz. Even visitors from war-torn Coventry would gasp with shock when they surveyed the scene. Coventry had been bombed and received world-wide attention, but Plymouth had been blitzed and endured her pains in silence. Yet despite the massive destruction, Plymouth welcomed the Athabaskans generously, as though she had said: 'My churches and homes have been shattered; my schools and pubs have been levelled; thousands of my citizens have been killed and injured; but I am not disheartened. My resources are limited, but what I have I will share; all I can offer are hope, a warm heart, and the right hand of fellowship.' To the Athabaskans, this was Tribal language, epitomizing the courage, resourcefulness, and kindness they strove to represent. From that time onward, Plymouth became a home-away-from-home for the Canadians.

Signalman William G. Stewart visits and photographs relatives of hometown neighbours, the Pulsford family of 5 Gerald Road, Bournemouth.

Chapter Five

The Bay of Biscay

HMCS Athabaskan *in Plymouth Harbour.*

BY THE MIDDLE OF 1943 the war had taken a more favourable turn for the Allies. In the East, the Germans were slowly but surely being expelled from the soil of Russia. Military supplies from Britain and the United States, shipped via the northern convoy route and Persian Gulf, were adding clout to the side of the Russian bear. Axis resistance had finally collapsed in North Africa, paving the way for the invasion of Sicily. United States forces in the Pacific were gathering momentum in their island-hopping campaign which would roll the enemy back to his homeland.

During this period *Athabaskan* was undergoing repairs in Plymouth as a result of the *Bargate* incident at Scapa Flow. Her company had been granted leave as the Canadian ship rested and recuperated from the stress of the sea. Meanwhile, an aggressive air/sea offensive had commenced in the war against the enemy's U-boats on passage to and from their lairs in the major French Atlantic ports, and the new offensive policy was designed to destroy the German submarines before they could attack Allied convoys. The war at sea was beginning to look brighter and more hopeful for the Allies. The monthly tonnage of shipping sunk had dropped dramatically from May 1943 with a corresponding rise in the rate of U-boat losses. Consequently, these marauders of the deep were forced to travel in groups, submerged and hugging the French and Spanish coasts in daylight and taking their chances of survival on the surface at night.

Coastal Command of the Royal Air Force, working in close support with the Royal Navy was to patrol two areas in the Bay of Biscay, code-named *Musketry* and *Seaslug*. Squadrons of *Sunderlands, Wellingtons,* and *Whitleys* ranging far out over the Bay were to report U-boat sightings to hunting groups of Allied units and call them in if an aircraft attack proved unsuccessful. It was an innovation which held great promise of success, and spelled ultimate disaster for the enemy's underwater offensive.*

*The Admiralty had received reports that the Germans were using a new weapon against surface craft—the radio-controlled glider bomb—and the naval striking forces were also assigned to find out if the reports were true, and if so, how the bomb operated, so that effective counter-measures could be devised.

Against this background of global warfare and local strategy, *Athabaskan* was repaired and made fit for service again. Her company, fresh from leave and itching for action, practised and prepared themselves for the battle at sea.

Athabaskan made a total of five voyages to the Bay of Biscay, slipping her lines and clearing Devonport Dock for the first one at 1730 on 19 July 1943. She sailed as Senior Officer, Force "W", in company with her sister RCN Tribal *Iroquois* and the Polish destroyer *Orkan*. The cruiser HMS *Glasgow* joined them on the 21st, providing additional support for the force while operating in South-East *Musketry*.

That evening *Iroquois* sighted the Spanish fishing vessel *Monolo* working in a prohibited area. The RCN Tribal immediately took aboard the crew from the ship and sank her by gun-fire. (The drastic action had been preceded by an announcement made by the Admiralty several months earlier that all ships, regardless of nationality or registry, would be sunk if found in certain prescribed areas of the Bay of Biscay. This was designed to prevent Spanish vessels from reporting Allied movements.) The next morning *Isolina Costrade* was sunk by *Iroquois*, while *Orkan* disposed of *Vivero*. Fifteen other Spanish fishing vessels were sighted during the patrol, but they were in a recognized area and were therefore not disturbed.

The following day a Focke-Wulf *FW 200* long-range reconnaissance aircraft was sighted, but it did not attack Force "W". *Orkan* was within range so fired on her with all armament, but no hits were registered and the aircraft withdrew. This was *Athabaskan's* first sighting of an enemy aircraft, and it provided her young ship's company with experience in the precise art of aircraft recognition. Although the ship's guns remained silent, fire control and gun crews had followed the bandit through all his movements, ready to fire at the first command.

With fuel running low, Force "W" steered for Plymouth on 24 July. During the homeward passage *Athabaskan* picked up five exhausted enemy sailors floating in the Bay on a life-raft. They proved to be survivors from *U-558*, sunk four days earlier by Allied aircraft. They were promptly hauled aboard and provided

Five fortunate survivors of U-558, sunk four days earlier, are rescued from the Bay of Biscay by HMCS Athabaskan *on 24 July 1943.*

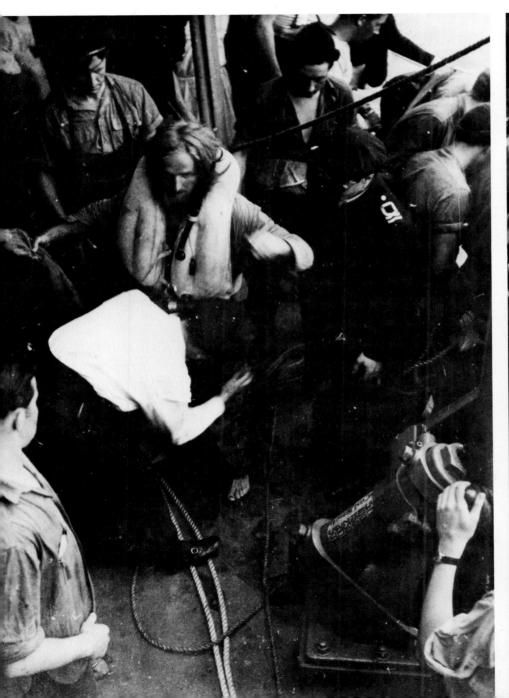

with blankets, food, and hot drinks. During this rescue operation a signal was received from a *Sunderland* that another U-boat was sinking in the vicinity. Force "W" closed the reported position and, in the early hours of the 25th, found thirty-seven survivors of *U-459* and one Allied airman. The latter was a tail gunner, the only survivor of *Wellington* bomber Q of 172 Squadron, RAF, which, with *Wellington* V of 547 Squadron, had sunk *U-459*. The bomber had been shot down in the engagement. While they were picking up the survivors, the rescuers tried to avoid looking at what appeared to be the bodies of seven German sailors floating on the water—a nauseating sight.

Iroquois picked up the airman and *Orkan* took on board the enemy. Landfall was made at Plymouth on the 26th and the Canadian ships berthed at No. 5 jetty, Devonport Dock at 1730. The prisoners were disembarked shortly afterward and turned over to the Shore Patrol; their war was over.

Athabaskan's second voyage to the Bay commenced on 31 July. She was accompanied by the destroyer HMS *Grenville*, and the two ships joined the sloop HMS *Kite*, Senior Officer, to form the Second Support Group. *Musketry* was again the area of activity, and the Second Support Group was backed up by Group EG-40 consisting of the sloops HMS *Landguard*, Senior Officer, and *Bideford*, *Hastings*, and *Waveney*. Their passage to the designated patrol area was uneventful, but on 2 August reports indicated that enemy destroyers from a French Atlantic port were nearby. At 1810 a *Sunderland* aircraft reported to Group EG-40 that enemy destroyers were sighted twenty-one miles to the north-east, bearing 270° at a speed of thirty knots. Unfortunately, Group EG-40 was not in a position of strength because its units were outclassed in size and speed. With his hand forced by this state of affairs, the group commander ordered a retirement to the south to join up with the Second Support Group.

The latter force, alerted to the enemy's position, pulled out all stops and raced to the scene, eager for battle. A confusion of signals erroneously indicated that Group EG-40 was the enemy, and the Second Support Group, with all hands at action stations, pressed on to meet the foe. When the two forces eventually met,

friendly recognition signals were effected, amidst loud wails of disappointment.

After the confusion had been sorted out the two groups took up night dispositions in an effort to trap the eastbound enemy destroyers. But radar contacts in the middle watch indicated that the enemy, travelling at high speed in the vicinity of Group EG-40, had successfully evaded the Allied forces.

The hunters continued the patrol in *Musketry* area, and *Grenville* obtained an underwater contact on 4 August. A concentrated depth charge attack was carried out, but it failed to yield any evidence of destruction. The contact was eventually lost and the two groups continued the patrol. They were shadowed intermittently by *Ju-88s* from French airfield bases, but no attacks developed. With fuel running low the patrol was terminated, and both groups returned to Plymouth on the 6th.

After an uneventful Biscay sweep on 8 August, *Athabaskan* and *Grenville* left Plymouth on 16 August for their fourth Bay patrol, pausing at Falmouth for refuelling. They were joined by HMS *Glasgow* for a limited time, and the trio drove off several enemy reconnaissance aircraft with gunfire. Several possible U-boat contacts were registered, but they proved negative. The patrol continued without enemy activity, and when the allotted time had run out on 19 August the two ships returned to Falmouth for a boiler cleaning.

By this time the Athabaskans had become more experienced, and the enemy presence in air and sea had strengthened their resolve and quickened their ability to respond to action. Team work, both aboard ship and with sister units, developed day by day, and the group gradually became a formidable foe for the enemy.

The *Musketry* and *Seaslug* operations were beginning to have a serious effect on enemy operations in the Bay of Biscay. U-boat sightings in the month of August dropped dramatically, and it became evident that Admiral Karl Doenitz was employing new tactics to evade the Allied hunters. U-boats were apparently sailing close to the coast of Spain and France, remaining submerged during daylight hours. So the Allied hunter groups also moved closer to shore, carrying on their patrols, ranging generally in a line

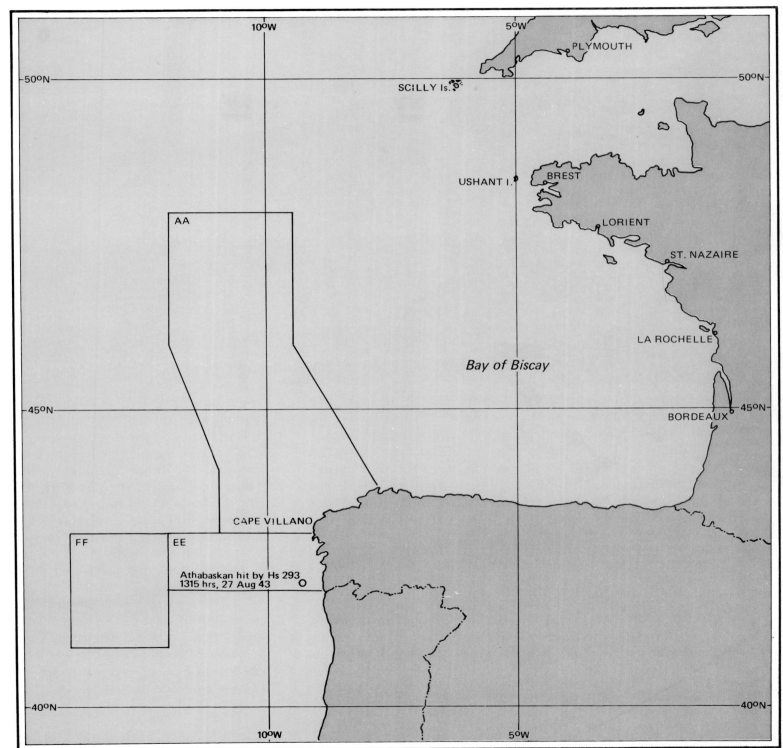

BAY OF BISCAY
PATROL AREAS
27 August 1943
Daytime 'Percussion'
Patrol Areas Marked

42

Bomb-aimer of Do 217
operating radio control unit
for glider bomb.

*The formation, led by
Major Bernhardt Jope, belonged to
Kampfgeschwader 100
of the Luftwaffe and was based
in Toulouse, France.

from Cape Villano north-east to Cape Ortegal, at the north-west tip of Spain. They patrolled from about 43°N to 44°N over the continental shelf, where the depth of water averages about seventy-five fathoms. It was hazardous water for U-boat operations, but it was even more risky for the hunters, for they were closer to land-based enemy aircraft.

Athabaskan and *Grenville* sailed on 25 August to operate in this new area of action. They cleared Falmouth Bay at 1930 on a southward course which would take them further south than they had ever operated before. The next day they paused briefly to investigate six tunny fishing boats, and then carried on. Four *Ju-88s* shadowed them throughout the day, but no shots were fired. At 0400 on the 27th *Athabaskan* and *Grenville* joined up with HM sloop *Egret*, Senior Officer, and HM frigates *Rother* and *Jed* to form the First Support Group. The group immediately commenced patrolling on a south-westerly course at fifteen knots in line abreast off Cape Villano. *Athabaskan* was on the port wing, the closest unit to shore. It was still dark, and Cape Villano light

could be clearly seen as it quietly signalled every few seconds, warning ships at sea of the rocky coast nearby.

The ships' companies were ready for action, because they knew it would not be long before the enemy became aware of their presence. The group continued on course and at 0646 a friendly *Liberator* appeared. Then, at 0727, two enemy *Do 217s* came out of the clouds to shadow the formation; *Egret* began firing and drove them off. RAF *Liberators* and *Beaufighters* circled the area for a time keeping in constant touch with the group commander. Then the alarm sounded—'Action Stations!'

At 1240 the group intercepted a signal reporting a formation of aircraft to the north. At 1300 a formation of eighteen enemy *Do 217s* appeared,* each carrying one HS 293 glider bomb. This newly-operational weapon was a radio-controlled missile guided by an operator in the aircraft, having a warhead weighing 650 pounds and a speed of 375 mph. This was the new weapon Admiralty had warned them about, and many suggestions were sent as to how to jam the control radio frequencies. Lieutenant-Commander Lantier tried plugging his electric razor into a high frequency Telecom, but neither the bombs nor the razor ceased to function. The enemy aircraft lost no time in attacking the group with their secret weapon. *Athabaskan* opened fire at 1303 and soon all ships were firing at the enemy, who were managing to keep their distance.

During a brief lull in the action, Able Seamen Ray Moar and Art Burgess at the Oerlikon gun on the starboard bridge sponson paused to wipe their brows. 'Art,' said Moar, 'look at that sailboat over there.'

'Sailboat!' his shipmate exclaimed. 'That's no sailboat; it's *Egret* going down!'

During the heat of battle, *Egret* had been hit by one of the glider bombs and had blown up. She sank quickly, a victim of one of the *Luftwaffe's* latest and deadliest creations.* In the bright sunlight of mid-day, her grey bow jutting out of the water had appeared to the young gunner to be a triangular-shaped sail.

Firing began again almost immediately as the enemy picked his targets carefully. Several glider bombs came close to hitting *Rother*. Five aircraft came down on *Athabaskan's* port side, three of them launching their glider bombs at the same time. One missile hit her at the junction of "B" gun-deck and the wheel-house at 1315. The glider bomb passed under the plot room, through the Chief Petty Officers' mess, and out the starboard side, exploding with a loud roar barely a few feet beyond. Flying bomb fragments pierced *Athabaskan's* side and bridge in a number of places, and the heat from the explosion scorched her steel plates and super-

structure. Commander Miles and the officers with him on the bridge were all knocked down by the impact, and several of the group were wounded, including Lieutenant-Commander Dunn Lantier and Sub-Lieutenant John A. Brebner, who had both legs severely injured. Fortunately, the German bomber crew had made an error in identifying the type of ship they were attacking. They had mistakenly labelled *Athabaskan* as a cruiser, which had a wider beam and heavier plating than *Athabaskan*, and the operator had set the fuse to explode the bomb in the centre of a cruiser's hull. To this technical error, *Athabaskan* owed her survival.

The crew of "B" gun bore the brunt of the explosion. Able Seaman Thomas Smith was blown overboard and a subsequent search revealed no trace of him. Able Seaman William Pickett was killed instantly. Petty Officer Ernest Latimer, in charge of "B" gun, was mortally wounded, so Leading Seaman John Gordon took charge and carried on despite the fact that he was injured and in severe pain. Able Seaman James Pike was knocked down, and there were several cases of men being burned, but they carried on, getting "B" gun firing again.

Several members of "A" gun's crew were burned and wounded, and others were badly shaken up. Commander Miles sent Sub-Lieutenant Jack Scott to take charge of "A" gun, and after a small fire had been subdued the men succeeded in getting the gun back into action. "X" gun lost all communication with the bridge; "Y" gun did the same.

*The bombs were powered by pulsating jet engines and were guided in flight by radio signals from the aircraft. On leaving the parent plane the wings of the bomb spread. Bombs were dropped as a rule from planes flying directly overhead, but these ones were released when the aircraft were flying a course parallel to the ship and at a distance of under two miles on her port beam. HMS *Egret* turned to avoid a bomb which passed astern of her. The bomb swung around like a boomerang and struck her on the starboard side. There was a tremendous explosion. *Egret* sank in a matter of seconds with the loss of 200 officers and men—only 35 were saved.

Fire rages on Athabaskan
while (below) another escort evades a bomb.

Two of the Oerlikon gunners, Able Seamen Thomas Crews and Henry Perrin, were in action all the time, and both were wounded by bomb splinters. When the enemy again came within range there was continuous fire from the pom-poms, directed by Gunner (T) George D. Sigston. Although each gun had to be operated independently, the gunnery control system having been damaged, Gunnery Officer Lieutenant Whiteley Eastwood kept his men pumping shells at the enemy until the last bandit disappeared over the horizon at 1330. Two aircraft had been shot down into the sea, and one had been damaged.

Parts of the bomb's wing flaps and fins had been left in the ship; others were floating alongside *Athabaskan*. They were fished out of the water, taken aboard, and eventually brought to England. In due course these important fragments were studied by experts, to try to find ways and means of countering this new menace. Some ratings who had watched these projectiles nicknamed them "Chase-me-Charlies", and the name was to stick.

A quick situation report from *Athabaskan's* Damage Control Officer revealed that she was in bad shape. Both forward magazines, the torpedo mess, and the number one boiler room were flooded. The signal office was wrecked, all but emergency lighting was out, and all electrical equipment in and forward of the three boiler rooms was unserviceable. The central fire-control station, radar communications, asdic, compass, and "B" gun mounting were useless. One man was killed, one lost overboard, and three fatally injured; twelve others were wounded. *Athabaskan* was on fire, had a fifteen-degree list, and was down at the bow by ten degrees.

With superhuman effort, the Athabaskans heaved to on the task of saving their ship. Fires were quickly extinguished and temporary repairs were made to electrical gear and circuits. In the lower decks, damage control parties were struggling successfully to slow the inrush of water which was dangerously pulling down *Athabaskan's* bow. The remainder of the support group had had better fortune than *Egret* and *Athabaskan*. *Rother*, *Grenville*, and *Jed* had experienced near misses, but had managed to escape damage. They picked up *Egret's* survivors and closed *Athabaskan* to offer help. By 1500 the damaged Tribal had managed to raise steam and was under way at fourteen knots. Steering was difficult, but, fortunately, there were no rough seas to complicate the situation.

German aerial photo sequence showing glider-bomb attack on Athabaskan
Ulf Balke, *Kampfgeschwader 100 "Wiking" (Motorbuch Verlag).*
Photos by Wolfgang Worpahl

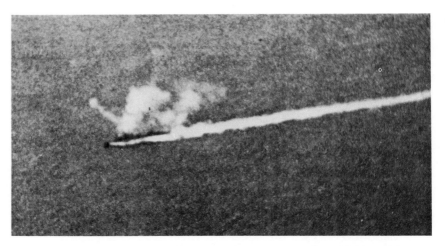

Grenville now assumed the position of Senior Officer as *Atha-baskan's* communication equipment was unserviceable, and the group departed from the unfriendly Spanish coast. The Captain of *Grenville* anticipated that the remaining three ships would have to screen *Athabaskan* to Gibraltar, the closest British base, but Commander Miles had other ideas. He knew that Plymouth was well-equipped and staffed to handle a damaged ship, besides being *Athabaskan's* home port. Telegraphist Len Woolsey had been ordered to send a signal to the Admiralty in London reporting the attack and the Captain's decision to try for Plymouth. An escort was requested for the long journey home, but the terse reply read, 'Proceed independently', with instructions to steer west out of aircraft range, then north, then east to Plymouth.

'How about them apples,' Woolsey muttered to his companion. 'It's going to be a long, hard grind. I hope we make it.'

With the decision made, *Athabaskan* took aboard *Egret's* thirty-five survivors and turned for home. *Grenville, Rother,* and *Jed* signalled 'good luck' and resumed their important *Musketry* patrol. The Commander-in-Chief, Western approaches, attached consider-able importance to maintaining the operation and leaving no gap, even temporarily, that a U-boat might slip through. It had been a definite victory for the *Luftwaffe* and their new weapon, and the surviving aircraft returned to their base at top speed, anxious to report the triumph in person. Herr Goebbels did not waste time announcing to the world what had happened, although the Berlin Radio's version of the battle was definitely wrong. The overzealous broadcaster was not content reporting the sinking of a destroyer, but also added that a cruiser had been sunk. The "cruiser" referred to was *Athabaskan.* Major Bernhardt Jope of the *Luftwaffe* received the Knights Cross, from Hitler personally, for his success in the action. Meanwhile, the First Support Group licked its wounds and prepared to resume the struggle; there was no fighter air cover for this particular operation and everyone realized the potential danger.

Shortly after *Athabaskan* was hit, Surgeon-Lieutenant William B. Wallace and Able Seaman Eric J. Mengoni, who had volunteered as medical orderly, were summoned forward to take care of and report on the casualties. As they made their way through the wrecked quarters, fire and smoke created an even more dismal

scene. The smell of cordite and burning rubber was almost over-powering, but they managed to assess the situation. Able Seaman William Pickett, who had been killed instantly, was moved aft along with the three mortally injured seamen. Several other Athabaskans who had received cuts, bruises, and contusions got attention at local first aid stations till the more serious cases could be dealt with. Commander Miles offered his day cabin as a combined surgery and dressing headquarters, as the Sick Bay was too small to accomodate more than a few seriously injured men. Here, Dr. Wallace and Able Seaman Mengoni proceeded to do their utmost for the stricken Athabaskans. Petty Officer Ernest Latimer died about twenty minutes after the explosion. As the doctor knelt beside him, Latimer smiled, but did not speak. 'I don't think he realized that he was mortally wounded,' said Dr. Wallace. 'In any event, I doubt if he was in much pain, either.'

Meanwhile, *Athabaskan* was proceeding on course at fifteen knots. Engineer Lieutenant J.B. Caldwell and his damage control party were below decks, sloshing around in water up to their waists, desperately trying to stem the inrush of water gushing from bomb splinter holes and sprung plates. They used anything suitable that came into sight. Hammocks, uniforms, cleaning rags, coats, underwear, pieces of wood, and other paraphernalia were stuffed and pressed into the gaps. Finally their efforts succeeded and the pumps gradually brought the water down to an acceptable level. The stokers in the three boiler rooms were sweating to maintain steam. Suction had been restored, enabling a steady flow of fuel to pass to the burners.

At 2000, Commander Miles conducted a burial service on the quarter-deck for seamen Pickett and Latimer. In the glow of the setting sun, and in the finest tradition of the RCN, all available Athabaskans mustered aft to pay their respects and last farewells. The First Lieutenant and a firing party of twelve men in full dress paraded aft and assembled on the quarter-deck. Beside the firing party lay the bier, consisting of a wooden grating with one end resting on the rail supported by two able seamen on either side. On the bier, enshrouded in canvas sewn and properly weighted by the loving hands of fellow shipmates, and draped in the White Ensign, lay the bodies of Athabaskans Pickett and Latimer.

HMS Egret *and her last moments*

Top to bottom: HM Ships Grenville, Jed, Rother

A prayer of safe repose was said for the souls of the fallen men, as well as a prayer for the safekeeping of the ship and her company, and a prayer of general thanksgiving to God. These were followed by the Lord's prayer, which was repeated in unison by all hands. Throats tightened and tears fell as those words of love and compassion were spoken. Then the firing party fired a volley of three saluting shots, the bier was tipped upward, and the canvas-clad figures lying side by side slid silently into the foaming waters of the Bay. The crimson rays of the setting sun, far out on the western horizon, added a warm, comforting glow to the sombre scene. After the brief but impressive service, all hands dispersed and bent once more to the task of saving their ship.

Athabaskan continued on course at fourteen knots. She was still listing seriously to starboard, causing much anxiety. Her port fuel tanks were flooded to correct the situation, and this helped prevent the inward surge of water below. She slowed and stopped during the night because suction was lost once again, but eventually it was restored, and she got under way.

At 0820 on the 28th there was another burial service. Able Seaman Joseph McGrath, a bridge lookout at the time of the blast, had died during the early morning hours despite the unceasing efforts of the Surgeon-Lieutenant and his assistant. They had been aided by *Egret's* medical officer, Surgeon-Lieutenant Charles E. Drew, but it had been a losing battle. Seaman McGrath was given the same burial honours as Athabaskans Pickett and Latimer.

The day wore painfully on for the ship's company. *Athabaskan* was forced to stop three times because of contaminated fuel. The drinking water had also been fouled, but this was soon overcome. The Officers' Wardroom facilities were operating, but they were inadequate to supply a large body of men, so meals were scant and cold. Water had soaked the labels off tinned goods, preventing identification of the contents—it was pot luck all around. At 1215 seven ships were sighted at a distance on the starboard beam, causing some apprehension until they were identified as a small fleet of Portuguese fishing vessels.

The stricken ship struggled on through the night at a steady rate of fifteen knots. Gloom in the mess decks deepened when it was announced that Leading Cook Frank Prudhomme had died. At

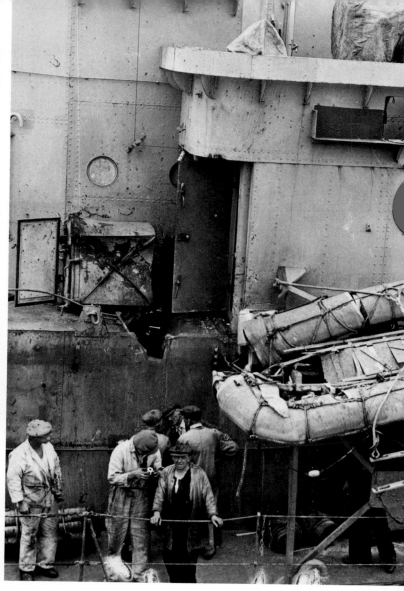

Above:
Glider bomb's point of entry,
port side. Dockyard maties
about to repair damage.

Left:
Leading Seaman George A. Lauder
surveys the scene, starboard side.

0930 on the 29th Prudhomme was accorded the same burial rites as his fallen comrades. Again it was simple but trenchant, filling the remaining Athabaskans with an overwhelming sadness; four of their shipmates had died and one was lost overboard, never to be seen again.

At this stage of her journey, all *Athabaskan's* injured were responding well to medical care—save one. Telegraphist Charles Kent had been severely injured in both legs and his condition was causing grave concern. He had bled rather badly and had been transfused three times, but toxin was beginning to spread. Surgeon-Lieutenant Wallace and *Egret's* Surgeon-Lieutenant Drew reluctantly agreed that amputation was the only hope of saving the young man's life, so preparations were taken in hand at once. Able Seaman Mengoni poured anaesthetic while the two doctors prepared for the ordeal. Dr. Wallace's official report of the incident was dramatic:

> The patient with both injured feet was a particular problem because with shock and the fact that he almost bled out, he appeared moribund twice, on one occasion requiring artificial respiration. Any thought of amputation seemed at first likely to be a lethal procedure. However, about forty-eight hours after the injury, having received 4000 cc's of reconstituted serum, 1000 cc's of 5% glucose and 3000 cc's of whole blood, it appeared that if anything was to be done, it must be done then. Accordingly, the patient was anaesthetized and placed on an improvised table in the Captain's day cabin. A guillotine amputation was performed on each leg as low down as possible. . . . Post-operative recovery was immediate and remarkable and the probability of recovery seemed assured from then on. Although the mangled feet were decomposing, there was no evidence of infection, but in view of his almost miraculous improvement right after the operation, I think he must have been absorbing tremendous amounts of toxin from them . . .

Surgeon-Lieutenant Wallace could not speak too highly of his assistants. He recalled:

> They were towers of strength to me at a very difficult time and all credit should go to them. *Egret's* Surgeon-Lieutenant, with more surgical experience than me, pitched in without hesitation. He was the only survivor from below decks on *Egret*. Apparently, after his ship was hit by the glider bomb, she exploded and capsized. The ship's doctor was stunned momentarily and when he came to, found himself in a flooding compartment with six ratings. Emergency lighting had come on and they had asked him, 'What should we do, Sir?' He replied, 'Deflate your life-jackets and follow me.' Since it was a bright summer day outside, shafts of sunlight were reflected down in the water and the plucky British Officer dived deep. He swam and swam and swam as far as he could go. When he finally broke surface near one of the other ships, there was no sign of his companions. They appeared to have shared the fate of their other 200 lost shipmates. Hours later, this same gallant man was standing beside me assisting with the operation on Telegraphist Kent. If ever a man deserved a medal, surely it must be him. Able Seaman Eric "Ike" Mengoni was a marvellous assistant too. This physically tough, case-hardened sea-dog was an RCN man who had knocked about the world quite a bit. He looked like a version of Anthony Quinn. His reputation as a fighter was well known in naval circles, but when the chips were down, that's when he shone. He moved about the injured Athabaskans like a mother hen, tending to their needs and offering words of comfort and help. He had a great sense of humour and was extremely helpful in the emergency.

At 1506 on the 30th, *Athabaskan* sighted HM ships *Goathland*, *Limbourne*, and *Tanatsyde* off the Scilly Islands. The three Hunt class destroyers had been sent out as escorts for the stricken Tribal. Commander Miles refused a tow, and for the last six hours of the journey steamed home independently at the remarkable rate of eighteen knots—the escorts were left far behind. *Athabaskan* passed through the harbour gate at 2031 and was taken in tow by the tug *Perth*.

The journey was nearly over. The two ships moved slowly through the Sound, past Drake's Island, and into Devonport Harbour to the sound of whistles, bells, and sirens. The welcome home was tremendous. Plymouth knew about the Bay of Biscay action, and proclaimed her feelings in no uncertain terms. Her citizens had heard Lord Haw-Haw's* announcement that a British cruiser had been sunk in the engagement and several ships damaged. True, the sloop *Egret* had been lost, but there was *Athabaskan*, Canada's Tribal, arriving home under her own power. Ship and company were battered, but not broken, and would live to fight another day.

*Lord Haw-Haw was really an American-born British subject by the name of William Joyce. He served as an announcer on German radio during the Second World War, and was executed in the Tower of London as a traitor shortly after the end of hostilities.

Survivors of HMS Egret

Athabaskan secured alongside No. 1 jetty at 2130. The seamen hurrying back and forth below the bridge were overjoyed to see a postman from the base waiting to come aboard—back mail had at last caught up with them. The injured were disembarked shortly afterward and moved to Stonehouse Hospital. A food barge moved alongside and commenced transferring hot meals aboard for the weary seamen. For three days and nights the entire ship's company had endured lack of sleep, rest, and proper meals. Added to their ordeal was the constant watch for enemy aircraft and the grim thought that they might not complete the passage. In his official report Commander Miles extended great praise to all ranks, and the report ended with the following statement: 'The conduct and bearing of a young and inexperienced ship's company during the short period of action and a return passage exceeding a thousand nautical miles left nothing to be desired.'

When Commander G.R. Miles, Engineer Lieutenant J.B. Caldwell, Chief Engine-Room Artificer E.G. Mills, and Acting Petty Officer F.R. Harbour were Mentioned in Despatches for their work during this action, the citation read: 'For courage and seamanship in bringing their ship safely to port after she was damaged.' Surgeon-Lieutenant William B. Wallace was also Mentioned in Despatches; his citation read: 'For service in caring for the wounded in HMCS *Athabaskan* after his ship was attacked by enemy aircraft.'

Signalman Rafe Chadwick recovering in Plymouth Hospital

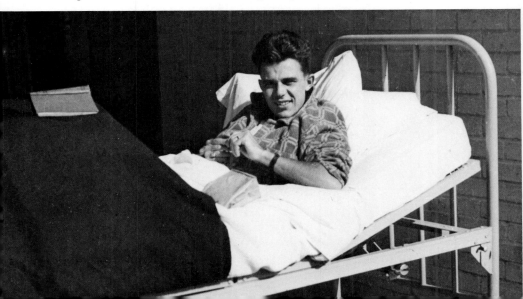

Chapter Six

Second Voyage to the Arctic

Convoy PQ18 under high-level air attack. RN Tribal HMS Eskimo *is in the foreground.*

FOR THE NEXT TWO months *Athabaskan* was laid up in drydock at Devonport undergoing major surgery to make her a fighting ship once more. The glider bomb had caused extensive damage which required considerable time to repair. Advantage was taken of the enforced stay in dockyard to fit the ship with a new lattice fore-mast which both enhanced her looks and supported the latest type of radar equipment, the Plan Position Indicator, which gave a continuous visual presentation of the area around the ship. Any object detected by the radar showed up as a blip of light on a screen. Twelve new Oerlikon 20-mm guns on six twin mountings were also fitted, replacing the six single-barrel Oerlikons.

Another new acquisition was an H/F D/F (High-Frequency Direction-Finding) set, nicknamed "Huff-Duff". This apparatus was capable of accurately taking the bearing of a high frequency wireless transmission, and could give warning of a threat from enemy submarines. U-boats normally sent a signal to their head-quarters upon sighting a convoy and before attacking. The form and nature of these signals, as well as their frequencies, had become familiar to the Allied monitoring stations ashore. An H/F ground-wave intercepted by a destroyer would indicate that the transmitter was inside twenty miles. As the bearing was obtained, an escort or an aircraft could be sent out to hunt for the U-boat.

Another installation was the latest refinement in TBS (Talk Between Ships). These VHF (Very High Frequency) sets eliminated the tedious process of call-up by lamp and the laborious spelling out of an order, or the insecure communication of high-frequency radio. It enabled each ship's captain to transmit information immediately to his fellow captains by simply speaking into a telephone handset, the message coming through on a loudspeaker or handset on the bridge. It could also be used to pick up the enemy's conversations during close actions, thus facilitating manoeuvering and evasive actions. This of course required inter-preters, and on *Athabaskan* these men were Austrian Jews. These were very brave men, for they knew that if taken alive they might be sent to a concentration camp like the others of their race in Hitler's Germany. They were among the missing when *Athabaskan* sank in 1944.

During the period of repairs the ship's company was sent on leave. It was a time for much-needed rest and recreation which the Athabaskans accepted with gratitude. It was a time for changes too. Some men were drafted to other ships and establishments, though they would always fondly remember the days served in *Athabaskan*. New drafts of men arrived and began to acquaint themselves with their ship and their duties as *Athabaskan* was slowly made whole again.

Toward the middle of October rumours began to spread through-out the mess decks that a change of command was coming. It was the principal topic of conversation, and Commander Miles' name surfaced many times.

'I wonder where the Old Man will be going?'

'They say he's up for promotion.'

'Anyway, if he leaves he'll have a chance to get home.'

'You can say what you like about his steering problems, but we're going to miss him.'

These and similar comments were heard during the next few days. They were the natural reactions of a concerned ship's company which looked to its skipper for leadership. They didn't appreciate the idea of changing the make-up of a team which was functioning reasonably well. Then the talk about a replacement added to the general shipboard buzz.

'They say a guy by the name of Stubbs is going to take over.'

'Who the hell is he? Never heard of him!'

'He was the Captain of *Assiniboine* when she rammed and sank that U-boat.'

'I heard he's a pretty smart cookie. They say he was demoted for trying to steal a swastika flag from the German Embassy in Iceland!'

'They say a new draft of guys is coming in from *Assiniboine*. I heard they made special applications for transfer to serve under the new skipper.'

And so the talk went back and forth as the Athabaskans busied themselves with routine tasks and helped to get their ship in shape once more. On 5 November an informal party was held in *Atha-baskan's* wardroom by her officers to bid goodbye to the Captain with toasts, handshakes, and personal farewells. Commander G.R. Miles was reluctantly leaving a ship and her company which he had grown to love and take pride in. In his new appointment as Director of Plans at Headquarters in Ottawa he would be faced with fresh challenges in the expanding war effort, but he would look back to the *Athabaskan* period as one of his happiest tours of duty.

The following day Lieutenant-Commander John H. Stubbs, DSO, RCN, walked on board *Athabaskan* as her Commanding Officer. This thirty-one year old permanent force officer, rising quickly through the ranks, had already achieved an exceptional reputation as a seaman and wartime commander. John Hamilton Stubbs had been born on 5 June 1912 in the small mining town of Kaslo, British Columbia. His early years were spent in this beautiful location, and the origin of his exceptional ability in steering and navigating warships can possibly be traced to his early days as a boating enthusiast on nearby Lake Kootenay. He was a member of the local naval cadet association, and family photographs portray him as the skipper of a small boat with his dog, Quest, at his side. His love for animals was further manifested when, as Captain of HMCS *Assiniboine*, he adopted a stray mongrel and promptly made it the ship's mascot.

The Stubbs family eventually left Kaslo to settle in Victoria. Young John completed his education there and then wrote his navy entrance examination, joining the RCN as a Cadet on 1 September 1930. He was eighteen years of age, strong and healthy, filled with a spirit of adventure, and anxious to get on the move with the Navy. After basic training in Canada he was sent to England for various courses, later serving in the Mediterranean Fleet. At the outbreak of the Second World War Lieutenant Stubbs was serving as Navigation Officer on the destroyer HMCS *Ottawa*, which was transferred at that time from Esquimault to Halifax. He later joined the destroyer HMCS *Assiniboine* as First Lieutenant under the command of Commodore L.W. Murray, RCN, who subsequently was appointed to the Canadian Naval Mission in London, leaving Lieutenant Stubbs in command.

John Stubbs sitting next to father, sister Margery, cousin, and friends, Kootenay Lake, British Columbia.

July 1919, 7 years old.   John with sister Margery, holding their catch, at Fry Creek.

John, right, with the Kaslo Sea Cadets.

The young officer-in-training.

Stubbs' service with *Assiniboine* was one of the highlights of a promising career. During the *Bismarck* episode in May 1941, *Assiniboine* was a short distance from HMS *Hood* when that powerful warship blew up. The Canadian ship was one of those which took up the chase after *Bismarck,* but she was forced to drop out when her fuel supply ran low. Prime Minister Churchill was aboard *Assiniboine* following his visit with President Roosevelt when the Atlantic Charter was proclaimed. The Prime Minister had made a courtesy call to Iceland on his way home aboard HMS *Prince of Wales.* He and his party boarded the Canadian destroyer about twenty miles out of Reykjavik and were borne into the Icelandic capital. When the visit was over, *Assiniboine* returned the distinguished group to the British battleship. The Prime Minister inspected *Assiniboine* from stem to stern, pleasantly commending her company for their good work, and told the men to 'keep it up'. Lieutenant Stubbs was the proud recipient of a later signal from the Admiralty which read: 'The Rt. Hon. Winston Churchill was most impressed with your handling of HMCS *Assiniboine* at Reykjavik.'

Winston Churchill comes on board HMCS Assiniboine.

On 6 August 1941 *Assiniboine* and five corvettes were escorting convoy SC-94 eastward in the North Atlantic when it was attacked by a wolf-pack of U-boats. During the engagement Lieutenant Stubbs led his ship in a spirited chase through fog patches, sinking *U-210* after a hard-fought, two-hour battle.

HMCS Assiniboine's *Battle with* U-210

In Stubbs' own words:

We caught up with the U-boat after chasing it in and out of fog and losing sight of it twice. We saw him again at half-mile range and tried to ram but lost him in a fog bank. Then we saw him again, right on the surface and almost a stone's throw away. We closed him at 200 yards and the submarine started an evading action. We kept moving in and just missed ramming his stern. It was so close we couldn't depress our guns but we were firing anyway. Then we drew parallel with him and the guns started to boom in earnest on both sides. From my perch on the bridge, I could see the German commander [*Kapitanleutnant* Lempke] plainly in the conning tower but a short time later he was killed by a shell from one of our 4.7s. The Nazis concentrated their fire on our bridge and the first few shots started a fire on the starboard side. This interfered with our fire-control and so we had to resort to quarter firing, each gun operating independent of the other. With all our guns blazing, our point-five gunners kept spraying the submarine decks. The crew stuck by their guns and everytime we scored a direct hit, they set up such a roar of cheering that I couldn't hear myself giving orders. We slapped right into them, then, and for good measure let go charges from our port and starboard thrower which exploded under him. By this time the Germans had had enough and lined themselves along the deck with their hands held high. They were all wearing their escape apparatus. As the Nazis plunged into the sea, the submarine went up by the stern, shook for a second and took the last plunge.

Congratulations on her victory came to *Assiniboine* from all sides. Acting Lieutenant-Commander Stubbs received the Distinguished Service Order for his part in this action, with the following citation:

Acting Lieutenant-Commander Stubbs' decoration is awarded for gallantry, devotion to duty and distinguished service under fire. He showed outstanding skill, inspired leadership and conducted a brilliant action against an enemy U-boat. This officer, in the face of enemy fire at 0-300 yards' range, and with the bridge structure on fire, handled his ship with dauntless resolution and courage, and pressed the attack with great determination to a successful conclusion.

Still wearing his Mae West following Assiniboine's *battle with U-210, Lieutenant-Commander Stubbs meets Admiral Murray at the dockside.*

Prior to his *Athabaskan* appointment, Lieutenant-Commander Stubbs had served for a year on the staff of the Flag Officer, Newfoundland Force as a desk man. This was not his idea of naval action, however, and now he looked forward to the fresh challenge of commanding *Athabaskan*.

When Stubbs assumed command of *Athabaskan*, he found to his dismay that he had inherited a commander's nightmare—an unhappy ship. He could sense an uneasy spirit prevailing throughout the ship, and morale seemed to be at a low ebb. The astute captain also noticed that the crew did not appear to smile, laugh, or sing; a complete change from his tour of duty with *Assiniboine*.

Calling a meeting of officers in the wardroom, he proceeded to mention his observations and told them that there had to be a strong team spirit between all ranks if *Athabaskan* was to become a first class fighting ship. He went on to say that he could get along just fine without officers, but that he needed the men who would run the ship for him. With this gentle threat, they were admonished to get on the job without delay, and dismissed.

Lieutenant-Commander Stubbs then asked the boatswain to pipe the order, 'Clear lower decks!' All seamen not on duty assembled at the waist of the ship where the Captain repeated his observations. After a short pep talk he dismissed them. His words had apparently had quite an effect. From that time on, *esprit de corps* rose by leaps and bounds.

On the second night after Stubbs had assumed command, Able Seaman Don Newman was on duty as Quartermaster's messenger. He was approached by Sub-Lieutenant Robert Annett with a message from the Captain requesting a pair of dice. Annett and Newman proceeded to the seamen's mess, where the officer discreetly inquired if any dice were available. Eventually, a set was produced. Annett signed a chit for them and quickly returned to the wardroom. Since gambling of any kind was frowned upon in RCN ships, Stubbs' gesture became another morale booster.

On another occasion, Lieutenant-Commander Stubbs came across one of his officers berating some seamen who were working alongside the ship at the boring task of chipping and painting. Apparently the work was not to the officer's satisfaction and he was letting them know in salty naval language. The interested Captain quietly suggested to the officer that perhaps he should don coveralls, slide over the side, and show the men just how the job should be done!

Repairs to *Athabaskan* proceeded steadily and were completed by the beginning of November. Canada's Tribal was again ready for action, her Captain and company eager to get under way. Her first assignment was to help escort the battlecruiser HMS *Renown*. This famous British warship was homeward bound from Alexandria, where she had conveyed Prime Minister Churchill and his party to the Cairo Conference for the meeting with President Roosevelt and General Chiang Kai-Shek. On her return to Plymouth *Athabaskan* required some hull repairs, which were completed by 6 December. Two days later, fully loaded with stores, victuals, and ammunition, she steamed around Land's End and headed north to rejoin the 3rd Destroyer Flotilla based at Scapa Flow.

From March to November, 1943, convoys to Russia had been suspended because the Royal Navy could not offer adequate protection for them. The battle against Admiral Doenitz's U-boats was reaching a climax and all available escorts were needed for the continuing Battle of the Atlantic. The remaining heavy surface units of the German Navy had been moved to Norwegian waters, and the phenomenon of perpetual daylight at that time of year added to the high risks faced by Allied convoys venturing into northern waters. It had been decided to resume operations in November, so the stage was set once again for a series of convoys to Murmansk. The Russians had been extremely annoyed by the suspension of convoys and cared little that Allied navies and merchantmen would be going to certain doom had the convoys continued throughout the summer. In fact, the Arctic convoy question became a serious problem in the Anglo-Russian relationship at this time, and at one point Prime Minister Churchill refused point-blank to accept a message from Premier Stalin.* But Novem-

* *The Second World War,*
Winston Churchill, "Closing the Ring", Book One, Chapter 15, p. 272.

ber saw a swing of the pendulum of war in favour of the Allies, and the convoys could now go out with at least a fighting chance for survival and success.

On 10 December *Athabaskan* arrived at Scapa Flow and prepared for her second voyage to the Arctic. She was allocated to escort convoy JW-55A eastbound from Loch Ewe, on the west coast of Scotland, to Kola Inlet, Russia. There were nineteen merchant ships in the group, and escorts included HM destroyers *Beagle*, *Meteor*, *Milne*, *Athabaskan*, *Ashanti*, and *Westcott*, HM corvettes *Dianella* and *Poppy*, *Acanthus* (Norwegian), and HM minesweeper *Seagull*.

The impressive array of ships departed Loch Ewe on 12 December under a dull, leaden sky. It was the third convoy to Russia since the revival of this important lifeline, and hopes were high because the two convoys in November had made their round trips without loss. As convoy JW-55A approached the Faeroe Islands, it was met by the 36th Destroyer Division, consisting of HM destroyers *Matchless*, *Musketeer*, *Opportune*, and *Virago*, to provide additional support. The tankers steamed in the inside lanes of the convoy, shielded to a certain extent from U-boat attack. As convoy JW-55A moved into the vicinity of Bear Island, where a German submarine base was located, the men took up defence stations, expecting action at any time. It was difficult to keep the convoy in formation in the limited visibility, and anti-submarine watches were maintained constantly, the operators listening intently for the sounds that would betray the presence of the enemy. The passage was uneventful until 1600 on the 18th, when *Athabaskan's* Huff-Duff operator sent a report to the bridge to the effect that a U-boat had just transmitted a message reporting the sighting of a convoy. Upon nearing the suspected sector *Athabaskan* fired starshells, and as the magnesium flares slowly descended they illuminated the sea beneath like sunlight. Up on the bridge the atmosphere became tense with excitement when the Captain caught a glimpse through his binoculars of the unmistakable outline of a U-boat conning tower. *Athabaskan* steadied her course, heading directly for the submarine at full speed. The Captain kept his gaze fixed on the U-boat, now brightly visible as the starshell flares fell. Suddenly there was a welter of white water all about the enemy U-boat toward which *Athabaskan* was charging. 'She's diving,'

Top to Bottom: HM Ships Matchless, Musketeer, Opportune, *and* Virago

muttered the Captain, and calmly took a bearing on her. In a matter of seconds she was gone, her position marked by a swirl of foam.

As the destroyer approached the diving position her asdic beam began searching beneath the surface for the vanished enemy. A full pattern of depth charges was dropped, but moments later the asdic operator reported, 'Lost contact, Sir.' As there were probably other U-boats in the area preparing to attack the convoy, Lieutenant-Commander Stubbs called off the attack and *Athabaskan* returned to her station.

There were no further threats during the voyage, although at one point *Athabaskan* picked up the wireless transmission from a damaged U-boat to its home base. The convoy finally reached Kola Inlet safely on the 20th. It had made the passage successfully under strong escort, with Force 2 in the background consisting of HM cruisers *Belfast, Norfolk,* and *Sheffield* keeping out of sight but within a couple of hours steaming distance.

Vaenga, close to Murmansk, offered little in the way of amenities to the Athabaskans and their brother seamen. It was a cold, dreary place with a constant, bitter wind blowing in from Kola Inlet. Nevertheless, most of the Canadians went ashore for a few hours to visit the town and pay their respects at the British canteen. Vaenga was populated by peasants, all of whom possessed a poverty-stricken, war-torn appearance. The Russian children begged the Canadians for chocolate and cigarettes. Fraternizing with the inhabitants was hopeless because of the language barrier, although some of the Athabaskans managed to exchange hats with their Russian counterparts, much to the new owners' eventual discomfort. A few Russians even ventured aboard the *Athabaskan*. In due course the Canadian sailors returned to their ship, glad to be back among familiar faces and surroundings.

On 23 December *Athabaskan* left Kola Inlet with her sister escorts. Their new task was to shepherd convoy RA-55A, consisting of twenty-two empty merchant ships, westbound to Loch Ewe. As this group of vessels moved slowly northward through the Arctic night into Barents Sea, the seamen on board little realized that they were shortly to take part in one of the war's most significant naval encounters. The convoy was a piece in a giant chess game which had already begun. The moves and contemplated moves are worth noting at this point:

·Convoy JW-55B departed Loch Ewe on the 20th, eastbound for Kola Inlet, consisting of nineteen loaded merchant ships and an escort of ten destroyers and three smaller vessels. Included in the escort were the other three Canadian Tribals, *Haida, Huron,* and *Iroquois.*

·Convoy RA-55A departed Kola Inlet on the 23rd.

·Force 1 commanded by Admiral Sir Bruce Fraser consisting of the battleship HMS *Duke of York,* the cruiser HMS *Jamaica,* and the destroyers HMS *Saumarez, Savage, Scorpion,* and HNMS *Stord* left Akureyri, Iceland on the 23rd, moving north-east at speed.

·Force 2 covering all convoy activities and within convenient range if needed.

·The German battle-cruiser *Scharnhorst* with five destroyers was to leave Altenfjorden, Norway on Christmas Day.

·Eight U-boats were ordered to form a north-south patrol line south-west of Bear Island.*

The War at Sea, Captain S.W. Roskill, p. 80.

HMS Belfast

The scene, the timing, the movement of ships in the Arctic darkness, signalled that a major encounter would take place within the next three days. Oblivious to this emerging pattern, *Athabaskan* plodded slowly through rising seas, alert and maintaining her station. Seamen on the upper decks cursed the weather as they sought protection from the searing wind and spray while their eyes strained for potential threats in the darkness ahead. Those below decks experienced a different brand of invasion, heralded by some particularly salty language. Apparently the Athabaskans who had gone ashore at Vaenga and traded hats with the Russian sailors had brought back more than they bargained for. As heads began to itch, it soon dawned on them that they had returned with a strong colony of Russian fleas!

Christmas Day 1943 found *Athabaskan* bucking heavy seas in company with her convoy somewhere north-west of Bear Island. It was Saturday and the most important Christian festival of the year, but for the Athabaskans it was just another routine day at sea. They were tired, fed up, had not received any mail, and their

nerves were stretched taut waiting for a possible attack. For all those whose duty took them above decks, every hour on watch was a harrowing experience. Fierce winds from the north-west shrieked continually, blowing cold spray and ice before them. The ship's bow rose and fell as it met the onrushing seas, burdening itself with a thick coating of ice. There was ice on the rigging, it coated the gun mountings and bridge with its dangerous weight, and it covered the decks, making every step treacherous. Cursing the elements, duty watches struggled and slipped as they went about their tasks.

In spite of the weather, the business of watching and waiting for a sign of the enemy had to continue. But all the lookouts saw were the blackness of everlasting night, the dark cold sea, and occasional snow squalls which reminded them of home. Able Seaman Roy Westaway sought shelter behind a ventilator housing and wondered about the folks at home. 'I can just see the gang now,' he murmured to himself. 'I'll bet they're having a damn good time.'

Able Seaman John A. King on the starboard Oerlikon was thinking of kinfolk too. 'But things aren't that bad,' he said to one

companion. 'At least we're on the way to home port and may be out of danger pretty soon. Think of the poor guys on *Haida*, *Huron*, and *Iroquois*. They're in that eastbound convoy and God only knows what'll happen to them.'

During the early hours of the 26th, as men slept heavily in the thick atmosphere of the mess decks, there was a tap at the door of the Captain's cabin. The petty officer telegraphist, signal pad in hand, said, 'From Admiralty, Sir. *Scharnhorst* is at sea and is probably going to attack one of the convoys.' The Captain looked at the clock. It was 0615. Shortly afterward alarm bells clanged urgently throughout the ship. 'Action stations! Action stations!' Weary sailors wakened from their deep sleep and came automatically to life, groping forward and aft to their stations. '*Scharnhorst's* out and attacking the convoy!' echoed the cry from deck to deck. This was grim news for the Canadians, because they knew that convoy RA-55A's escort was no match for the enemy battle-cruiser, which could tear them apart like the proverbial fox in the chicken house. It was a thought too devastating to imagine, but nevertheless the Athabaskans were prepared.

On the bridge of Athabaskan *in Arctic waters*

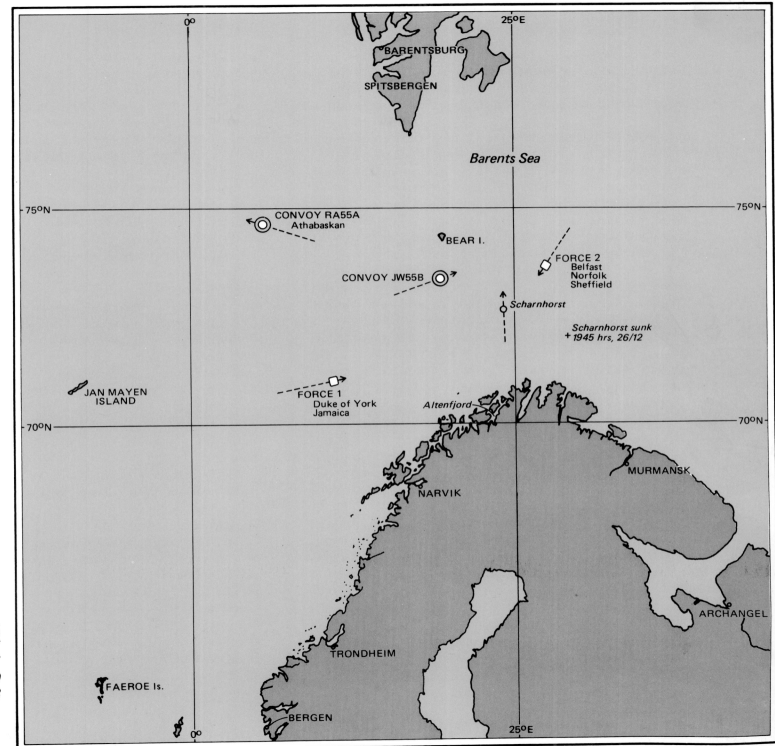

0° · 25°E

BARENTSBURG

SPITSBERGEN

Barents Sea

75°N · 75°N

CONVOY RA55A
Athabaskan

BEAR I.

FORCE 2
Belfast
Norfolk
Sheffield

CONVOY JW55B

Scharnhorst

Scharnhorst sunk
1945 hrs, 26/12

JAN MAYEN
ISLAND

FORCE 1
Duke of York
Jamaica

Altenfjord

70°N · 70°N

MURMANSK

NARVIK

ARCHANGEL

THE
SCHARNHORST
INCIDENT
*Situation at 0400
26 December 1943*

TRONDHEIM

FAEROE Is.

BERGEN

0° · 25°E

26 December was St. Stephen's Day, and the giant chess game had changed significantly in the past sixty hours. At 0400 the dispositions of all elements in the fast-moving drama were as follows:

·Convoy JW-55B eastbound loaded, about fifty miles south of Bear Island.

·Convoy RA-55A westbound empty, approximately 200 miles west of Bear Island.

·Force 1 approximately 200 miles south-west of the loaded convoy, steering a course East by North to close.

·Force 2 about 150 miles east of the loaded convoy, steering South-West to close.

·Scharnhorst with five destroyers at sea, steering North somewhere between the North Cape and Bear Island.

·Eight U-boats forming a north-south patrol line, south-west of Bear Island.

All signs pointed to an early action as radio silence was broken by hurried signals. Convoy JW-55B had been shadowed by enemy aircraft and U-boats during Christmas Day, so there was not much doubt that it was going to be the enemy's main target.

Meanwhile, aboard *Athabaskan*, all hands bent to the task of preparing for action. Lieutenant-Commander Stubbs addressed the ship's company over the public address system, saying something like this: 'Well, it may be a busy day for us and I'm hoping that we'll get a slice of the action. It's anybody's guess what's going to happen, so stand by for immediate orders. I'll keep you posted from time to time on the course of the battle. Four destroyers have already been detached from our convoy to strengthen convoy JW-55B so our turn may be next.'

At noon the Captain again came on the blower to give a situation report. 'Captain here, men. This is a report of what's going on out there. Since shortly after 0400, radio silence has been broken so the signals have been flying thick and fast. The Commander-in-Chief ordered the other convoy to steer north and signalled Force 2 to close. Rear-Admiral Bey in the *Scharnhorst* ordered his five destroyers to search to the south-east for the convoy, but they don't seem to be having much luck finding it. At 0815 Force 2 had reached the convoy and was supporting it. At 0840 *Belfast* picked up *Scharnhorst* with her radar and was commencing to shadow. *Sheffield* reported that the enemy was in sight at a range of 13,000 yards. Shortly after, Force 2 engaged the enemy and *Norfolk* got in some hits. *Scharnhorst* tried to make an attack on the convoy but drew away to the north-east. I guess the heat was too much for her. Force 2 lost contact and around 1000 *Scharnhorst* had another go at the convoy but didn't do any damage. She broke off again for some unknown reason and now Force 2 is in close support of the convoy. That's all for now, but I'll be back to you later.'

'He was damned good,' said Able Seaman John Laidler. 'The Captain's blow-by-blow description of the battle kept us all agog and we forgot about any danger. He would have made a good hockey broadcaster.'

Convoy RA-55A plodded slowly westward at eight knots. It was an agonizingly slow speed but every turn of the ships' screws was taking them out of danger. The sun, still well below the horizon, offered no welcome light in that season of eternal darkness.

'Captain here, men,' came the familiar voice as Lieutenant-Commander Stubbs gave forth another battle report. 'It's 1410 and this is the latest. *Scharnhorst* turned away from the convoy and the cruisers lost contact. At 1215 *Belfast* regained contact and *Sheffield* reported the enemy in sight. Soon after, Force 2 engaged at 11,000 yards for a few minutes, but the action was broken off when *Scharnhorst* turned away. She's now steaming west and Force 1 is moving east so it looks like they're on a collision course. More later.'

As the day wore on all hands strained for any scrap of information about the battle. There were still no orders to detach from the convoy and move south-east to the action zone, which created impatience and frustration.

At 1750 Lieutenant-Commander Stubbs resumed his play-by-play description. 'Rear-Admiral Bey ordered his five destroyers to make for the Norwegian coast, so it looks like they're out of the picture. At 1615 *Duke of York* made radar contact with the enemy at twenty-two miles and was closing fast. *Saumarez, Savage, Scorpion,* and *Stord* were ordered to take up positions for a torpedo attack. I sure wish we could get in there and help. At 1650 *Belfast* fired starshell and *Duke of York*, with *Jamaica*, opened fire at 22,000 yards. They pursued *Scharnhorst* which gradually drew away. Both destroyer divisions tried desperately to close but the enemy was still making headway. *Duke of York* kept up her fire at a range of 20,000 yards and they're both going at it hammer and tongs this very minute. So that's all I can say at the moment.'

The tension aboard *Athabaskan* by this time was almost at the breaking point. A fierce naval battle was in progress yet the Canadian Tribal was not called upon. It was an exercise in total frustration for her company, who knew full well that their first duty was to cover the convoy. But in a couple of hours it would all be over.

'Good news, men,' said Lieutenant-Commander Stubbs. '*Scharnhorst* has been sunk! Ball game's over! I know you're just as disappointed as I am that we didn't get into it, but that's the way the ball bounces. Here's what happened. At 1820 the enemy's guns went silent and Rear-Admiral Bey signalled to Hitler that he would fight to his last shell. *Scharnhorst* was still making good headway and the destroyer divisions were trying their utmost to close. It looked like the enemy was going to escape, but *Saumarez*, *Savage*, *Scorpion*, and *Stord* gradually closed. The enemy turned away but the destroyers hung in there and managed to fire torpedoes. Hits were scored and the German ship's speed was reduced. This enabled *Duke of York* and *Jamaica* to close and they opened fire at 10,000 yards. Then the cruisers were ordered to close and finish the enemy off. *Matchless*, *Musketeer*, *Opportune*, and *Virago* got in some hits too. At 1945 *Scharnhorst* sank, so it's all over. I guess we can stand down now and relax.' With these words, all hands cheered.

Scharnhorst

And so ended the giant chess game. Checkmate. The bold gamble by *Scharnhorst* to attack convoy JW-55B had ended in total failure. Grand Admiral Karl Doenitz had sustained a crushing defeat, while for the Allies it was an overwhelming victory. The 32,000-ton battle-cruiser had carried a complement of 1968 men, including Rear-Admiral Bey, Captain Hintze, and forty naval cadets who had joined her for training. *Saumarez* suffered casualties when a shell from *Scharnhorst* which did not explode passed through the Director Control Tower, killing three men and putting the tower out of action. There were no Allied warships nor merchant ships lost in this brilliant operation, which proved to be a classic example of ideal battleship, cruiser, and destroyer co-operation in a fleet action. Cruisers and destroyers searched the area for survivors, but only thirty-six were picked up. *Scharnhorst* sank at position 72° 16' North 28° 41' East in 255 fathoms; and thus ended a major threat to the Arctic convoys.

Lieutenant-Commander Stubbs went to his sea cabin below the bridge and pondered the events of the last twenty-four hours. He was disappointed that his ship had not been called to action. With a fine ship and keen crew, he knew that *Athabaskan* could have done more than her share in the battle. His thoughts turned back to the days of the *Bismarck* affair and the successful encounter with *U-210*. Direct encounters with the enemy had been scarce all through his sea-going career and he brooded on the latest lost opportunity to come to grips with the foe.

Although the Athabaskans were bitterly disappointed not to have participated directly in the *Scharnhorst* affair, they had one consolation. The major enemy threat destroyed, men could relax and celebrate Christmas, and this is how it came about. A few days after the battle, *Athabaskan* was tied to chummy ship HMS *Ashanti* in a cove of the Faeroe Islands, north of Scapa Flow. The ship's company was using this brief respite to repair minor damage caused by the heavy seas and to deal with *Athabaskan's* recurring condenser trouble. (The latter may have been the reason she was ordered to remain with the convoy during the *Scharnhorst* action.) An inspiration struck Lieutenant-Commander Stubbs. He asked Lieutenant-Commander J.R. Barnes, RN, of *Ashanti*, 'What's Christmas without a party?' Lieutenant-Commander Barnes replied that it was a marvelous idea—and so the party began.

(1)

Observing the trad-itional Christmas routine the youngest member of the ship's company becomes C.O. for the day. Athabaskan did not overlook this rule-there was much confusion as this O/D'S sympathies laywith the lower deck rates, consiquently there were a number of officers who stopped a blast from this stroppy seaman...

What have we here? Ah, yes, this beautiful hunk of man, believe it or not, started the day with full intentions of staying in the rig but it seems that a Gremlin stepped in and slipped him a Mickie. As the alcohol made Borris feel quite warm he began to disrobe but fortunately this is as far as he got....

(2)

Christmas dinnerwas an interesting event for us this year. The one and only Connolly took it upon himself to carve the turkey, which inciden--tally wasn't really as tough as the illustration shows, but he sure did wade right into that bird. There was a good deal of cussing coming from the head of the mess table but finally we all put on the feed bag, tucked the ears back and dug out...

It's odd in the Navy to have the leading hand of a mess to dish up after the mad scramble of gannets. This being a special occasion though it was the case. They kinda' took the strain as we had a few Sigs and Coders from a Juicer ship as guests. The killicks didn't seem to mind as every--one had the Xmas spirit (5 pts. of beer)...

(3)

Christmas day itself was spent out on that green rolling stuff but this handicap didn't prevent us from exchang--ing small gifts. They weren't much actually but it did help us to remember that the folks at home were doing the same thing.- Joe said he wanted to get rid of the sweater his gal sent anyway...

Some folk are under the impression that lockers are a stowage place for gear only- not a bit. One of their many uses is for tired ratings who are toolazy to sling their carts and prefer to recline on top of these lockers. Scanlon, who is now growing a beard, (it says here) decided he would crash for awhile before starting in again on the liquid refreshment...

Christmas mail was not brought aboard until we arrived at our home port during the latter part of December. The mailman thought he was having a nitemare when 119 bags- (don't get me wrong!),were waiting to be sorted and distributed but some of the boys gave a very willing helping hand.

67

Canadian and British Tribals roamed from ship to ship, exploring and visiting the several messes. Makeshift Christmas trees were put up in different places and simple gifts were exchanged. Parcels of food were shared to make it a festive occasion. There was loud singing and laughter all over as the Athabaskans and Ashantis joined in a spirit of fellowship. Before leaving Plymouth, Lieutenant-Commander Stubbs had acquired a substantial supply of beer and liquor for his men, and now it was beginning to flow. 'They're not feeling much pain,' remarked a duty petty officer, who was bravely trying to join the fun, while at the same time attempting to keep his wits sharp and clear for action.

The youngest man aboard *Athabaskan*, Able Seaman John W. Fairchild, became Commanding Officer for the occasion and walked around the decks wearing the Captain's uniform. As the day wore on and the food and liquor disappeared, the shouting and noise subsided. Sporadic bursts of activity flared up here and there, but in the main, they had really "tied one on" and most of the revellers sought sleep and rest while the duty watch carried on.

Convoy RA-55A arrived safely at Loch Ewe on 31 December 1943. On New Year's Day 1944, *Athabaskan* proceeded to Scapa Flow, where she went into a floating dry dock for hull inspection and minor repairs. It was a welcome break for the Athabaskans, who relaxed and caught up on the many chores and tasks left in abeyance during the passage from Kola Inlet. Then the mess deck buzz started all over again:

'We're going on some secret mission. It's all very hush-hush.'

'Someone told me we're going to Canada. Gad sir, I'd sure like to set my eyes on Halifax.'

'The Old Man's supposed to be making an announcement tonight.'

'I don't give a damn where it is so long as we don't have to take another convoy to Russia.'

'Bermuda anyone?'

'They say we're going to the Med.'

The buzz continued long after *Athabaskan* put to sea with *Ashanti* on 8 January 1944. They steered a southward course and joined up with HM destroyers *Antelope*, *Brilliant*, and *Anthony*, forming a screen for HMS *King George V*. With the battleship in their midst, the Athabaskans began to realize that something was

An illustrated letter to Miss Sarah Burrell of Hamilton, Ontario gives Signalman W.G. Stewart's impression of Athabaskan's *last Christmas.*

up. The warships continued on a South-West by South course at twenty-five knots, but their destination remained a mystery. Able Seaman Don W. Newman, who was standing watch during the early hours of the 11th, reported something unusual. He remembers, 'As daylight was breaking, I could see a group of strange lights dead ahead. Then as we approached closer, we could make out land and buildings. All of the buildings seemed to be white. On entering the harbour to tie up at the jetty for fuel, we were told that we were in the Azores.'

Shore leave was granted to half the company, who lost no time getting into Ponta Delgada. The Medical Officer's warning 'to be careful' was lost in the noise and bustle and excitement. It was like casting a straw to the wind. Naturally, those who remained behind were disappointed and envied their shipmates who had managed to get away. But their envy later turned to joy when a group of natives pulled alongside *Athabaskan* in their bumboats and dories, loaded with oranges, pineapples, bananas, grapes, wine, and other goodies. 'It was like manna from Heaven,' said Leading Coder Norris J. Legh:

There we were, basking in the tropical sunshine only a few days after leaving the cold weather of the Arctic. We bartered back and forth for about an hour. Cigarettes, silk stockings, British shillings, and the odd Russian rouble were used as exchange for the fruit. Later we sat on the warm deck and gorged ourselves with the island's fresh products.

Athabaskan and *Ashanti* were the only ships of the group which were detached for the Azores. *King George V* and the other three destroyers had continued on to Gibraltar, leaving the two Tribals to follow later. Fuelling completed, the Tribals reluctantly slipped their lines and made for Gibraltar. It was then that the real purpose

of the voyage began. Although those on *Athabaskan* and *Ashanti* didn't know it, they were escorting Prime Minister Churchill and his party from Gibraltar to Plymouth.

King George V cleared Algeciras Bay on the 15th and the two chummy Tribals quickly took up their screening positions, *Athabaskan* on the port quarter. The passage to Plymouth was uneventful and provided a restful voyage for the Prime Minister after his serious bout with pneumonia. Included in *King George V's* company was a group of Canadian sailors who had been drafted for special training, amongst them was Stoker George T. Phillips:

> I was one of ten stokers attached to *K.G.V.* for special service and we got along well with the Brits. The food was no hell—sour sausages and mash, powdered eggs, cabbage, pilchards, and grey-coloured tea. But *K.G.V.* was well organized and the Old Man ran a pretty tight ship.

There were about 150 in the PM's party including Geraldo's dance band from London. I didn't see the Prime Minister because he spent a lot of time on the bridge, but Mrs. Churchill visited our mess once, accompanied by two Royal Marines. In addition to my regular work, I had to make an extra hundred pounds of ice cubes per day for the party—there sure must have been a lot of headaches on that trip! It was a happy boost to our group though, knowing that *Athabaskan* and *Ashanti* were with us.

The special armada with its distinguished passengers arrived safely in Plymouth on the 18th, and the Prime Minister was welcomed by the War Cabinet and Chiefs of Staff. The two escorting Tribals received a message which finally let them know who the VIPs had been: 'Well done destroyers: P.M.' The important task finished, the Tribals immediately closed on Devonport Dockyard for rest and further orders.

Delighted with their fresh fruit buys during the Azores stopover of early January 1944, these Athabaskans gleefully display their purchases.
Back, l to r: Stu Kettles, George "Buck" Parsons;
Middle, l to r: Don Newman, unidentified, Ray Meloche, Bill Hayes;
Front, l to r: unidentified, Tom Eady.

Chapter Seven

In the Footsteps of Drake

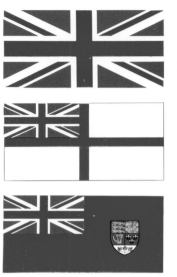

This "D" class MTB 726 was one of a Canadian-manned flotilla of eight boats on patrol in the English Channel. They fought hazardous, high-speed actions almost nightly.

AS THE WAR MOVED relentlessly forward into 1944, the pace of Allied activity began to accelerate. Russia, in the east, was in ferocious combat with the enemy and gradually driving him westward. Premier Stalin had been pressing for a second front by the Western Allies since the moment his country was attacked in June 1941, and his pressure continued. The convoys of precious war materials *via* the Arctic Ocean and Persian Gulf routes were but a drop in the bucket as far as he was concerned, and he had little sympathy or understanding for those who risked the dangers of enemy air and sea activity and the cruelly capricious weather.

General Dwight D. Eisenhower had been appointed Supreme Commander of the Allied Expeditionary Force and he and his staff were deeply involved in planning the long-awaited invasion of Europe. As Supreme Commander of *Overlord*, his duty was to lead and direct the largest amphibious operation ever conceived in the history of mankind. This cross-channel expedition would call for the highest level of skill, imagination, and ingenuity by British and American leaders of the three services and their civilian counterparts if it was to succeed. Hundreds of thousands of soldiers, sailors, and airmen were to be involved in this gigantic operation, and their combined efforts were to zero in on a time in the not too distant future called "D-Day".

Before the vast armies of men and their supplies and equipment could be transported safely across the Channel for a successful invasion, the dangerous Channel waters would have to be cleared of all enemy activity by the Allied navies. It was a formidable task to face, for the enemy still had many surface warships available. One of the most deadly of these was the E-boat, and it could create havoc at incredibly short notice. Although limited in number they caused a great deal of damage, for with skilled crews the E-boats could dash in here and there along the south coast of England, attacking and sinking vessels in the growing fleet of coastal convoys, and their minelayers were ever active. Apart from enemy activity, the Channel itself posed continual problems to the Allied navies. The Channel's general configuration was complicated. It was confined, mine-infested, and strewn with shoals and wrecks, highly dangerous waters for an invading army to cross.

The Allied navies' task called for the utmost skill in seamanship. The Channel left no margin for mistakes, and every man and ship was expected to work in close harmony and confidence with one another against the formidable combined challenge of the enemy and the elements. Should the need arise however, each ship was fully prepared to operate independently. Most of the action was to take place at night, entailing the added stress of sailing into the darkness of the unknown.

In preparation for the Allied invasion, a series of naval operations were planned to destroy enemy sea power in the Channel. These convoy interception patrols were known by the code word *Tunnel,* and *Athabaskan,* along with her Canadian and Allied sisters, participated in a number of these sweeps. The first *Tunnel* operation took place on the night of 19/20 January 1944, and consisted of HM destroyers *Ashanti, Brissenden, Talybont,* and *Tanatside,* and HM Canadian Tribals *Athabaskan, Haida,* and *Iroquois.* This initial patrol took the force as far as the French coast near Ushant, but no enemy ships were sighted and the ships returned to Plymouth.

As *Athabaskan* was under the orders of the Commander-in-Chief, Plymouth, she became involved in further *Tunnels* and in escorting the all-important British coastal convoys. By herself, *Athabaskan* was a complete Canadian entity of which her company was proud. She was a smart ship with a respected Captain, and was quite capable of carrying out operations on her own. But her role now was that of a valuable team member, working in close support with the Royal and Allied navies, altogether one of the strongest offensive naval forces of their size in the world.

For the last ten days of January *Athabaskan* was temporarily detached for boiler cleaning, giving her crew the opportunity for a much needed three-day leave. Following this, the three Canadian Tribals, *Athabaskan, Haida,* and *Iroquois,* sailed to join the Home Fleet at Scapa Flow, to take part in the *Posthorn* operation. The object of this raid was to attack enemy shipping in the dangerous waters along the Norwegian coast between Ytteroerne and Stadlandet. Aircraft from HMS *Furious* were to carry out the strike, but a strong force consisting of HM battleship *Anson,* HM cruisers

Belfast and *Nigeria*, HM destroyers *Serapis*, *Impulsive*, *Oribi*, and *Onslaught*, plus *Athabaskan*, *Haida*, *Iroquois*, and the French battleship *Richelieu* was standing off to provide strong support should the German battleship *Admiral Von Tirpitz* decide to sally forth from Kaa Fjord, where she lay ready to pounce.

Posthorn was delayed for a few days as fierce gales swept across the Orkney Islands and North Sea. The force finally sailed from Scapa at 0945 on 10 February. The following day an air strike consisting of ten *Barracudas* with twelve *Seafires* as fighter escort made landfall on the coast and swept down past the head of Stadlandet. Unfortunately, only small coastal vessels were sighted, so the aircraft flew to an alternative target, the beached SS *Emsland*. The *Barracudas* made a successful attack, losing one bomber and one fighter for two *Messerschmitts*, and returned to *Furious* at 1100. During the airborne attack *Athabaskan* and her sister destroyers patrolled the shoal-studded waters, maintaining a constant alert. It was a tense time for all the ships, and when the raid was completed the force withdrew at twenty-four knots, arriving at Scapa Flow on 12 February.

Shortly afterward the three Canadian Tribals returned to Plymouth to join the 10th Destroyer Flotilla, which consisted of the British Tribals *Tartar* (Captain D), *Ashanti*, and *Eskimo*, the Canadian Tribals *Athabaskan*, *Haida*, and *Iroquois*, HM destroyer *Javelin*, plus the Polish destroyers *Blyskawica* and *Piorun*. Together with HM cruisers *Bellona* and *Black Prince*, the 10th DF formed Force 26. HMCS *Huron* joined this powerful hunting group later.

Athabaskan had barely settled down to her new life as a 10th DF member when the rumours started up once again:

'Did you hear the latest? We're going home!'

'Good old Attaboy, she'll soon be on her way.'

'Boy, do we ever deserve it.'

'I'll believe it when I see Chebucto Head.'*

The buzz continued periodically for a few days until the news broke that it was *Iroquois* that was to go home for a refit—not *Athabaskan*. The Athabaskans were disappointed, but in the final

*Chebucto Head is a point of land near Halifax, N.S.

HMCS Iroquois *lays a smokescreen.*

summing-up they had to admit that their sister ship had been the Canadian Tribal longest in service. *Iroquois* slipped her lines on 17 February and slowly moved out of Devonport Dockyard to the cheers and waving of all the Canadian Tribals.

'So,' argued the Athabaskans, 'by all rules and regulations of naval procedure, it should be our turn next,, what a day that'll be. We'll turn Halifax inside out and show'em what real sailors are like.'

During the remainder of February *Athabaskan* participated in two more *Tunnels,* but did not sight the enemy. She was also involved in several exercises designed to bring Force 26 to a high pitch of night-fighting efficiency. On the 18th *Huron* returned from Scapa Flow and assumed *Iroquois'* place in the 10th DF.

HMCS Huron 1944, Plymouth.

As the Athabaskans settled down to the busy task of preparing for D-Day, it was inevitable that the strain of day and night reconnaissance would surface somewhere. Lack of sufficient sleep, hours of ceaseless watch, and confined quarters for work and rest, combined with the fickle state of the sea and weather, created a spirit of tension aboard ship. Plymouth became the undeserving outlet for this emotional build-up, and a few Athabaskans, like other Canadian sailors before them, by their inconsiderate conduct ashore, created a bad reputation for all.

The culprits were punished in the course of regular naval discipline, but naturally some negative feelings persisted. The threat of being drafted from the ship was always a possibility, and it helped to neutralize the situation. The Plymouth folk, who over four centuries had acquired a vast knowledge of the ways of sailors, drunken or otherwise, tolerated the wild Canadians and understood that their rough behaviour was largely attributable to the pressures of war.

In an effort to put an end to these unhappy circumstances and to re-establish a spirit of goodwill, Lieutenant-Commander Stubbs organized parties and receptions aboard ship whenever the demanding schedule of Channel activity allowed. Plymouth people were invited aboard on several occasions, and some lasting relationships developed as a result. Some Athabaskans met girlfriends and became casual acquaintances, while others fell deeply in love with

*Three Tribals (*Haida *on right) and light cruiser HMS* Black Prince *(second from left) manoeuvre at high speed.*

local girls and were subsequently married. But the Captain's efforts to promote friendship weren't always successful. A guest who attended one party that was interrupted by a sudden call to action came away with rather mixed feelings:

> It was a Saturday evening, and a bunch of girls from the office had been invited. We were thoroughly enjoying ourselves with spirited conversation and cocktails in the officers' wardroom. As the party progressed, we didn't realize that some of the officers had disappeared, and a short time later the ship started to vibrate and hum. Someone said, 'We're moving' and everyone froze in surprise. We made our way up on to the deck and to our shock and dismay watched *Athabaskan* slowly edging away from the dock. 'It's all right, Ma'm', said a cheery Petty Officer, 'We're only taking on fuel oil.' But the ship kept moving down Devonport Dock to the harbour and others were following us. She swung around Drake's Island and kept moving towards the sea. By this time all we girls were in a state of fear and excitement, not knowing what was going to happen. I suppose by some pre-arranged signal the ship was to stop near the outer gate—which it did—thank God. We were then told that all visitors were to go ashore in the harbour boat. So there we were struggling to go down the ship's ladder to a small craft which was bobbing like a cork on the water. I was wearing a summer frock and had a broad-brimmed hat. The wind was blowing briskly and it was quite a tricky job trying to go down. I was hanging on to my hat and the ladder at the same time, and my skirt was up over my head exposing panties and bare legs, much to the enjoyment of the sailors. We finally struggled aboard the harbour boat and *Athabaskan* pulled away, disappearing into the twilight. We eventually reached the dockside and an angry bunch of girls gratefully went ashore.

March was an extremely busy month for *Athabaskan* and her sisters. Few nights were spent in harbour as Force 26 worked up to a high degree of efficiency and readiness. Canada's second Tribal destroyer shared in two more *Tunnels*, three patrols protecting Channel shipping, and a number of night exercises. On 24 March *Athabaskan* was privileged to have the visit of Vice-Admiral Percy W. Nelles, RCN, Chief of Naval Staff. The ship had been polished from stem to stern for the occasion. After he had been piped aboard Admiral Nelles inspected the ship. The entire ship's company then fell in amidships to hear him give a brief speech, in which he mentioned, among other things, that there was not the slightest doubt in his mind as to the ultimate outcome of

Admiral Nelles inspects Athabaskan's *crew.*

*Monument to
Sir Francis Drake
on Plymouth Hoe*

the present struggle. He felt that everyone on board knew the job that lay ahead and would do it effectively when the time came.

Despite the rapid and intense pre-invasion program, there were a few precious moments of relaxation. Petty Officer George W. Casswell was one who took advantage of them. He had been with *Athabaskan* since commissioning and had developed a deep love and admiration for her—he was born near the ocean and was an old sea-dog at heart. He recalls:

> Chief Petty Officer Don I. Metcalfe built a scale model of *Athabaskan* complete in all details including a clock-work motor. It was painted the same colours as the real thing and was a beautiful piece of workmanship. I bought it from him for $150 and did trials with her in the basin at Devonport. The maties watched her go through her paces with keen interest and excitement. They seemed to be enjoying the show more than myself. I took pictures of her which turned out sharp and clear. It was my intention to take her back with me when *Athabaskan* sailed to Canada for refit. She sure would look good in a glass case on the mantle shelf over my fireplace.

By the end of March, Force 26 was a most highly trained unit, ready and able to meet the enemy head on. It displayed the same indomitable spirit that Drake and his men had demonstrated in July 1588 when they waited at Plymouth for the great Spanish Armada to strike. History has recorded the finale to that perilous threat to Britain, and 355 years later, an equally crucial confrontation with the enemy was about to take place.

*14 April 1944, Plymouth.
Aboard HMCS* Athabaskan, *Vice-Admiral Percy W. Nelles,
standing on a catwalk straddling the torpedo tubes,
tells the crew of Canada's pride
in their achievements, but advises them that further efforts
will be required before the Channel waters can be
freed and mentions the possible price.*

Chapter Eight

The Hunters

The crew of Athabaskan's *"X" gun.*

Athabaskan alongside HMCS Prince Robert, *Devonport.*

BY THE SPRING OF 1944 preparations for the invasion of the Continent were building up to a grand climax. The southern region of England was a vast armed camp with thousands of soldiers, sailors, and airmen converging on the many staging areas. Soon the entire region would be sealed off to the outside world as the strengthening of men, stores, and equipment reached a maximum, awaiting go-ahead orders from the Supreme Commander.

Force 26 based on Plymouth still had important business to complete in the Channel before the huge armada could sail. April was even busier than March, and by the third week, as D-Day approached, the tempo of exercises, escorts, and operations against enemy shipping had increased significantly. On the night of the 22nd, *Athabaskan,* accompanied by *Haida* and *Ashanti,* took part in her first *Hostile* operation. These were operations in which fast minelayers laid minefields near the enemy coast with a covering force in support. In this particular operation, the minelayer HMS *Apollo* was screened by the three Tribals. When they later returned to Plymouth the ships' companies were amazed to count no less

than thirty-five destroyers and fifty landing barges in the harbour.

On the 24th the same Tribals, along with *Black Prince* and *Huron,* carried out another *Tunnel* operation, but no direct contact was made with the enemy, although some gun flashes were seen over the horizon as they were on their way home. Returning from this patrol, Lieutenant-Commander Stubbs displayed his typical "no-nonsense" approach to the business of war. Able Seaman Jack Carr was on deck preparing for going alongside and witnessed the altercation:

Athabaskan entered Devonport Dock at daybreak and steered to come along the starboard side of HMCS *Prince Robert*. There was no duty watch to receive our lines so Captain Stubbs conned *Athabaskan's* bow in so that some of our men could jump aboard the *Robert* and tie up. Her Captain, out on deck for his morning constitutional, stopped dead in his tracks and bellowed out to our bridge: 'Get those men out of the rig of the day off my ship!' Unperturbed by this rude welcome, Lieutenant-Commander Stubbs retorted loud and clear, 'Captain—Sir, my men are tired and hungry. They've been standing to action stations all night. Where is your duty watch to receive our lines? This is a fighting ship—not a banana boat, like yours!'

This "let's get on with the job" attitude was typical of all Canadian servicemen and was the spirit which spurred them on to victory. Spit and polish was necessary to a certain degree, they admitted, and perhaps there were some finer points involved, but there was a war to be won and it couldn't be done in Number Ones.

Justification for the long days and nights of ceaseless exercise and patrols came on 25 April. Force 26 sailed for another *Tunnel* that night, clearing Plymouth's outer harbour gate at 2100. It was not just another routine patrol, however. Aerial reconnaissance and naval intelligence had reported that three enemy destroyers were sighted in St. Malo preparing to put to sea. Consequently, Force 26 was to position itself seventeen miles East/North-East of Ile de Batz and steer on this course until 0330. If the enemy had not been contacted by that time, the force was to return by the most direct route, bringing it within twenty miles of the English coast by dawn.

The night was dark and moonless, with about two miles visibility, as the marauders stealthily approached the French coast in close order. *Black Prince* formed the First Sub-Division, *Athabaskan* and *Haida* the Second, and *Ashanti* and *Huron* the Third, with the destroyer sub-divisions disposed forty degrees on the cruiser's starboard and port bows. The flashing light from Ile de Batz lighthouse was visible at 0100, and the force altered course to 070° at 0130. About this time flashes from gunfire were sighted southwest of Ile de Vierge, but no explosions were heard nor fall of shot seen. The Senior Officer presumed that Force 26 had been the target of shore batteries.

The patrol continued without incident until *Black Prince* picked up radar echoes at 21,000 yards. The contact, confirmed by *Haida* and *Ashanti*, indicated a force steering directly toward Force 26 at about twenty knots. Moments later, the radar blips showed that the approaching force had altered course 180° and increased speed to twenty-four knots. Force 26 began to increase speed also, ultimately reaching thirty knots. An exciting stern chase eastward now began. Stokers and Engine-Room Artificers in all units bent to their tasks energetically as they realized that this was a golden

HMS Black Prince

opportunity to catch and destroy the enemy. Action stations had already been sounded, and gun crews were assembled and waiting impatiently for the order to open fire.

Black Prince illuminated the enemy with starshell at 0219 at a range of 13,000 yards, and in accordance with night-fighting policy, the destroyers closed the enemy at full speed. The Third Sub-Division opened fire at 0223 and the Second three minutes later. *Black Prince* continued firing starshell. The range was now down to 10,900 yards. The enemy countered by laying a smoke screen, and within two minutes opened fire with both starshell and main armament, which luckily was inaccurate.

Ashanti claimed a hit on the left-hand target at 0231. Five minutes later there was another bright flash which indicated a hit

although it was impossible to tell which destroyer had scored. In the meantime *Black Prince* opened fire from "A" turret, while still using "B" turret for starshell illumination. By 0250 the range was down to 7300 yards, and at 0257 *Haida* could only detect two blips instead of three on her radar. Unfortunately, "B" turret on *Black Prince* had jammed, thus putting her out of action as an illumination ship. She was also forced to take evasive action to avoid torpedoes, and finally withdrew westward to avoid further attacks of this kind. At 0307 she altered course again to the east.

The four Tribals continued the hectic chase eastward, *Athabaskan* providing starshell illumination. Following the coastline, *Haida* and *Athabaskan* found themselves near the enemy smoke screen. One of the British minefields was in the area, but when the

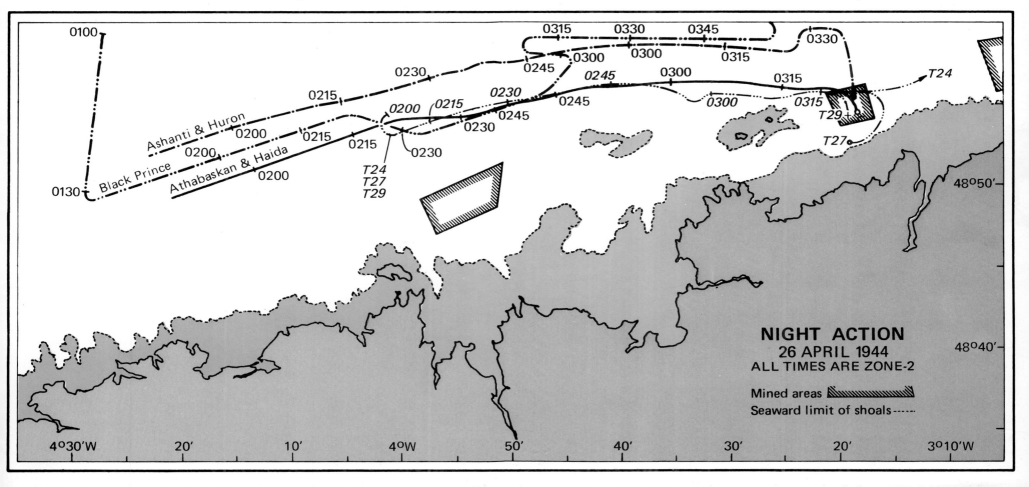

NIGHT ACTION
26 APRIL 1944
ALL TIMES ARE ZONE-2

Mined areas ▨▨▨
Seaward limit of shoals -----

enemy vessels started to go through it the Tribals followed. By this time the enemy ships had been identified as Elbing class destroyers. The Elbings, so known to the Allies because the entire class was built at Elbing, Germany, were classified by the Germans as Fleet Torpedo Boats (the smallest vessel the Germans would call a destroyer was the size of a Tribal). The Elbings had approximately the same size and armament as the River class destroyers with which the RCN entered the war, but were a more modern design.

A tremendous steaming effort by Force 26 gradually worked its speed up to thirty-two knots, thereby closing the range substantially. By 0310 it had been reduced to two and one-half miles, and it became apparent that the enemy was altering course southward, hoping to find protection in the nearby, rock-strewn coast. The chase had been going on for one and one-half hours with no clear-cut victory or loss, but a change in the situation was imminent.

At 0324 *Haida* sighted an enemy ship 45° to her starboard bow, about five miles from shore. She presented a fair target under the canopy of starshells and *Haida* scored a hit. Another Elbing turned broadside to engage *Haida*, firing explosive and starshell ammunition, which was brighter than *Haida's* but burned out quickly. Immediately *Haida* signalled a 90° turn to starboard for the Second Sub-Division, and *Athabaskan* and *Haida* raced on, hot on the heels of the enemy. *Haida* knocked out the enemy's main forward armament with her first salvo and started a fire amidships with the second. Great geysers of steam rose from the enemy destroyer's midships section and she slowed down, her main deck a blazing inferno. *Athabaskan's* salvoes were hitting her too. Shells smashed through the high bows where more fires broke out, until only the upper bridge and the after deck still showed black through the flames which engulfed her. Even from their distance of about two miles, the bridge watches on *Haida* and *Athabaskan* could hear the roar and hiss of the Elbing's escaping steam.

Torpedo Boat T-27 *built by F. Schichau, Elbing, near Dantzig. Commissioned 17 April 1943. 1512 tons. 97 metres long. Speed—32.5 knots. Captains—Korvetten Kapitan Wilhelm Verlohr and Kapitanleutnant Gotzmann.*

During this spirited chase the Third Sub-Division (*Ashanti* and *Huron*) had altered course to the north to avoid suspected E-boats in the area. They lost contact with the other two enemy units they had been chasing amongst the treacherous rocks and shoals of the French coast. At 0329 they altered course to 175° and rejoined the Second Sub-Division.

The Elbing, later identified as *T-29*, was now cornered by all four Tribals, but gallantly attempted to maintain firing, particularly with her close-range armament. Survivors could be seen trying to get clear of the burning ship on a life-raft, but since her guns were still firing, *Haida* fired a salvo in return, intended to strike below the waterline. It crashed into the enemy's hull and sent the raft and its occupants hurtling skyward. By this time the other two Elbings had fled, leaving their sister ship to her fate. At 0332 *T-29* appeared to be stopped with all guns evidently out of action. The only sounds coming from her were the roar and crackle of the flames and intermittent small explosions. The Tribals opened up at about 350 yards with their Oerlikons and pom poms, and in reply two streams of tracer spat with unexpected suddenness from points high on her bridge and far back on her quarter-deck, sweeping along *Haida's* after superstructure, spattering *Athabaskan's* length, and beating a devil's tattoo on *Huron's* and *Athabaskan's* bridges. As the Tribals came in for their next attack, the enemy ship blazed from stem to stern, illuminating the seascape for a good mile around. One of *T-29's* after magazines suddenly blew up, throwing debris and a sheet of flame high into the air. Two German sailors could be seen floundering on the water with a Carley float. A shell fell directly on them, and when the splash of water receded, neither was to be seen. The Tribals continued firing, and this time were answered by a lone 20-mm gunner, shooting from a position amidships with flame and flying shells all around him. He made a gallant last ditch fight and strafed the Tribals' decks with unrelenting fury, forcing many men to take cover. His shells hit *Huron's* bridge and upperworks, smashing the port navigation lights and the port side of the stoker's mess. Another shell shot away the pom pom feed rail, killing one of the gunners, Leading Seaman Henry W. Gosnell* and injuring four others.

*Leading Seaman "Salty" Gosnell, RCN, had served on *Athabaskan* from 25 March to 21 May 1943. His loss was keenly felt by the many shipmates who had served with him. He was buried at Weston Mills Cemetery, Plymouth.

Shore batteries opened up on Force 26, but *Black Prince* returned their fire, forcing them to cease. The Tribals were continuing to hammer the doomed *T-29*. A stream of coloured tracer spat from *Haida's* Oerlikons and swept the enemy's deck, probing and ricochetting throughout her bridge and after structure. The Elbing's fire had finally ceased, but still she remained afloat, even though aflame from bow to stern. She seemed unsinkable, and the Tribals closed again to fire torpedoes. While *Haida* was in the act of firing, Commander De Wolf observed that *Athabaskan* was also firing and would almost certainly hit *Haida*. *Haida* was compelled to alter course, and consequently only one of her torpedoes scored. All *Athabaskan's* torpedoes missed. *Ashanti* then fired, scoring no hits, but while concentrating on this she rammed *Huron* amidships, damaging *Huron's* hull and buckling the main bulkhead between Nos. 1 and 2 boiler rooms. The port cutter and its davits were smashed, the guard rails and stanchions bent inward, and the torpedo-davit damaged. *Ashanti's* bow was split 19 feet back from her stem. The Tribals altered course again for another attack, but suddenly *T-29* rolled to port. Her bow dipped, and the fires went out as she sank, a few miles off St. Malo, Brittany, at 0421.

Shore batteries opened up again as the Tribals departed, but fortunately their shells all missed. The Tribals closed on *Black Prince* at daybreak, and Force 26 steamed home at twenty-five knots. It had been a successful night's hunting, and all units proudly and triumphantly entered Plymouth Sound with battle ensigns flying at the peak. As they proceeded up the harbour they were saluted from both sides by ship after ship.

This extract from the war diary of the German No. 4 Torpedo Boat Flotilla sheds additional light on that night's action from the enemy's point of view:

> The evaluation of this action is incomplete because of the death of Lt. Comd. Kohlauf, CO of the Flotilla, killed on board T-29. As a result, his own ideas and decisions have, for the most part, remained unknown.
>
> The No. 4 Torpedo-Boat Flotilla, consisting of the ships T-29 (Flotilla Leader), T-24, and T-27 lay in the roadstead of St. Malo. The Flotilla was supposed to set up a field of contact mines during the night of the 25th/26th of April and to take over the visual protection of a convoy on the coast of northern Brittany; Brest was the port of destination.

The formation weighed anchor at 2130 hours on the 25th. A northern wind, strength 2-3, blew, sea 2, visibility was good in spite of the dark night. The mines were laid at 0130 hours. At 0200 hours the formation proceeded on a westerly course, ten miles north of Ile de Batz. According to reports so far received from our radar, an enemy force had been located in grid square BF 2861 on a course of 210°. A further direction-finding signal received at 0201 hours reported the enemy in grid square BF 2862 to the left, so that they were still eleven miles from our formation. Thus, the CO of the Flotilla ascertained that the enemy, whose strength was unknown to him, was straight ahead. Due to the threat arising to the safety of the convoy, the CO decided to divert the enemy from the former, in as much as he had to assume that he had already been spotted by the enemy's radar and that a surprise attack was not possible anymore. At 0202 hours, he decided to make an about turn and to change course by 90°. At 0214 hours the Flotilla moved in line ahead, course 80°, speed thirty knots. Starshell fired from the right, aft, burst on top of the Flotilla. Muzzle flashes could not be seen but all ships are well illuminated. Shortly afterward, shells exploded in the vicinity of the ships. The enemy could not be sighted during the initial minutes of the engagement but muzzle flashes could now be seen on a bearing of 190°. Tactical No. 3 was T-27 which is straddled by several salvoes, receiving two hits in her after-canopy, one hit in the port 3.7 cm gun position and one hit in the forward engine-room. She is detached by the CO of the Flotilla, a withdrawal under the protection of the coast could be carried out successfully, thanks to the throwing of several smoke buoys provided with lifebuoy flares which deceives the enemy. Our own starshell illuminates the enemy insufficiently but they seem to keep outside the range of our guns and are safe from our torpedoes because of the too acute angle. T-24 received a direct hit at 0238 hours which put the entire radio installation out of commission. In the meantime, the enemy drew closer from the port side. At 0320 hours, their position is bearing 220° and T-24 fires a spread in the direction of the largest shadow which is thought to be a cruiser. Torpedoes about to be launched by the after group of tubes, misfire because the tubes had been swung too far by the Torpedo Officer in charge. By 0330 hours, T-29 is straddled by enemy salvoes. Her rudder is out of commission as the result of a hit, she is on fire and is forced to reduce speed. Her position is the grid square BF 2929. This is the beginning of her death struggle which is fought to the bitter end under the fire of a far superior enemy. The behaviour of the ship's company was exemplary. The CO of the Flotilla, the Captain, all officers, and most of the crew lost their lives. Evaluating the situation correctly, T-24 breaks off contact and withdraws eastward, a decision made by the CO with great reluctance. She reached St. Malo at approximately 0700 hours.

CONCLUSION

The enemy force consisted of the cruiser *Black Prince*, the Canadian destroyers *Haida*, *Huron*, and *Athabaskan*, and the destroyers *Ashanti* and *Tartar*. [In fact, *Tartar* was not present, as she was under refit at the time.] Thanks to his radar-operated fire-control equipment and to the wide range of his starshell, the enemy was able to carry on the fight while staying for a long time beyond the effective range of our ships. The insufficient speed of his ships presented the CO of the Flotilla with a difficult problem in this action because he was unable to break off contact. In retrospect, he was in an extremely difficult situation. A headlong attack launched without changing the westward course, might have brought hard-fought success. The CO of the Flotilla was, however, unable to arrive at such a decision because he did not take the enemy's radar-controlled fire into account, because he was tied down to the convoy which he had to protect, and because a surprise attack was not possible. He found a hero's death in action for which he was awarded the Knight's Cross.

The lack of a quarter-deck radar warning set was detrimental. Uncertainty as to the enemy's position prevailed for a long time. The low speed of the Torpedo-Boats proved to be extremely harmful. Demands concerning the installation of a built-in jamming device against enemy radar-operated fire-control and the provision of rockets able to deflect enemy radar must be met.

Athabaskan and *Haida* took part in a pre-invasion exercise code-named *Tiger* the following evening. There was no enemy activity in their area until 0200 on 27 April. Action stations were sounded when radar got an echo directly ahead of the two Tribals at a range of eight miles. The Tribals increased their speed, reducing the range to four miles. Starshell was fired, illuminating what appeared to be E-boats, but while the destroyers were training their guns, the enemy entered a fog bank and escaped. The Tribals returned to Plymouth at 0800. Shortly afterward they learned that *Ashanti* had requested to be withdrawn from the 10th DF, claiming that the Canadians were too savage in their attacks and describing them as "wild Indians" and "very blood-thirsty".

Athabaskan stood down on the night of the 27th for a well-deserved rest. All hands were weary from hard work and lack of sleep. This break would restore them for the next item on their busy schedule.

Athabaskan returns to Plymouth after the night action of 25/26 April. HMCS Haida *is on her far side.*

Athabaskan's *company
(plus a dockyard matey)
pose for what was probably
their final photo together,
April 1944*

88

Back row, l to r: PO Russell N. Knight, PO RadMech Norman Rutherford, EA (3) Donald I. Metcalfe, Stk. PO Claude A. Mancor, unidentified, Stk. PO Douglas T.L. Laurie, ERA Kenneth W. Williams, Cook (S) James Tyrie, Stk. PO Edgar E. Bieber, unidentified, unidentified.
Middle row, l to r: ERA (2) Victor H. Brighten, Shipwrt (4) Charles Young, CYS Thomas H. Goldsmith, unidentified, Stk. PO G.E. Cooper, ERA (4) Leonard K. Mumford, SBPO Robert B. Ogilvie, PO J. Yourke.
Front row, l to r: CPO E. Calverly, unidentified, EA (3) Harry B. Neaves, CPO S. Colvin (Torpedo Gunner's Mate), SyCPO Hector H. Cooper, ERA (3) John T. Shea, Chief Stk. William D. Mitchell, Lieut.-Com. John H. Stubbs, Lieut. Ralph M. Lawrence (1st Lieutenant), CERA Ernest G. Mills, ERA Walter M. Love, SyPO Joseph V.W. Veinotte, OA (2) Stephen T. Dunnell.

Lieut.-Com. John H. Stubbs with Chiefs and Petty Officers, Plymouth, 1944

Communications

Top row, l to r:
    Tel. James A. Martin, Westmount, Quebec
    Sgm. Thomas G. Eady, Welland, Ontario
    Tel. Reginald J. Watson, New York, N.Y., USA
    Sgm. William G. Stewart, Hamilton, Ontario
    Tel. Walter R. Sheppard, Vancouver, B.C.
    Tel. William S. Lambert, Montreal, Quebec

Centre row, l to r:
    Sgm. Delbert D.H. Scanlon, Toronto, Ontario
    Tel. William M. Martin, Hamilton, Ontario
    L. Sgm. Allen Ray Chadsey, Vancouver, British Columbia
    L. Sgm. Allen B. Thrasher, Toronto, Ontario
    Sgm. G. Johnstone Norris, Nelson, British Columbia
    L. Tel. Henry J. Bennetts, Esquimalt, British Columbia
    L. Tel. J.A. Emile Beaudoin, Quebec City, Quebec
    Tel. Irvin V. Amiro, Pubnico, Nova Scotia
    L. Tel. George C. Quigley, Toronto, Ontario

Bottom row, l to r:
    Coder Paul E. Soucise, Montreal, Quebec
    L. Coder Norris J. Legh, New Westminster, British Columbia
    CYS Thomas H. Goldsmith, Victoria, British Columbia
    Lieut. Douglas M. Brown, Vancouver, British Columbia
    Lieut. John W. Scott, Halifax, Nova Scotia
    Tel. Alfred T. Cross, Armdale, Nova Scotia
    Sgm. John Downey, Montreal, Quebec
    L. Coder William Hayes, Hamilton, Ontario

Signalman William G. Stewart at the 24" signal lamp.

Carrying a telescope is Chief Yeoman of Signals Thomas H. Goldsmith
Signalman Rafe G. Chadwick works the Aldis lamp

Specifications/1944

Dimensions: Length—377' overall
               355' 6" between perpendiculars
               Beam—37' 6"
               Depth—21' 6"
Draught: 9' light, 15' fully loaded
Displacement: 1990 tons (trial)

Armament: Main—six Mk XI 4.7" QF guns firing 50-lb shell,
           on three twin CP Mk XIX mountings
           (maximum elevation 40°).
           Two hundred rounds per gun (low angle ammunition)
           plus fifty rounds of starshell.
           High Angle—two 4" guns on a twin HA/LA mounting,
           four 2-lb "M" pom poms on a quadruple mounting,
           twelve Oerlikon 20-mm guns on six twin mountings,
           two Lewis and two Bren .303" machine-guns.

Torpedoes—single quadruple, centre-line mounting (power-operated) for four 21" Mk IX torpedoes.
Depth Charges—single set of stern rails, two depth charge throwers, forty-six depth charges.

Complement: Wartime—254 officers and men.

Machinery: Propulsion— two sets of Parsons single reduction geared turbines, 44,000 SHP, designed speed 36 knots, trial speed 30 knots.
Boilers—three Admiralty three-drum water tube boilers, working pressure 300 lbs per sq.in. at 620°F.
Oil Fuel—524 tons
Endurance— 5700 nautical miles at 15 knots
3200 nautical miles at 20 knots

Athabaskans at ease

Communications, l to r: Bill Hayes, George Quigley, Bill Stewart, Del Scanlon, Al Cross, Walt Sheppard, and Reg Watson. The four-barrelled two-pounder pom pom and a twin Oerlikon are visible behind them.

Athabaskan's three sister ships at Greenock. Photo taken by J. Winnick of HMCS Haida.

Athabaskans at ease:

*Sunning on the way home to Plymouth after a Channel patrol, March '44.
Back row, l to r: Sub-Lieut. (E) R.I.L. Annett, Surg.-Lieut. W.B. Wallace, Lieut. R.B. Hayward, Lieut. (E)
T.D. Izard. Front row, l to r: Lieut. J.G. Dykes, Lieut. W. Clark, Lieut. J.W. Scott, Lieut.-Com. D. Lantier.*

*Athabaskan's Captain's cutter forms
a backdrop for Able Seaman J.F. Andre Audet*

l to r: Isabel Robinson
Sgm Rafe Chadwick
Sgm Bill Stewart
Sarah Johnson

AS Raymond Miller
L/Tel Emile Beaudoin
Devonport Dockyard

Rafe Chadwick on Nelson's
Monument, Trafalgar Square,
London

Left: Sgm. D. McGrath stands in front of signal flag locker.

Right: Mess deck scene in Athabaskan. Telegraphists J.B. O'Connell, A.T. Cross, and W.S. Lambert enjoy a mug of cocoa. Note personal belongings stowed behind them.

Below: Sgm. W.G. Stewart in his Arctic duffel coat.

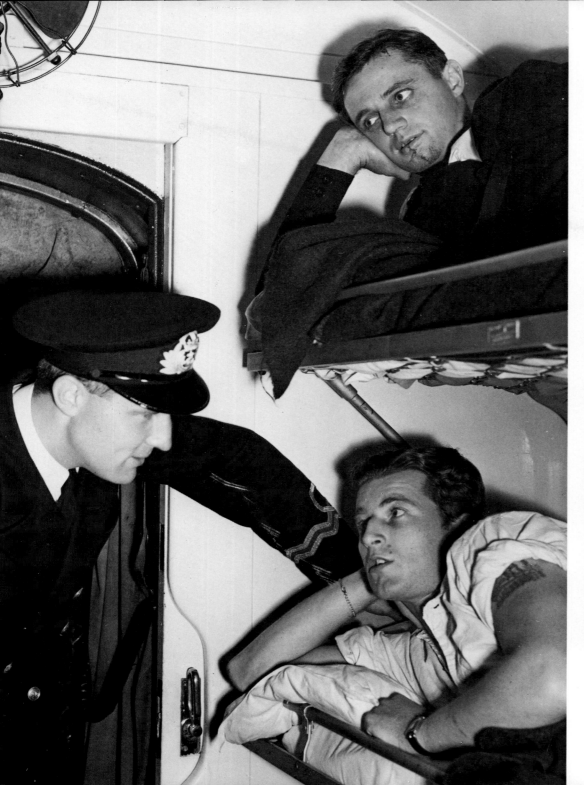

Two signalmen about to go ashore on leave in South Shields, W. E. Connolly and W.G. Stewart.

Surgeon-Lieutenant W.B. Wallace speaking with two survivors from the 27 August glider-bomb attack on Athabaskan, September 1943.

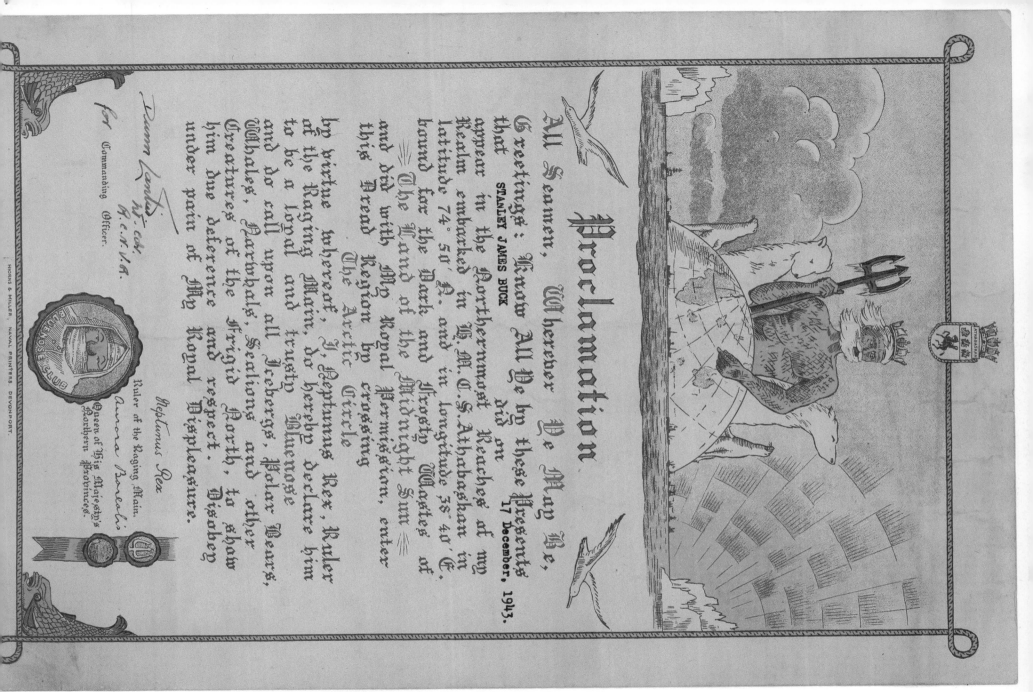

The coveted Bluenose Award, issued to those aboard Athabaskan *when she sailed into Arctic waters.*

Above. Top row, l to r: Able Seamen Herman C. Sulkers, Maurice Waitson, Ordinary Seaman R.F. Moore, Able Seamen John O. Gordon, unidentified, Raymond L. Roberts, Leading Seaman Joseph W. L'Esperance. Bottom row, l to r: Able Seamen Vincent L. Myette, R. Ray Meloche, (Victor Millar?), Arthur E. Barrett, Eugene M. Fuller.

Left. Top row, l to r: Able Seaman (Daniel H. McLean?), John W. Fairchild, (Norman V. Ryan or Ordinary Seaman Paul V. Bandick?), Louis Ledoux. Bottom row, standing, l to r: Able Seamen Samuel M. Fillatre, George C. Howard, Lester B. McKeeman, Ordinary Seaman Joesph R. Miller, Able Seamen Walter B. Saunders, Earl H. Sanderson, R. Ray Meloche, J.S. Capson, G.J. Parsons. Kneeling: Petty Officer J. Yourke.

September 1943, No. 3 Dry Dock, Devonport.
Back row, l to r: AB Stanley J. Clarke, (AB Raymond L. Roberts?), AB Harold L. Fleming, PO Tel. Donald A. Lynch, LS Joseph W. L'Esperance,
AB J.O. Gordon, unidentified, AB Francis L. Sampson, L Stk. William McGregor, AB Vincent G. Corbiere.
Front row, l to r: AB Hibert J. Peart, unidentified, PO E. Calverly, CPO James E. Evans, (AB Lloyd E. or John Edwards), LS M.A. Jennings.

The engine-room staff of Athabaskan *in September 1943. Standing, l to r: Stk. PO W. Berry, Stk. (1) Edwin A. Polson, L. Stk. C.J. Brick, L. Stk. Leonard W. Jako, Stk. (1) C. Faulkner, Stk. Wm. Cripps, unidentified, ERA (5) Wm. S. Howard, unidentified, Stk. (1) Henry Stark, unidentified, Stk. (1) P.A. Woolley, Stk. (1) Harry Thompson, Stk. (1) J.C.M. Guy Theriault, Stk. PO Douglas T.L. Laurie, Stk. PO J. Derby. Sitting, l to r: Stk. PO G.E. Cooper, Chief Stk. Wm. D. Mitchell, ERA (3) Walter M. Love, Sub-Lieut. W. McBride, Lieut. (E) J.B. Caldwell, ERA (3) John T. Shea, Chief ERA Ernest G. Mills.*

H.M.C.S. ATHABASKAN

SECTIONS

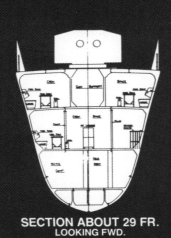

SECTION ABOUT 29 FR.
LOOKING FWD.

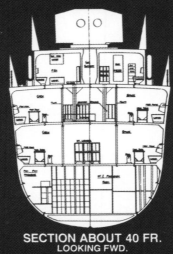

SECTION ABOUT 40 FR.
LOOKING FWD.

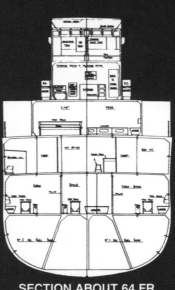

SECTION ABOUT 64 FR.
LOOKING FWD.

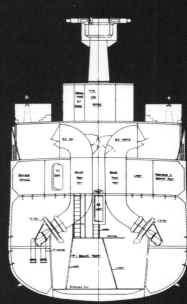

SECTION ABOUT 76 FR.
LOOKING FWD.

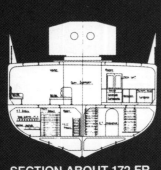

SECTION ABOUT 172 FR.
LOOKING AFT.

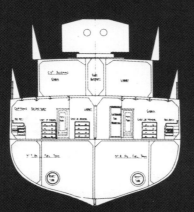

SECTION ABOUT 155 FR.
LOOKING AFT.

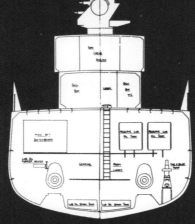

SECTION ABOUT 138 FR.
LOOKING AFT.

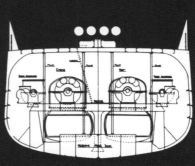

SECTION ABOUT 118 FR.
LOOKING AFT.

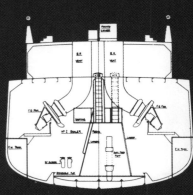

SECTION ABOUT 98 FR.
LOOKING FWD.

Chief Yeoman of Signals Thomas H. Goldsmith semaphores, observed by Lieutenant-Commander John Stubbs.

CAMOUFLAGE

HMCS *Athabaskan* as she was before her last battle. She is wearing the camouflage pattern that she carried through most of her career. This was designed for the British war- built "emergency class" destroyers.
The Canadian Tribals, though of pre-war design, were laid down and built during wartime, and so were painted in a modified version. *Athabaskan* did carry another scheme at intervals during her brief career, both before refit (see pages 33 and 36) and after (see page 112).

Athabaskan at speed
Bay of Biscay

Chapter Nine

Journey's End

THE 10TH DESTROYER FLOTILLA'S situation report at 1200 on Friday, 28 April was far from satisfactory. The action between Force 26 and the enemy three nights before, although very successful, had created some temporary problems. *Ashanti* and *Huron* had damaged themselves during the battle and were subsequently laid up for vital repairs for several days. *Tartar* was undergoing a short refit and was still unavailable. The absence of these ships left the 10th DF with less than half its offensive power; the brunt of responsibility fell on the shoulders of *Haida* and *Athabaskan*.

At 1500 the twin Tribals were ordered to two hours' steaming notice, arousing a vociferous reaction from the ships' companies. They were expecting some relief from the past few weeks of constant pressure, lack of sleep, and little recreation, and their arguments seemed to be well justified.

'Who the hell do they think we are?'

'Those guys at HQ don't know if it's punched or bored.'

'What kind of a war do they think they're running?'

'My name's Simpson, not Samson!'

'Gad, man. I could sleep for a whole week.'

Many Athabaskans had gone ashore before the warning notice to relax in a variety of ways. Some made a bee-line for their favourite pubs for a glass of scrumpy, some headed for the dance halls, and others went to movie theatres. It was in one of the latter, toward evening, that Stoker John J. Dolan saw, flashed on the screen, 'All members of *Athabaskan* return to your ship.'

'God Almighty!' he muttered. 'They can't leave us alone for five minutes!'

At the same time, in the seamen's mess of *Athabaskan*, a crowd of sailors were watching the tail-end of the movie *Wake Island*. They appeared to be contented, but the thought of another night patrol certainly didn't sit too well with them.

An enterprising Athabaskan had painted the name "Canada House" on the Canadian Tribals' mooring buoy, and it was from this buoy that *Athabaskan* and *Haida* slipped their lines at 2000. They had been berthed side by side for several hours, permitting sociable visits between the two companies, who were a closely-knit body of men, welded by the bonds of comradeship, language, and the threat of danger. They understood one another completely and were united in tackling the job that had to be done. When *Athabaskan* and *Haida* sailed that night, they went forth as sisters, with a spirit between them which two ships of war had rarely experienced before.

As they slowly separated, *Athabaskan's* pet cat made one last vain effort to jump aboard *Haida*. 'For some strange reason,' said *Haida's* Petty Officer Cook George H. Goodwill, 'it had been coming over to our ship, and every time we gently tossed it back. As the distance between our ships increased, the cat poised to try again but hesitated. As I waved goodbye to MacAvoy and Manson* of *Athabaskan*, they grabbed the cat to stop it from falling in the water. Someone behind me said, "That's not a good sign."'

The two Tribals left their moorings and took up position in line ahead with *Haida* leading. They moved downstream fairly quickly. Sporadic waves and signals from ships and shore marked their departure. They steered to port of Drake's Island, past the rows of grey houses and buildings of Plymouth, then out into the Sound. On shore, people, cars, and buses were moving about. Couples were strolling across the Hoe enjoying the balmy night air, oblivious to the shouts and screams of young children. The soft glow of the evening suggested peace with the world. Overhead, keeping their constant vigil, were the barrage balloons, straining at their cables. Sir Francis Drake's statue stood proudly on its podium and smiled approvingly on the scene as the Canadian warships hastened toward the harbour gate. In a few minutes they had passed through the gate into the Channel. This was their stomping-ground, and it was here that they were to hunt the enemy destroyers, pursue them, engage them, and finally destroy them in a bold effort to clear the treacherous waters for D-Day.

Tonight's commitment was another *Hostile* operation, to be carried out by the 10th Minelaying Flotilla with the two Canadian Tribals in support. A minefield was to be laid approximately ten miles north-east of Ile de Batz, and the Tribals were to go on an east-west patrol about twenty-three miles north/north-east of Ile de Batz, in order to prevent any interference by the enemy while the operation was being carried out. The fast minelayers had

*Petty Officer Cook Gerald W. MacAvoy and Cook John L. Manson.

proceeded to their destination earlier so that they could lay their mines in total darkness and turn for home by the early hours of the 29th. The weather was ideal for the operation: a clear sky, a waning moon, a north/north-west wind at force 3, visibility about two miles, and a smooth sea with a low swell.

As *Athabaskan* and *Haida* pressed onward to their rendezvous position the current watch closed up to defence stations. They had done this many times before and it was accepted as routine procedure, but tonight—tonight it was somehow different. There was a strange tension in the air that they hadn't felt on previous patrols. Nervous bursts of laughter could be heard as duties were carried out in the various stages of readiness.

Some Athabaskans, available and waiting in the seamen's mess, were filling in the time playing cribbage, writing letters, repairing uniforms, arguing back and forth, or just quietly meditating.

Able Seaman Harry C. Blinch was tidying up his locker; he glanced now and then at his favourite poem, which he had attached to the inside of the door. He almost knew the words by heart; they were the lyrics from Joyce Kilmer's well-known poem "Trees". An incongruous prelude for a man about to go into battle perhaps, but no doubt Able Seaman Blinch was thinking about the majestic forests near his home in British Columbia. On the bridge Lieutenant-Commander Stubbs was discussing the possibility of enemy action with his First Lieutenant, Ralph M. Lawrence, and his Navigation Officer, Lieutenant Robin B. Hayward. 'I hope they come out,' he said, 'because we're ready and willing.' Occasionally he would disappear into his sea cabin below the bridge, and return again to resume the conversation.

Deep down in the engine-room Lieutenant Theodore D. Izard was checking the logbook. During rare inactive moments he permitted himself the luxury of thinking about his wife Pam, now safely settled with his parents in Victoria. They had met and married in Plymouth barely six months before, and now she was on the other side of the world. 'It shouldn't be long before *Athabaskan* goes to Canada,' he pondered. 'Admiral Nelles said it would be soon, and then we'll have a real honeymoon. Boy! What a day that'll be.'

At 2200 Leading Telegraphist Oswald "Ozzie" R. Burkholder had been making his way through Devonport Dockyard to join *Athabaskan* at No. 5 jetty. He had been on a special course for three weeks in London and was now returning wearily home. He was challenged by two members of the Shore Patrol who wanted to know where he was going. 'You're adrift,' they said, 'she's gone hours ago.'

'Damn,' muttered the Canadian. 'Now I'll have to find a place to sleep.'

'Never mind,' said one of the Shore Patrols. 'The Church Army hostel will fix you up. Turn right at the main gate, bear left, first turn on your right, and you can't miss it.' Burkholder, in all likelihood, would have been on duty in the after wireless telegraphy office of *Athabaskan* if his train had not been delayed.

By 0200 on the 29th the two Canadian Tribals had reached their allotted position and commenced patrolling at sixteen knots on a mean course of 260°. Radar plotting conditions were unstable, despite the excellent weather, and all watches were alert for any sight or sound of the enemy. A signal from HQ Plymouth indicated that two enemy ships had been detected, proceeding westward at twenty knots, between St. Malo and Roche Douvres. This information was attributed to Admiral Rene Georgelin and his men of the French Maquis forces, who were keeping the surviving ships of the German 4th Torpedo Boat Flotilla, *T-24* and *T-27*, under close surveillance at St. Malo, and who notified London of the ships' departure.

At 0258 these vessels were picked up by radar, now in a position north-east of Morlaix and still moving westward. As they continued to move toward *Athabaskan* and *Haida*, the two Canadian Captains planned their battle strategy. A second signal from HQ Plymouth at 0307 ordered the two destroyers to proceed south-west at full speed. Without further prompting they altered course to 225°, steaming at maximum speed to intercept the enemy. By this time there was no doubt in the minds of all the Tribals that they were going to have the opportunity for a repeat performance of the battle fought on the night of 25/26 April. All hands were now at action stations and ready for the confrontation with the enemy.

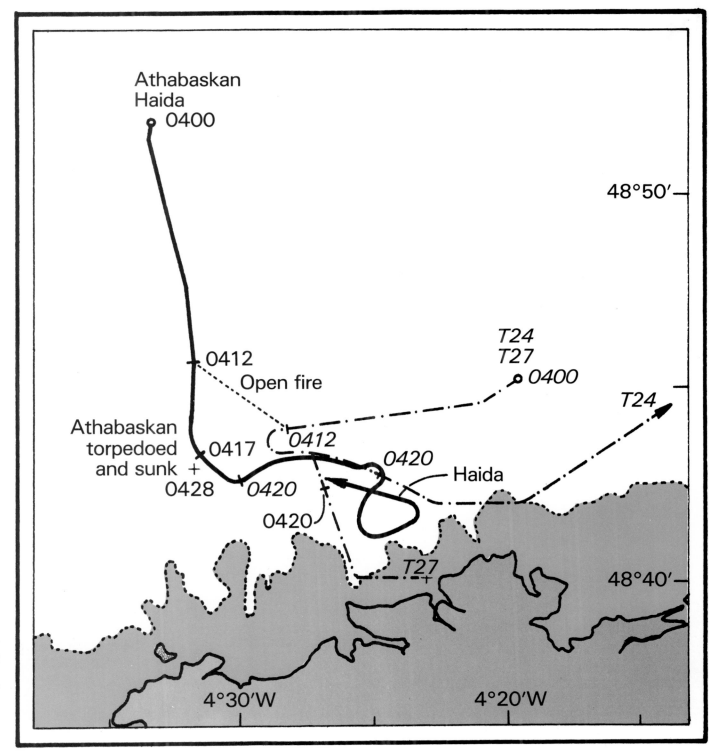

Athabaskan
Haida
0400

48°50′

T24
T27
0400

0412
Open fire

T24

0412

Athabaskan
torpedoed
and sunk +
0428

0417

0420

0420

Haida

0420

T27 +

48°40′

HMCS ATHABASKAN'S
LAST PATROL, 29 April 1944

All times are Zone-2

4°30′W

4°20′W

HMCS Athabaskan's *Last Fight by war artist Thomas H. Beament.*

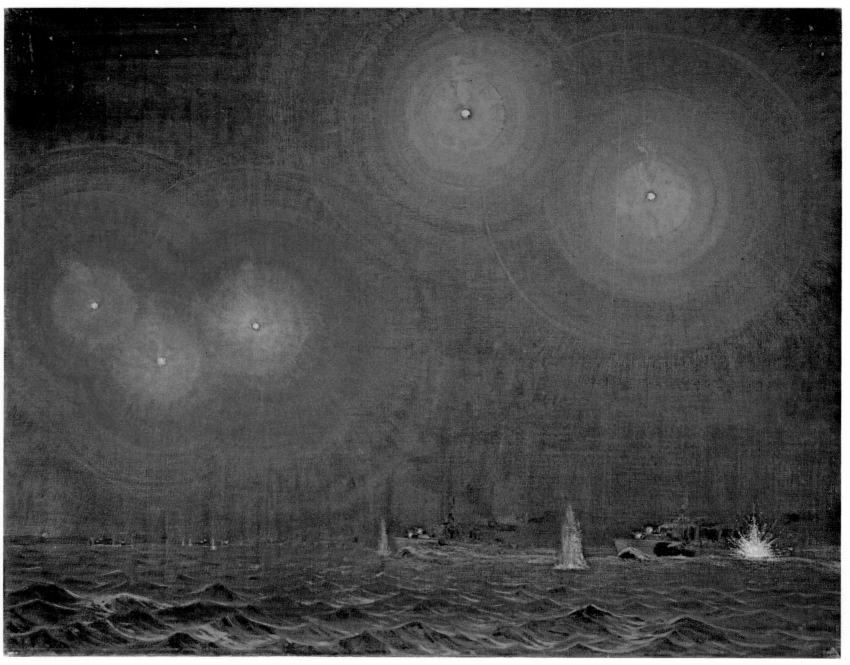

At 0332 the Tribals' course was changed to 205°, and was adjusted at 0343 to 180°.

The two opposing forces were now on converging courses and contact appeared imminent. *Athabaskan's* radar detected an echo bearing 133° at fourteen miles which was confirmed by *Haida* at 0400. Course was adjusted to keep the enemy ships 45° on the port bows and at 0412 *Haida* opened fire with starshell at a range of 7300 yards. Two minutes later *T-24* and *T-27* were sighted moving westward bearing 115°.

Able Seaman C. Owen "Digby" Deal was standing by *Athabas-kan's* "Y" gun when he received an order from the bridge to proceed to "B" gun, after being relieved by Leading Seaman John R. Kobes. Digby was a starshell specialist and no doubt his services were needed forward. 'As I made my way past the bridge,' he recalled, 'Captain Stubbs kept urging me on:'

'C'mon Digby,' he yelled, 'get the lead out, we gotta get cracking.' When I reached "B" gun, he called again. 'Digby, are you on the gun? — Then take the bearing and proceed with our starshell pattern.' That's all I was waiting for, because I knew the drill just like the palm of my hand. In seconds we had the whole sky lit up like real daylight.

The two German destroyers were brightly illuminated. The range was 7000 yards. *Athabaskan* and *Haida* opened up with all guns as the enemy swung away desperately to the east, firing main armament and torpedoes as he ran, and seeking temporary shelter by laying a smoke screen. A spread of six torpedoes was launched by *T-27*, but they all ran in the wrong direction, greatly endangering her sister ship. *T-24* managed to get a spread away too, but three of these ran in the wrong direction!

At 0417 the Canadian Tribals, steaming in line ahead about four cables apart, altered course 30° to port to avoid the torpedoes, maintaining their volume of fire as they manoeuvred to the new position. *Athabaskan* seemed to be on the receiving end of the enemy's fire; starshell was bursting over her and salvoes whined through her rigging, splashing in the water about her. Lieutenant-Commander Dunn Lantier, as radar officer, was informed by his radar operator that there were two objects starboard quarter, travelling at high speed. The close station-keeping and the speed of the radar blips indicated the presence of E-boats. (*T-24* and *T-27*

were taking evasive action on the *port* side.) Thirty seconds afterward, when *Athabaskan* had almost completed her turn to the new course, she was struck astern on the starboard side.

John Laidler, a radar operator, was the first man to leave the ship. He was blown overboard by the force of the explosion. When he rose to the surface of the water, coughing and choking, *Athabaskan* was 300 yards away and still moving. Laidler found a Kisbie buoy and hung on to it grimly.

The explosion was most probably caused by a torpedo fired by one of the E-boats on *Athabaskan's* starboard side. The powerful blow wrecked "X" and "Y" guns, decimated their crews, and started a fierce fire. *Athabaskan's* propulsion gear was also damaged, so that she lost way as she steered to port, and eventually lay dead in the water.

Meanwhile, *Haida* continued the chase, pouring rapid fire on the fleeing enemy. From her bridge Commander De Wolf was following the quickly changing scene. The first word he got from Lieutenant-Commander Stubbs after *Athabaskan* was hit read: 'We seem to be badly damaged aft.' There was a burst of gunfire from the enemy ships as they sighted the burning *Athabaskan* and attempted to finish her off. Then *Haida's* Torpedo Control Officer turned to his Captain and asked, 'Why don't we make smoke?'

'That makes sense,' he replied.

Soon *Haida* was belching forth white clouds of chemical smoke, providing a temporary screen for *Athabaskan* from the enemy's concentrated fire. *Haida* steered between the stricken ship and the enemy as she laid her protecting blanket, meanwhile pressing the attack home with vigor. She obtained her first hit at 0418, and at 0422 the two enemy vessels parted company; *T-24*, badly hit, dashed to the east, while *T-27* broke away to the south with *Haida* in hot pursuit.

While *Athabaskan* drifted helplessly on the Channel swells, her men struggled valiantly to save her. The fierce fire at the stern, fed by exploding ammunition, began to spread. Smoke and flames climbed high into the sky, revealing her position to the enemy. *Haida's* smoke screen was a partial palliative for the situation, but it failed to hide her sister ship completely. So *Athabaskan* became a target for shore batteries, E-boats, and the fleeing *T-24* and *T-27*.

There was no panic aboard the battered Canadian Tribal. Damage Control parties were at their stations assessing the damage, and a steady stream of reports and orders flowed to and from the bridge:

'Torpedo hit near the gearing room. Heavy damage aft. "X" and "Y" guns smashed. Steering gear out of action, Sir.'

'After pump shattered. Forward pump sent for, Sir.'

'Try the after steering position.'

'After steering out of action and the ship is flooding in the stern.'

'Turn out the seaboats but don't lower them. Haida will take us in tow later.'

'Turn torpedo tubes inboard and secure.'

'Torpedo tubes secured, Sir.'

'Prepare to be taken in tow.'

After this order Lieutenant-Commander Dunn Lantier requested permission to clear "B" gun of starshell. Permission granted, "B" gun was fired.

It was Athabaskan's last round.

The seventy-ton pump was by this time in position amidships and was almost ready to commence its vital job. The feedline was hoisted overboard and several men made their way aft to help quench the raging flames. Others, burned and stunned by the initial blast, were ordered forward to seek help. On the bridge Lieutenant-Commander Stubbs was handling the situation calmly, but he must have been worried. Athabaskan was settling deeper into the water and her time seemed to be running out. Finally, reluctantly, he gave the order: 'Prepare to abandon ship! All hands stand by their Abandon Ship Stations!' The men had begun to proceed slowly to their respective stations, scarcely able to believe the order they had just been given, when suddenly it happened.

Approximately ten minutes after the first hit, Athabaskan was ripped asunder by a torpedo just abaft the break of the forecastle, starboard side. First Lieutenant Ralph Lawrence, on his way to the bridge, was killed instantly. A split second later, Athabaskan's after magazine, fuel tanks, and high-pressure steam supply combined to create a giant blowtorch, shooting flames skyward with a terrible roar. Firebricks, gratings, piping, steel plates, and other debris were hurled high into the air by the blast. Men were dashed to the decks or blown into the water by the force of the scorching convulsion.

Crews on the fast minelayers returning to Plymouth from the Hostile operation reported seeing a white cloud of smoke from thirty miles away. Stoker Ernest Takalo was lying on Athabaskan's deck facing the bridge section, and the flash was so bright that he could see brush marks in the paint on the steel plating. Lieutenant William Clark, who was climbing down from the bridge to the signal deck, was engulfed in flames and blown over the side. Observers on Haida, still pursuing the enemy, saw the bright light and heard the explosion from five miles away. With one voice they gasped, 'My God—it's Athabaskan!'

From No. 1 boiler aft, Athabaskan was a blazing inferno. Burning oil showered down upon the decks while the confused sailors tried dazedly to shield themselves.

It was then that Lieutenant-Commander Stubbs gave his final command as he stared at the devastation around him: 'Abandon ship. All hands abandon ship.' Ordinary Seaman James O. Aikins had been on duty in the Carpenter's Shop when someone peered through a porthole and told him to prepare to abandon ship. He tried the deck door, but it was jammed tight, so he turned and raced through the seamen's mess and reached the passage-way. From the starboard side he ran across to the port side, reaching No. 2 boiler room watertight door just as the explosion erupted. Superheated steam shot up from the boiler room, completely engulfing him. He tried to shield himself with his hands, and they became terribly burned. The blast tossed him against the guardrail, where he hung momentarily before dropping into the cold waters of the Channel.

Leading Seaman Victor A. Bushie was at the range finder on the bridge with Lieutenant Jack W. Scott when he was ordered to go forward and help to rig for towing. He was working on the forecastle when the explosion came. 'It was like a huge steam locomotive crashing through a large, plate-glass window,' he remarked later. He was blown into the water complete with heavy sea boots, duffle coat, steel helmet, and life-preserver. He remembers that, as he struggled to get rid of his helmet and boots, 'I looked back and saw our ship ablaze. I knew it was the end of her.'

Stoker Robert B. Gracie was on duty in No. 1 boiler room during the heat of the battle, oblivious to the action going on above. The first sign of trouble came when the lights went out. Emergency lighting came on, and soon afterward Stoker Petty Officer Edgar E. Bieber hollered down a port hatch, 'Abandon ship.'

Stoker Gracie and his shipmates moved like greased lightening when they heard that frightening order, and they emerged on deck in record time; seven seconds was safe maximum time limit. From a boiler room temperature of 90°F, the stokers soon found themselves swimming in water about 55°F. The shock effect was traumatic, but the bold Athabaskans gamely struggled away from their doomed ship. Stoker Gracie swam about a hundred feet away and prayed that he was clear of the mast which was beginning to fall toward him—thankfully, he was safe. Then he felt an odd sensation in his right leg. Wondering if it had been smashed or otherwise injured, he carefully felt down with his hand, and to his joy and relief discovered that he had simply lost one of his boots during the fast exit.

Meanwhile, the fire on *Athabaskan* continued to rage, and she began to assume a dangerous cant as her stern sank deeper into the water. Chief Petty Officer William D. Mitchell was still aboard, and he had ugly visions of going down with his ship. He was wounded in both legs, and pinned to the main deck by wreckage; help seemed far away. Suddenly Able Seaman Donald W. Newman and Leading Signalman Allen B. Thrasher appeared out of the smoke to lend a helping hand. They freed the injured chief petty officer and slid him gently over the side. Able Seaman Newman yelled apologetically as Mitchell hit the water, 'That's all we can do for you.'

Able Seaman Russell E. Phillips was in a similar predicament. He was in the group trying to launch *Athabaskan's* cutter, which had jammed in its chocks. When he crawled underneath to investigate, it suddenly moved and fell on him, breaking an arm and dislocating a shoulder. For a few anxious moments he thought it was the end, but he too was rescued by shipmates, and shortly thereafter found himself floating in the water.

Able Seaman Roy A. Westaway was at his Abandon Ship station when the big explosion erupted. A Carley float fell on him, trapping him beneath its heavy weight. Fortunately, his call for help was answered by Chief Petty Officer Evans, who extricated him. Offering a steady hand to the apprehensive young seaman, who was still in his late teens, Evans ordered Westaway to jump into the water at once.

Able Seamen Samuel M. Fillatre and Lester B. McKeeman of "A" gun refused to leave the forecastle until they got their gun captain, Leading Seaman George J. "Buck" Parsons, safely over the side.

The weight of the water pouring into *Athabaskan's* compartments had now dragged her down to the point where she was almost perpendicular. The last men to leave were sliding down her bow into the chill water.

Able Seaman John Laidler, holding tightly to his Kisbie buoy, watched *Athabaskan* through her final ordeal. He could hear the sounds of her destruction, as ruptured watertight bulkheads caved in under the deadly weight of water, and machinery tore away from normally secure bedplates. The sound was almost human to him; it was like watching a friend dying in agony. She had guarded and protected him from the very beginning, and now he could do nothing to save her. Sad, and choked with emotion, Laidler turned his face against the buoy.

Many strange noises echoed from the ship. As the stricken destroyer canted slowly to a vertical position, all loose gear and equipment began to fall from their normal places. Sounding like stones and boulders cascading down the side of a mountain, pots and pans, tools, boxes, and other paraphernalia clattered and banged as they slid and tumbled. Two of the Athabaskans floating near the foundering ship could hear the racket quite clearly, and paused briefly in their escape to listen.

Suddenly, above the cacaphony, came a loud and very distinctive crash. 'There goes the piano,' shouted one of the seamen to his friend. And there wasn't much doubt about it. Loosened from its deck lashings, the heavy ship's piano, located in the forward section of the seamen's mess, had broken free and crashed with a resounding musical roar onto the now horizontal No. 1 watertight bulkhead.

In a matter of seconds, *Athabaskan* had vanished from sight, going to her last resting place without fuss or complaint. There was little suction of the water as she slid beneath the waves, and not much wreckage marked the position where she sank.* Her intense fires, now quenched by the cold water, left only a haze of smoke on the still night air.

Except for clusters of bobbing life-jacket lights spread over a wide area, the scene appeared quiet, desolate, and forlorn.

Athabaskan lies in position 48° 43' North, 04° 32' West, about five miles north/north-east of Ile de Vierge.

Chapter Ten

Brave Partner

HMCS Haida *with HMCS* Huron *(stern visible to left) and HMS* Black Prince, *April 1944.*

WHILE *ATHABASKAN* WAS ENDURING her agony, *Haida* lost no time in pursuing the enemy ships, which had fled in separate directions. Harrassed by the Canadian Tribal's fire, *T-24* sped eastward while *T-27* made off to the south. *Haida* had registered her first hit on the enemy at 0418, and she continued to concentrate her rapid fire on *T-27*, scoring frequent hits.*

Faced with a rapidly changing situation, Commander De Wolf decided to concentrate on *T-27* and ordered all fire to be directed onto the fleeing ship. Salvo after salvo was rewarded with a succession of hits and it soon became evident from her erratic return fire that she was in deep trouble.

Suddenly, in the heat of battle, *Haida* was illuminated by a strange bright light, which was followed by a rumbling noise astern. Her busy men above deck paused momentarily to look aft at the apparation. It was far brighter than standard starshell and cast an ominous reflection on a rising column of white smoke.

'My God!' the Haidas cried in sudden, terrible understanding. 'There goes *Athabaskan!*'

Able Seaman David Gold was stunned by the awful sight, and he gazed in disbelief. 'We're next for sure,' he groaned to his shipmates. It was a frightening moment for everyone in the frantic chase to bring the enemy to bay. The distance between the two ships was closing quickly, and *T-27* was beginning to show the effects of *Haida's* devastating fire. Flames were beginning to appear in her hull and superstructure as the fleeing enemy came dangerously close to the French coast. Suddenly, without warning, she turned toward *Haida* in a bold attempt to escape the trap. But then *T-27* slowed and stopped completely, leaning to port at an ever-sharper angle. The grim, rocky shoals of Finistere had snared the quarry, *Haida's* accurate gunfire helping to bring swift retribution for the loss of *Athabaskan*.* Realizing that further action was pointless, and that *T-24* was too far away to overtake, Commander De Wolf ordered all fire to cease, and *Haida* proceeded at once to

the position where *Athabaskan* had stopped. His next signal to HQ Plymouth was painfully terse: '*Athabaskan* has blown up.' The time was 0428.

As *Haida* approached the fateful area, Commander De Wolf became concerned about the wreck of *Athabaskan*. Was she still afloat, and if so, in what condition? Could she be wallowing just below the surface of the Channel as a possible danger to her sister ship? Had anyone survived that horrifying explosion? These and other questions crossed the worried Captain's mind as he cautiously advanced to the scene. Disregarding the possible presence of enemy ships, he ordered his Illumination Officer to fire one starshell for a better look at the situation. It revealed nothing. Suddenly they sighted the bobbing life-jacket lights of scores of Athabaskans, now desperately trying to group themselves together in the cold water of the Channel. *Athabaskan* had definitely gone. *Haida's* radar sets failed to locate any floating object whatsoever, although her asdic operator could clearly detect the motion of water created by the struggling survivors.

As an encore to her victory, *Haida* commenced a mission of mercy, and a rapid stream of orders followed in quick succession: 'Steer to the centre of the largest group.—Rig for scramble nets.—Cast off Carley floats.—Lower the whaler.—Lower the cutter.—All available men on deck for rescue.—Sick Bay prepare for survivors. —We'll stop for fifteen minutes.'

Like a mother hen gathering her brood, *Haida* eased slowly and gently into the mass of struggling seamen and stopped. For those on the lee side, it was comparatively easy to climb aboard, but for those on the other side, it was a different story. A light wind was causing *Haida* to drift faster than the men could swim to her, and rescue seemed beyond their grasp. The friendly ship's propellers were put in motion to manoeuvre closer, but the cries from astern of 'Stop the engines!' warned the bridge that men were being drawn into the deadly clutches of the screws.

---

*During a lull in the action, Commander De Wolf admonished several men for failing to wear their protective hats, little realizing that his own had been blown off by a gun blast, and he was only wearing the inner band!

*T-27, commanded by *Kapitanleutnant* Gotzmann, ran aground at Meneham, off Kerlouan. A salvage operation by the 24th German Minesweeping flotilla failed. On 7 May 1944 *T-27* was sunk by British Torpedo Boats.

124

Leading Cook Bernard Laurin had managed to swim clear of the scene and was floating on his back. He had swallowed oil and water during his hasty exit, which made him retch and cough. Oil on the sea is a shipwrecked mariner's curse. It burns his eyes, corrodes his lungs, and hinders movement with its evil coating. Laurin fought it with all his strength, thinking about his wife, son, and parents back home. What would they think when the news arrived? After floating and swimming for several minutes, he finally reached a crowded Carley float. His fingers felt as if they were twice their normal size, and he had difficulty hanging onto the lifeline. Lieutenant-Commander Stubbs appeared beside him briefly and said that he had been blown off the bridge. Laurin noticed that the Captain's face and hands were burned, but that he otherwise appeared in fair condition. That was the last time the young cook saw his captain. Soon afterward *Haida* came out of the darkness, and almost before he could realize it Laurin was safely aboard.

Lieutenant William Clark and Sub-Lieutenant Robert Annett were sharing a Carley float when they saw *Haida* appear out of the darkness. Both decided to swim toward her, but she was too far away to reach. They turned back toward the float, but when Clark reached a broken cork net and looked around, his companion had disappeared. There were fourteen men hanging onto the net at this point, but by dawn only four men were left. Clark then saw a nearby Carley float, swam over to it, and paddled back to pull in the remaining three survivors from the cork net.

Leading Writer Stuart A. Kettles found himself close to *Haida*, but was powerless to reach her because he was not on her lee side and he could not swim. A shipmate tried to tow him to her but it was useless. The rescuing ship just kept drifting further and further beyond their reach.

Petty Officer George W. Casswell was one of the men in the water who had drifted some distance from the main group. He was totally alone and couldn't see the rescue operation that was under way. Casswell was quickly beginning to feel the effects of the deadly, cold water. How long could he stand the paralyzing torture of its embrace? He kept repeating the Lord's Prayer over and over

German Torpedo Boat T-27, Haida's *unlucky antagonist.*

again, with intermittent foul invectives against the war, the Canadian Navy, the British Navy, and everyone else who had gotten him into this mess. Suddenly *Haida's* cutter appeared and the half-frozen sailor was hauled aboard. 'Canadian or German?' he questioned. Following the assurance that it was *Haida's* cutter, the exhausted seaman promptly collapsed.*

High up in *Haida's* Director Control Tower, Petty Officer Fred Polischuk gazed down on the dismal scene. He was torn between duty and emotion as he watched the oil-covered survivors struggling in the water. Many of them were former shipmates from his previous service aboard *Assiniboine,* and he wanted to jump into the water to help. But he had to contain himself because his station was of paramount importance to *Haida;* he was responsible for sighting the enemy and for rapid firing of guns during battle. At this critical moment E-boats were believed to be in the area and the enemy's shore batteries were not far off, but fortunately they did not open fire.

As the rescue operation continued the Haidas toiled and struggled to help their comrades. The minutes slipped by all too quickly as they worked like Trojans, ever mindful that the next instant might bring disaster. A rescue line of strong young hands and arms reached out and grasped the oil-soaked survivors:

'Atta boy, up you go.'
'Rocky—for God's sake, grab this guy!'
'Take it easy, Sir; we'll soon have you aboard.'
'Jack—get a rope around this man.'
'Art, this guy's slipping out of my hands, for Christ's sake—grab his hair!'
'C'mon men, you can make it.'
'Hurry guys. We're leaving in five minutes.'
'Swim you SOBs—swim like hell!'

The work of recovery continued, despite *Haida's* drift and the false assumption of many of the Athabaskans that they were being rescued by a German ship. The outcome of the battle was unknown to them and they feared that *Haida* had been sunk. Other exhausted Athabaskans managed to reach *Haida's* side, but were too far

*Casswell's model of *Athabaskan* went down with the mother ship, and both rest together on the sea bed in the English Channel. The model's creator, Chief Petty Officer Donald I. Metcalfe, was later listed as Missing Presumed Dead.

forward to be helped. They were severely chilled, fatigued, and injured, so pulling them up was out of the question. Fortunately, Petty Officer Thomas M. Cotterell of *Haida* heard their cries and organized a party to lower individual lines so that the survivors could be towed to the scramble nets.

From time to time Lieutenant-Commander Stubbs could be noticed moving about from float to float, offering words of encouragement to his men, urging them to sing and to keep their arms and legs in motion. At one point he drifted to within several feet of *Haida's* side and shouted his final command: 'Get out of here *Haida!* E-boats!' The youthful Lieutenant-Commander, acutely aware of the imminent danger to hundreds of men and their ship, had uttered a selfless warning of concern. At that point he might have been rescued quite handily, but he elected to stay with the remainder of his company, now dispersed over a wide area of the cold, dark Channel waters.

Those oil-sodden Athabaskans who reached the safety of their sister ship were met by energetic Haidas armed with large butcher knives who rapidly cut the men loose from life-jackets and saturated uniforms. Other willing hands wiped down their cold bodies and covered them with blankets.

Engine-Room Artificer Jack Owens of *Haida* was on deck pulling men aboard when he recognized a buddy: 'Bill! No kidding? It's really you?'

'Yea-ah,' mumbled the wet sailor. 'I used t-to s-s-st-t-tutter be-before, bu-bu-but I s-s-sure s-s-s-stut-t-ter m-more n-n-n-now.'

The fifteen minutes *Haida* had allotted for rescue work were up, but her job was far from completed. Bobbing lights, spread far and wide, indicated that many Athabaskans would never make it. They were simply too far away. On the bridge, Commander De Wolf was pacing back and forth, torn with indecision. Occasionally he stopped and leaned over the side, shouting words of encouragement to the shipwrecked men. Argument and counter-argument raced through his mind: 'How much longer can I stay? I can't leave these men to die! But what if the enemy has spotted us? What about mines and aircraft at daylight? The survivors are depending on me, but endangering the lives of my own men won't help.' It was 0510 and the first light streaks of dawn were showing to the east. Sunrise was not far away.

126

Finally the worried Captain announced that *Haida* would wait another five minutes. 'I'll warn you every minute,' he added. His compassion, bolstered with the fellowship of the sea and his strongly religious background, had won through. The Athabaskans would get a short reprieve.

Rescue operations at sea were not uncommon to Commander De Wolf. He had distinguished himself during the evacuation of Allied forces from French Channel and Bay of Biscay ports after the German Army breakthrough in May/June 1940. As Commanding Officer of *St. Laurent*, in co-operation with *Fraser, Restigouche*, and units of the Royal Navy, he was responsible for helping to save thousands of soldiers. Shortly after this evacuation on 2 July 1940, he had conned *St. Laurent* amongst the lifeboats and wreckage left by the British liner *Arandora Star* which had been torpedoed west of Ireland by a U-boat, and successfully took aboard 860 enemy nationals, mostly Italian. It was a brilliant act of seamanship on the part of the Canadian destroyer and her company, and it ultimately proved to be one of the greatest life-saving actions of the entire war.

For the Haidas, the five-minute delay seemed unending. Gun crews scanned the horizon for signs of the enemy. Stokers, engine-room artificers, and seamen, far below decks, sweated and cursed the pause. 'Let's get the hell outta here,' they cried. Most of the Athabaskans could not take advantage of the reprieve, and they too cursed as the minutes flashed by.

Able Seaman C. Owen "Digby" Deal was one of the lucky survivors to be hauled aboard during the final fleeting moments. He had helped to get Lieutenant Jack Scott safely on deck and was now home free himself. 'Cut his gear and take him below!' ordered a Petty Officer.

'Are you kiddin'?' yelled the seaman. 'My friend Moar's down there.' In an instant he was over the side, quickly scrambling down between the men being pulled up. He reached a Carley float and began to tie a line to Able Seaman Raymond "Pony" Moar, who was sprawled, moaning, on the float. Moar's back had been broken in the second explosion.

'Four! . . . Three! . . . Two! . . . One!' The mournful calls echoed throughout *Haida* as the seconds ticked on. 'Are you ready, Sir?'

Haida's *Captain, Commander H.G. DeWolf, in 1944.*

asked the First Lieutenant after the extra five minutes had passed. 'Just a little longer,' said Commander De Wolf.

Eventually the tension was broken as he reluctantly ordered, 'Slow ahead.' *Haida's* asdic operator had picked up signals astern and he assumed them to be approaching enemy craft, so Com-

Lieutenant-Commander John H. Stubbs in 1944.

mander De Wolf was compelled to abandon further rescue. Those aware that they were being deserted begged to be saved or cursed *Haida* for leaving them. Commander De Wolf had already disregarded three orders to retreat, but to remain longer would surely have been disastrous, especially as all lifeboats and Carley floats

had been lowered for use by the Athabaskans. *Haida* trembled and vibrated as her twin screws bit into the water, and soon she began to get under way. Two of her men, Petty Officer H.P. Murray and Telegraphist S.A. Turner, were still on one of the scramble nets trying to rescue the survivors. They started to climb back up, but the movement of the ship washed water heavily over their legs. The men held on tightly with both hands, but were unable to cope with *Haida's* increasing speed, and were torn loose from the net. They were last seen bobbing in the boiling wake dangerously near the ship's screws.

Able Seaman George C. Howard was swimming close to *Haida* when she began to move. Slowed down by the weight of his duffle coat, he tried frantically to get rid of it, but his arms became stuck in the sleeves. The harder he tried, the further he sank, gulping in blobs of oil and water. As *Haida* pulled away Howard's spirits fell in a welter of disappointment. He began to pray, trying desperately not to think about the cold water and his fear of drowning.

Meanwhile, Able Seaman Deal, struggling with his friend on the Carley float, had almost secured him when *Haida's* wash pitched them into the sea. 'Wait a minute,' he bellowed. 'I've almost got him.' But his calls were drowned in the noise of *Haida's* departure. Digby Deal's heroic effort in this instance earned him a year as a prisoner of war.

Able Seaman Ted C. Hewitt was sure that his life was just about finished. With one final heave he managed to grab one of *Haida's* lines, and he hung on with all his strength. Hewitt was pulled like a log through the water as the ship quickly gathered speed, but held tenaciously to the slim lifeline till strong arms hauled him up and brought him safely on board. Able Seaman Hewitt was the last of forty-two Athabaskans rescued by *Haida*.

At 0448 an order was sent from HQ Plymouth to the two Motor Torpedo Boats with the minelaying force, instructing them to proceed to rescue the *Athabaskan* survivors. *Haida* had received this signal and had passed it on to the struggling men before she departed. So when Commander De Wolf ordered all sea-boats to be lowered, he did not intend them to be manned by men from his own ship. He thought that the craft could be of some use to the surviving sailors, and certainly *Haida* could get along very well without them. But true to the tradition of the Tribals and the RCN, three of *Haida's* men took matters into their own hands.

As soon as the cutter touched the water, Leading Seaman William A. McClure, Able Seaman Jack Hannam, and Stoker William Cummings jumped in and commenced their own rescue operation. They started up the cold engine and quickly pulled away from the mother ship. Leading Seaman McClure assumed command and ordered a watchful eye for survivors. Petty Officer Casswell was the first to be picked up, followed by Able Seamen Andre Audet and Stanley J. Buck, Torpedo Gunner's Mate Charles T. Burgess, and Signalmen Thomas G. Eady and G. John Norris.

Then the cutter's engine began to vibrate and sputter. It backfired several times and suddenly quit altogether. 'Oh, no!' groaned the crew. 'Not now!' Feverishly they worked over the balky machine, trying vainly to get it running again. But months of inactivity had affected its vital moving parts, and it simply refused to fire. As the helpless craft drifted on the tide, the high hopes of both rescuers and rescued quickly evaporated. Their waning spirits were distracted momentarily when two flashing objects were sighted. As the objects floated closer to the cutter, they were seen to be survivors and were quickly hauled aboard. On closer examination, and amid howls of delight, they turned out to be Petty Officer Murray and Telegraphist Turner, who had miraculously avoided *Haida's* churning screws and had drifted out on the tranquil sea, awaiting the next turn of events. They had been rescued barely five minutes after the terrible departure from their ship.

Meanwhile, *Haida* had set course for Plymouth and was quickly leaving the grave of her sister ship far behind. *Athabaskan's* survivors had been stripped of their gear and were safely ensconced below decks. All had been wrapped in blankets and given hot grog and biscuits; the more seriously burned and injured had been taken to Sick Bay or the Captain's day cabin for treatment by the Surgeon-Lieutenant and sick berth attendants.

There was bunker oil everywhere, and *Haida* reeked with its stench. The decks were slippery as ice; steps and handrails were covered with the oil, creating a perilous passage for everyone. Every spare hand was ordered to attend to the survivors and see that they were comfortable and warm.

Far below, *Haida's* stokers were labouring to keep steam flowing to the whining twin turbines, now revving at maximum speed. In the engine-room Chief Petty Officer James Cameron surveyed the engine's numerous gauges. At one point, he stared at them in utter disbelief. 'My God!' he said to a shipmate. 'We must be doing at least thirty-five knots!'

Able Seaman John J. Carr, one of the survivors, was beginning to warm up and had started to count his blessings. Just before *Athabaskan* had sailed he had had a violent argument with Chief Petty Officer Laurent J. Bertrand about switching his action station from "Y" gun to "B" gun. Able Seaman Carr was fond of his regular position on "Y" gun because it was out of the weather. He couldn't understand why a new man should take over his comfortable spot so he objected strongly. But the Chief stood on his rank, and finally the stubborn seaman was forced to move. "Y" gun had been destroyed in the first explosion, and Carr was doubtful that any of its crew outlived the holocaust.

After checking the welfare of the Athabaskans, his own men, and the state of his ship, Commander De Wolf was finally able to repair to his cabin. The past harrowing few hours had allowed no time to rest from continuous strain. The victory over *T-27* was satisfying, but the loss of *Athabaskan* and her company heavily overshadowed *Haida's* excellent work.

Commander De Wolf wondered about young Johnny Stubbs and his men. The worried Captain harked back to peacetime days in the service when the spectre of war had seemed remote. They had been happy, halcyon days coloured with parades, special courses, winter cruises, new vistas of Canada, precious leave with loved ones, and an interesting social life. And if a man behaved himself and worked hard, there was always a chance for promotion. He remembered the youthful Stubbs as a popular lad, well known for his ability to beat any officer at the fast-moving game of squash.

Coming back to earth De Wolf remembered that he was a Senior Officer with a grim report to prepare, with precious few hours left to be completed. 'In any event,' he thought, 'the two Motor Torpedo Boats should have arrived by this time to pick up *Athabaskan's* men, and with their superior speed might even beat *Haida* back to Plymouth.'

When *Haida* had disappeared into the gloomy night, she had left a scene of utter desolation behind her. *Athabaskan*, the once proud Tribal class destroyer, had sunk to the Channel bottom and was at rest. There were few signs of her former presence, save for some Carley floats and cork net floats drifting silently on the water. Nearby, the lighthouse on Pointe de Pontusval flashed every few seconds, warning of her rocky shore. To the east, the light on Ile de Batz stood out clearly, and westward, far along Finistere's coast, Ile de Vierge's light winked out its message of caution. The silently blinking signals added a haunting note to the sombre setting. There was little hope or comfort to be gained from these sentinels on the shore as they continued to flash their muted warnings.

Haida had also left behind a large proportion of *Athabaskan's* company, now trying desperately to get and stay together. They were scattered about half a mile around on the easy swell, some swimming, some floating, and others apparently lifeless. Lights attached to their life-jackets pin-pointed their positions. *Haida* had managed to rescue forty-two survivors, and her cutter had picked up six more, but over 200 Athabaskans were still in the chill grip of the Channel.

Some had definitely gone down with the ship—there could be no doubt about it. Many of those in the lower regions of the ship had not stood a chance, and it could only be hoped that the end was mercifully quick for them. It was impossible to tell how many men had still been with *Athabaskan* when she went down. The Channel revealed nothing but a countless number of shipwrecked sailors fighting for their lives.

The Athabaskans could not at first believe that *Haida* would really leave them. After all, she was their chummy ship, and she would soon circle back, they thought. It wouldn't take long to pick up the rest of the gang, especially with daylight near at hand. And what about the Motor Torpedo Boats? They shouldn't be long in coming.

But *Haida* never returned, and the Motor Torpedo Boats never came. Plymouth Command had assumed that the latter could not arrive before dawn, and apparently the important order to proceed was scrubbed because it was felt that the Motor Torpedo Boats should not be left unsupported off the enemy coast in daylight.

For a while the Athabaskans were filled with hope and confidence—help would soon arrive to free them from their cold, oily bondage. Slowly it dawned on them that they had been deserted and would have to make it on their own. In plain language, it was sink or swim. This bitter realization was an ugly blow to morale. Cries of anger and despair echoed on the still night air. Men gave vent to heartfelt, abusive imprecations, mainly hurled at *Haida*. Rarely had seamen uttered such oaths against any ship, friend or foe. They plumbed the depths of human emotion in a turmoil of denunciations, enveloping many in their wrath. *Haida*, the Royal Canadian and Royal Navies, fathers and mothers, even God and His Son Jesus Christ did not escape their fury.

But the outburst could not last; it sapped the survivors' precious strength. Violent emotion gave way to quiet hope or absolute despair. Someone in Able Seaman Vincent L. Myette's group of survivors suggested that they should all pray. One disconsolate seaman hollered out, 'It's too late to pray now.' His voice was never heard again.

This same strange phenomenon had happened before in every sea and ocean. A shipwrecked sailor, floating on the waves with shipmates, would suddenly say, 'I've had it', or 'to hell with it', and quickly disappear from sight. The flame of hope had apparently burned out for them, taking with it the will to live. Others hung grimly on. Neither age nor physical condition indicated which way any man might react.

While some Athabaskans were giving in to the strange forces about them, many others were riding them out. One Athabaskan, standing upright on a crowded Carley float, held a flaming red flare high over his head, like the Statue of Liberty. The pathetic glow of its light created some measure of hope. Another seaman suddenly brought out a bottle of rum, and shared it with his shipmates.

Able Seaman Wilfred O. Henrickson was staunchly hanging on to the lifeline of a Carley float, but he did not know how much longer he could last. His head kept drooping into the sea, causing him to swallow oil and water. Exhausted, he was beginning to believe that life was over; there was no room on the float, and why bother any longer. But Able Seaman William B. Bint, from his spot on the float, noticed the young man's difficulties and promptly went over the side to help him. 'Take my place,' he said. 'You'll be alright.'

As the men in the various groups struggled to stay together and assist one another, attempts were made to keep flagging spirits up. Some broke into song, which lasted for about half an hour until tired voices could no longer sing. Others quietly hung on and debated what they should do next. One bunch started to talk about home and their families, and what they would think when *Athabaskan's* loss hit the news wires.

The Carley floats and cork net floats gradually became less and less crowded. As the long hours dragged on many men slipped from their holds and drifted away on the tide. Floating bodies bumped lightly against the living, adding a touch of the macabre to the scene. Gently they were pushed aside to make room for others trying to gain fresh hand holds.

Far away from the main groups, two lonely figures bobbed serenely on the Channel swells. Thirty-four year old Able Seaman Lester B. McKeeman (an old man in the eyes of his shipmates, who called him "Pappy") was supporting a young, injured sailor on his back, gamely trying to encourage the boy and sustain his spirits. They babbled about home, families, friends, shipmates, and a host of other things. Occasionally there was silence as the teen-aged Athabaskan lapsed into unconsciousness, his laboured breathing the only sign of life.

These quiet moments gave McKeeman an opportunity to wonder about possible rescue. The desperate pair had seen *Haida* come and go, and now the older man began to question his endurance. When darkness eventually gave way to dawn and the first rays of sunlight broke across the water, McKeeman's precious burden grew very still. Realizing that his young charge was dead, he slowly untangled the stiffened fingers and hands from around his neck and let the lifeless form drift silently away. 'Christ Jesus Almighty—forgive me!' sobbed the seaman. It was one of the most agonizing things he had ever had to do.

A long-service Petty Officer tried to cheer his group along by relating tales of other ships' companies in even harsher circumstances. 'I had a friend on *Matabele*,'* he said. 'They didn't stand a snowball's chance in hell of making it. At least we're not far from shore and should be picked up soon.' Whether this eager Petty Officer succeeded in his mission of cheer is debatable, but he was at least making an effort to turn thoughts away from the immediate situation.

When Leading Seaman Stanley R. Dick entered the RCNVR in 1940 he selected Gunnery School, and it was there that he met up with Instructor Petty Officer Laurent J.L. Bertrand. Right from the beginning the two men were at odds with one another. After leaving Gunnery School, Leading Seaman Dick went to sea and his feud with Laurent was forgotten.

In 1944 the young gunner was drafted to *Athabaskan*, and as he climbed the gangway to board her who should he meet but his old adversary, now a Chief Petty Officer. The long-forgotten feud erupted again as the two men faced each other. It was a strictly personal confrontation; somehow, the two individuals couldn't communicate on normal, friendly terms.

Now, in the early hours of the morning of 29 April 1944, Leading Seaman Dick found himself wearily holding on to a Carley float wondering what was going to happen in the next hour or so. He turned to speak to the oil-soaked seaman beside him, and who should face him but his old foe Bertrand. In good times and in bad the two seaman were fated to meet. But now there was neither time nor strength for verbal battles, and the long-standing quarrel suddenly seemed quite petty. The two men forgave each other and agreed to start afresh. Bertrand grew silent after expressing his regrets, and sometime later died beside his former antagonist.

As the early morning hours wore on, the Athabaskans continued to resist the cold water and its vicious coating of oil. Able Seaman John Laidler was joined on his Kisbie buoy by Able Seaman Walter Simaluk, one of the few survivors from *Athabaskan's* stern, who explained that he had been blown overboard from "Y" gun during the first explosion, but was apparently unharmed. The pair clung precariously to the buoy which helped to support them and save their waning strength.

'Johnny, what time is it?'

'How the hell would I know. Seems like we've been in the water for hours.'

Matabele, a British Tribal class destroyer, was torpedoed in the Barents Sea on 17 January 1942. She sank in two minutes and all but three of her company were frozen to death in the icy waters.

'God, this water's cold.'

'Yeah—cold enough to freeze the balls off a brass monkey.'

'Did you see the Old Man?'

'I saw him about half an hour ago. He seemed to be in fair shape.'

'Johnny, do you hear Mengoni over there trying to cheer up some young kid?'

'Yeah—the poor bastard's been crying all night.'

'Let's go over and see them.'

'Okay—grab this smoke float; they may be able to use it.'

Slowly the two men swam to the place where the voices had come from. By the time they arrived, the crying had stopped and Mengoni's familiar dialect could be heard no more. Both men were dead. They drifted quietly on the water, their signal lights still blinking. Mengoni's death was a heartbreaking blow to Laidler, for he had admired Mengoni as a first-rate seaman and had valued him as a good friend. They had shared many happy experiences from *Athabaskan's* early construction and throughout her career, and now it was all over.

Time dragged on, and Laidler and Simaluk held on to the smoke float until the sun began to beam over the horizon. Several times one of them had tried to break away and make for shore, and each time the other had held him back with quiet persuasion. The loneliness of the long night proved to be their salvation, because they were afraid of the unknown and gained inner strength by holding fast together.

Northward, far out in the Channel, *Haida's* cutter was painfully making her way toward England. After many starts and stops the tiny craft had finally settled down, her engine chugging with a steady sound that was beautiful to hear. 'With a streak of good luck, we should make it,' muttered the young skipper.

By 0730 on 29 April the first bright rays of the sun had begun to shine over the water where the Athabaskans drifted. Those fortunate enough to be squatting on Carley floats were shivering, and huddled close together in an attempt to keep warm. Others, still moving about in the water or holding on to cork floats, were also striving desperately to keep the spark of life glowing. But many, bobbing silently on the swells, would never see the sunrise again, for they were cold and lifeless. Injuries, burns, and exposure

had weakened them to the point of complete exhaustion. They had fought their last battle.

The desolate calm of the morning was suddenly broken by shouts from two or three groups: 'Look—over there!' All eyes looked to the south, where three dark objects were growing steadily larger. Five minutes passed, and the objects became recognizable as a destroyer and two smaller vessels. One of the latter parted from the others on a more northerly course, away from the Athabaskans, who were all trying to identify the approaching ships.

'I'll bet they're German Navy units.'

'No doubt about it.'

'Do ya think they'll pick us up?'

'Christ, they'd better, 'cause I won't last much longer.'

'The smaller ones look like minesweepers to me.'

'Friend or foe, I'm ready for anything.'

'Will you bastards pipe down. Let's play it by ear and see what happens.'

As the ships closed on the Athabaskans it became apparent that they were enemy ships coming to the rescue. German flags were clearly visible waving in the breeze and German commands were distinctly heard, leaving no doubt in the survivors' minds as to the origin of their rescuers. The smaller ship looked like a minesweeper, and the larger was recognized as an Elbing class destroyer. It proved to be *T-24*, which, but a few hours before, had been battling against *Haida* and *Athabaskan*. Now, she was on a mission of mercy.

Athabaskan's former antagonist carried a smaller vessel which looked like an Air/Sea Rescue launch. As the ships slowed to a halt near the largest group of Athabaskans, an officer on *T-24* called out in English through a megaphone, 'Approach, we are taking you aboard!' Then the work of rescue commenced. The smaller vessel had a fast and efficient system for picking up survivors. A rubber dinghy with a line attached was let down to the surface with one rating. He would paddle out to a survivor and take him quickly aboard, and the dinghy was then pulled back to the Air/Sea Rescue launch. When the launch had a good load of passengers they were then taken to *T-24*. The German sailors also had long-handled nets with which they were fishing any pieces of paper they saw out of the water.

Meanwhile, the minesweeper moved slowly through the water, stopping now and then to take aboard a shivering Athabaskan. The other minesweeper, which had veered northward, picked up seven Athabaskans, Able Seamen Deal and Moar, Chief Petty Officer Cook Raymond B. Stenning, Cook James Tyrie, Leading Seaman Joseph W. L'Esperance, Leading Telegraphist Emile A. Beaudoin, and Stoker Edwin A. Polson, who were trying to row toward England in a Carley float. The minesweeper then began to chase the fleeing *Haida* cutter, but abandoned the effort when the cutter entered a minefield. By the time the minesweeper rejoined the other two German ships all survivors had been picked up, so the little flotilla moved off at speed. *T-24* and the minesweepers set course for Brest while the Air/Sea Rescue launch made haste for the small fishing village of L'Aber-Wrac'h.

As soon as the shivering Athabaskans had been hauled aboard the German rescue ships they were ordered to take off their oil-soaked life-jackets and uniforms. These were stripped from their bodies and cast ignominiously into the sea, to quickly disappear from view. The loss of the life-jackets was almost a personal blow to the men, for they had sustained the weary sailors during the long night hours and had proven themselves over and over again. All Athabaskans who had survived that perilous night unanimously felt that they owed their lives to these life-jackets,* which had been issued just prior to leaving Plymouth.

The survivors picked up by the two minesweepers were taken below decks and given hot showers to remove the oil from their bodies. Most of them were too weak to stand, and lay huddled under the comforting spray of the water. Some of the German seamen, understanding their difficulties, came in under the showers and wiped the pathetic Athabaskans clean. They were then issued blankets and given macaroni with prunes, dry bread, jam, and ersatz coffee. Precious cigarettes were later distributed to the fortunate seamen, who were informed that the German ration was four per day!

---

*These new life-jackets were manufactured by the Gutta Percha Rubber Company Limited of Toronto, and were a Mae West jacket design filled with kapok material for buoyancy. The jacket was fitted with a special crotch

P.O.
Today the ships company were issued the new Canadian life belts and believe me they are quite the thing.

Excerpt from Signalman William Stewart's last letter
20 April 1944

piece to prevent injury from underwater explosions and included a special head gear for support. A flashing light attachment was fitted for visual sighting. Although somewhat cumbersome, it proved itself beyond doubt on this occasion. Further improvements were made to the design, and when HMCS *Clayoquot* was torpedoed in December 1944 the jacket demonstrated its lifesaving quality. Only seaman without life-jackets were injured by the underwater blast. Those wearing them at the same distance from the explosion were protected.

Conditions on board *T-24* are best described by Lieutenant-Commander Dunn Lantier's diary written in prison camp:

I was picked up at about 0715 and told in no uncertain terms to take off my oil-soaked clothes, including my life-jacket, which were then thrown into the water. It wasn't a happy idea but I managed to save my monkey jacket, which, although wet, didn't have much oil on it. We were then herded aft and taken below. There I was glad to see Nobby and Steve* who looked a bit worse for wear but very much alive. Our group consisted of about forty-five men and after a hot soapless shower, a cigarette, and a hot drink of sorts, all felt a little better. I managed to get a few blankets from the guards for those who were in bad shape and asked for a medical officer or sick bay attendant. Some sort of medical orderly came down later but it seemed to me that either he didn't know much or was not interested, because he did very little for the sick and wounded. I tried to ask for clothes or more blankets but met with no success whatsoever, and thus had to remain virtually naked. Not a very comforting feeling after a few hours in the cold water. By this time, I was able to get around to see everyone and cautioned them not to give out any information except name, rank, and number.

Later, two officers, who were both wearing white cap covers, came down to look us over. My first reaction was, 'what were two Captains doing aboard ship?' One disappeared and the other, who had a wounded hand, stayed behind and asked me if we had been sunk by gunfire or torpedoes. I told him I did not know and that reply apparently ended the conversation. One of the guards, a junior officer, spoke English and I asked him how come the ship had two Captains; realizing of course that only CO's wore white cap covers. He answered that the wounded one was the Captain of another Torpedo-Boat. What joy it was to know that we had been hitting the enemy ships and perhaps *Haida* had sunk one of them. This speculation did a great deal to bolster our low spirits. After the officer had left I did a bit of thinking and realized that they were in an even greater quandary as to who had sunk us. This captain seemed to wish that we had been sunk by gunfire. . . . A short time later a guard brought us a bottle of brandy with the Captain's compliments, for the wounded.

All of a sudden there was a heavy explosion off our port quarter and I was told that it was only a mine exploded by their minesweeping gear. . . . Shortly after, alarm gongs went off and we were assured that it was only *Spitfires* and that there was nothing to worry about. However, the Germans blew up their life-belts and if anything, this made us feel even more naked. Soon there was much firing from the upper deck and it sounded to me like 3-inch guns as well as 20-mm. (I later noticed that this ship carried three mountings of quadruple 20-mm.)

However, we did not seem to be attacked and this flurry passed off with little excitement.

At about noon, they brought us a sort of leek soup, warm at least, and some greyish bread. . . . It must have been about three o'clock when they opened the scuttles and we saw that the ship was coming into port. The guards had no objection to our looking out, but I must admit that there was very little to see. I did notice that there was a boom and that we were warped in by a tug. This turned out to be Brest.

*Lieutenants William Clark and Richard H. Stevenson.

*Captain
Wilhelm Meentzen
of the T-24.*

German Torpedo Boat T-24, *built by F. Schichau, Elbing.
1754 tons. Speed: 33.5 knots. Commissioned 17 December '42.
Captains: Kapitanleutnant Hofmann and Wilhelm Meentzen.
Date of loss: 24 August 1944 at Le Verdon near Bordeaux
through air attack by twenty Mosquitoes. Eighteen dead.*

Leading Seaman Stanley Dick was one of the Athabaskans who had been rescued by *T-24*. He now found himself huddled with several companions on the tiller flat messdeck, mostly naked, and vainly trying to keep warm. A young Athabaskan was beside him, shivering badly and in apparent shock. No one seemed to be concerned with the young man except Dick, who tried to comfort him. Sometime during the voyage to Brest his trembling companion died, and the body was slipped quietly over the side to the tune of a boatswain's call. It was war, the enemy was under fire, and there was no time for a formal ceremony.

The first rescued Athabaskans to land on French soil were the stragglers taken aboard the Air/Sea Rescue launch. There were twenty-eight of them in the party, all in various stages of physical and mental distress. The motor launch had made haste for the quiet Breton fishing port of L'Aber-Wrac'h, crossing the Baie des Anges to dock at the local jetty at about 0900. The forlorn Canadians were herded ashore and left under guard on the dock, waiting for further developments. Some of the French fisherfolk, who were aware of the night's action, stood by uttering words of sympathy as the Canadians were disembarked. Stoker John J. McNeil, who was badly burned and who had fought valiantly to stay alive, succumbed quietly on the quay beside his shipmates. His body lay there under a ship's blanket for a time, and was later taken to the village to be prepared for burial. The remaining Athabaskans were escorted to one of the hotels in the village and ordered to stay in the courtyard.

Under the vigilant eyes of armed guards, the prisoners waited in that little enclosure, hidden from the townsfolk and wondering about their eventual fate. The penetrating rays of the sun began to burn the oil-covered men, but when they took shelter in the shade they trembled with the cold.

An eager young French fisherman was allowed to bring fresh water and cigarettes to the men, and also to help change their clothing. Two young mademoiselles arrived later to minister to the prisoners. At one stage in their merciful mission they ran short of towels, but they continued to wipe the oil-covered faces with their white petticoats.

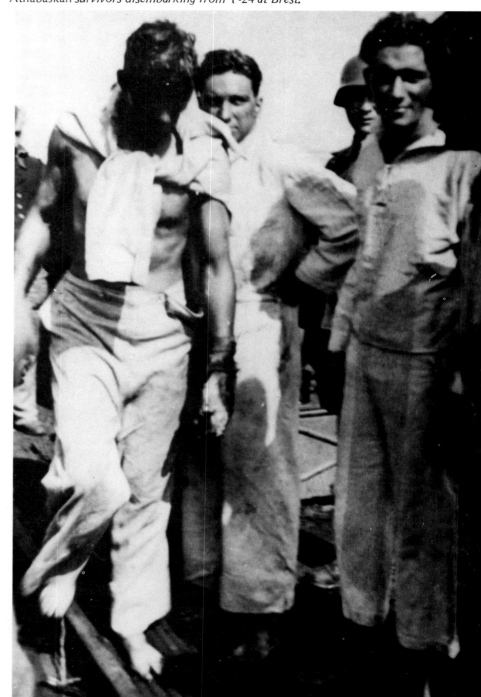

Athabaskan *survivors disembarking from* T-24 *at Brest.*

Meanwhile, far out in the Channel and making steady progress, *Haida's* cutter continued on her northward course. The cutter's balky engine had settled down to a steady rhythm and the sound of it was sweet music to the eleven seamen aboard. Later in the day the small craft was spotted by two enemy Messerschmitt *109s*, which flew in low over the cutter but did not attempt to fire and soon disappeared to the south. That brief, terrifying moment brought the dangers of their position home to the seamen, who prayed and hoped for a miracle to save them. England seemed a thousand miles away. Shared emergency rations of hard tack, malted milk tablets, candy, and chewing gum helped to sustain their flagging spirits. The course for the cutter continued at due North and the injured, tired, thirsty, and hungry band aboard repeated their prayers, finding comfort and fellowship in each other's presence.

When the main group of Athabaskans landed in Brest they were ordered to give up the ships' blankets which had been given to some of the more seriously injured men. Consequently, most of them were practically naked, bare feet burning on the hot deck plates, as they stood waiting to be escorted down the gangplanks to the quay. *Kapitanleutnant* Wilhelm Meentzen saluted the survivors as they left the ship. In a short speech he said that it was a time of war, and he hoped that there was no ill-feeling between them. As the half-naked, bedraggled Canadians struggled ashore they were met by a group of German Army and Gestapo personnel. Newsreel cameras were grinding away, capturing a graphic record of the scene. The films were no doubt soon on their way to Berlin. Apparently, it was a festive occasion for that particular group of victors; they gloated, chatted, and giggled as the pathetic prisoners disembarked.

The Athabaskans' spirit was far from quenched. One bold seaman raised his lusty voice to the crowd and shouted so that all could hear, 'Now you lousy bastards—take a good look at some real he-men!' Moments later, a Gestapo officer rushed up to one of the Canadians and berated him loudly for the bombing of Germany. He was ferocious in his attitude, but the Athabaskan stood his ground and said nothing, staring icily at the German.

Athabaskans with their German guards in the back of army trucks on the jetty.

Athabaskan *survivors disembarking from T-24, Brest, 29 April 1944. l to r: Dunn Lantier, Jim Evans, Samuel Willock, Milton Bower (face hidden), Walter Sheppard, Ray Meloche, John Fairchild, Ray Beach, Lloyd Edwards.*

In enemy hands: a wounded Athabaskan is treated by a German surgeon, Dr. Springorum. On the left in the white lab coat is Dr. Eitel W. Marechaux.

The more badly injured prisoners were laid on stretchers, placed in ambulances, and taken to a naval hospital, where they received minimal treatment and little sympathy. As the remainder prepared to board trucks, the Free French Maquis shot at the Germans. Leading Seaman Dick heard three shots being fired from a nearby building. One shot ricochetted off the pavement in front of the trucks, but no one was hit. The Germans did not fire back, but they did get the vehicles moving out of the area as quickly as possible. The Athabaskans rode in the backs of two army trucks, which were fitted with wooden benches. Armed guards sat between every second man, their rifles at the ready. This amused several of the Athabaskans, for they were in no mood to stage an escape and in any case lacked the physical strength to do so. The enemy, however, was apparently not taking any chances. After twenty minutes of touring the streets of Brest, the convoy finally passed through the entrance of a four-storey brick building into an open quadrangle. As they entered, one of the prisoners noticed a sign at the side of the gate which read "Couvent Ste. Louise".

The closing of the convent doors behind the Athabaskans marked the beginning of a new and highly unpleasant chapter in their lives. As soon as they were incarcerated, incessant orders, threats, and the ever-present armed guards became an integral part of their lives. Immediately after they arrived they noticed a dozen German ratings standing in a doorway to the courtyard. From their wounds and from the gloating expressions on their faces, some of the Athabaskans surmised that they were the survivors of the Elbing destroyer sunk on the morning of 26 April. This was confirmed later, as well as the fact that some of their guards were survivors from the *T-27*.

At 0840 that same morning *Haida* arrived at Plymouth after a record-breaking Channel crossing. She had been met by HM destroyers *Offa* and *Orwell* at 0635 and 0650 respectively in mid-Channel and the two had escorted *Haida* to Eddystone. The Canadian Tribal entered Plymouth Harbour to a warm welcome with her battle ensign flying proudly at the yardarm, but she arrived alone, her victory tempered by the loss of *Athabaskan*. All Plymouth knew about the night's encounter, and Lord Haw-Haw

Cook (S) T. Glen Newlove and Leading Seaman Frank J. Savage from Athabaskan *with a* Haida *crew member after the sinking.*

lost no time in broadcasting to the world news that a British cruiser had been sunk by the victorious German Navy. He overlooked mentioning the loss of *T-27.**

Ambulances were waiting at Devonport Dock to whisk the survivors to hospital. Soon they would be bathed, their injuries and burns tended, and they could enjoy the comfort of soft beds and clean, shite sheets. Able Seaman James C. Aikins was lying in one of the ambulances beside Lieutenant Jack Scott; both had been badly burned. 'The officer turned to me,' recalled the young sailor, 'smiled, and asked, "What's your name?"'

Meanwhile, on *Haida's* quarter-deck, the Commander-in-Chief, Plymouth, Vice-Admiral Sir Ralph Leatham, and his staff were in consultation with Commander De Wolf, going over details of the night's action. The tired Captain, still wearing seaboots and a white scarf around his neck, painfully reviewed every stage of the encounter to the eagerly listening party from Headquarters. He was still unaware that the Motor Torpedo Boat rescue mission had been abandoned.

**Kapitanleutnant* Wilhelm Meentzen, Commanding Officer of *T-24*, was awarded the Knight's Cross, First Class for the sinking of *Athabaskan*.

Meanwhile, many miles to the north, a far happier situation was developing. *Haida's* cutter had been sighted by a squadron of RAF planes south of the Lizard, and the exhausted survivors had been picked up by an Air/Sea Rescue launch and taken to Penzance. By midnight they were resting, warm and comfortable, and thankful that their prayers for safety had been answered. But a disquieting thought would not leave them: "What about the rest of the gang."

Top: Haida's *Stoker William Cummings, Leading Seaman William MacLure, and Able Seaman Jack Hannam in* Haida's *motor cutter in Penzance after the exhausting Channel trip. The six grateful Athabaskans who owed their rescue to these three Haidas were:*
Able Seaman Jean F.A. Audet of Montreal, Quebec;
Able Seaman Stanley J. Buck of Toronto, Ontario;
Chief Petty Officer Charles T. Burgess of Victoria, British Columbia;
Petty Officer George W.T. Casswell also of Victoria;
Signalman Thomas G. Eady of Welland, Ontario;
Signalman Guy J. Norris of Nelson, British Columbia.

A group of Haida's *men after the rescue of 45 Athabaskans, their relieved faces and oil-soaked clothes starkly outlined by the rising sun.*

A variety of expressions are seen on the faces of these Athabaskan *survivors as* Haida *nears Plymouth, with an escorting Hunt class destroyer in the background.*

Athabaskan *wounded are brought on stretchers down* Haida's *gangplank to waiting ambulances.*

In a sombre mood, Athabaskan survivors watch their wounded disembarking from Haida.

The disembarkation of helpless Athabaskans, including one badly burned and one soaked in fuel oil is watched by part of Haida's company and two other survivors.

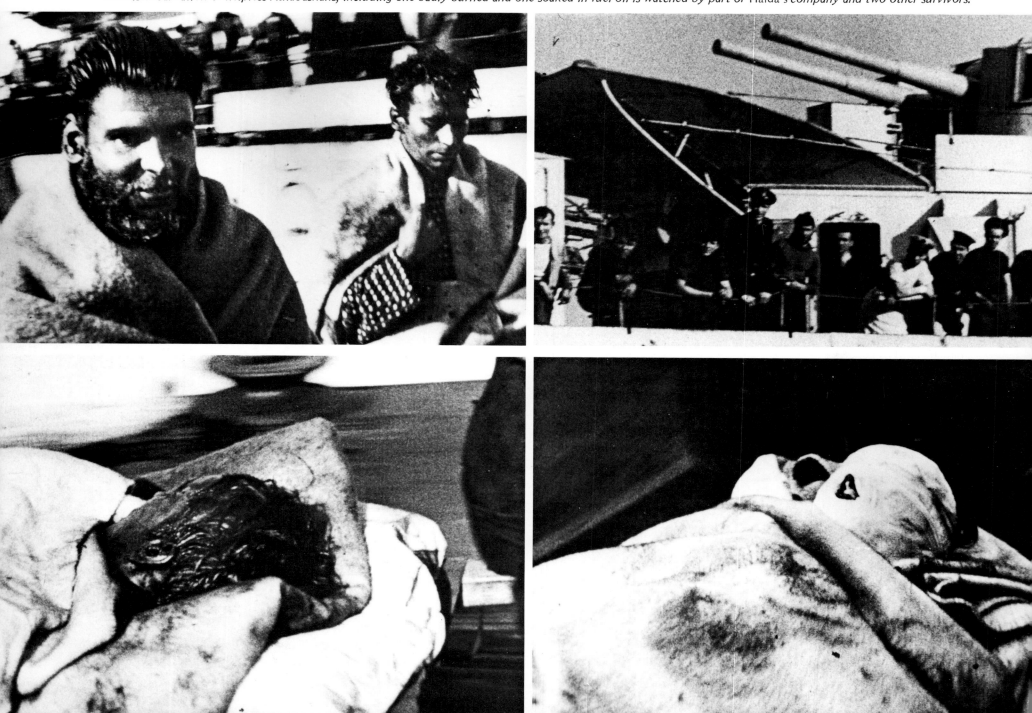

During their sojourn most of the Athabaskans tried to catch some sleep. Others moved about to improve their circulation and keep warm. One resourceful sailor had managed to retain his money-belt, and he proceeded to lay out seventy-five pounds of British money in the hot sun to dry. Unfortunately, one of the German guards noticed this treasure and immediately took possession of it. The angry young seaman was in no position to object and never saw his money again.

Able Seaman Herman C. Sulkers peered into a courtyard window, using it as a mirror while attempting to wipe his oil-covered face. The head of a woman appeared behind the glass, watching the young man with apparent interest. As Sulkers continued his unpleasant task, the woman's countenance suddenly twisted to a look of horror. She threw up her hands and quickly vanished from sight. Sulkers couldn't understand the strange reaction until he realized that he had been burned in the second explosion, and in the shelter of the hotel's enclosure he had unwittingly wiped away shreds of raw, red skin from his face.

Late in the day the pathetic band of survivors, tired and hungry, was hustled aboard German army trucks and taken to Brest. They had not eaten for over twenty hours and many of them desperately needed medical attention.

In due course the Canadians were issued with very used working clothes, fed after a fashion, and segregated to prevent the opportunity for ordinary conversation. One group was given the sorrowful task of identifying before burial the bodies of those Athabaskans washed ashore.

Within a week the survivors were all entrained for the long, tedious railway journey to Bremen, and eventually Marlag und Milag Nord, two prisoner of war camps for captured Allied naval and merchant seamen. Some seriously burned and injured men were diverted to an Orleans army hospital, Front-Stalag 133A, for hospital treatment and care. This small group was fortunate enough to be liberated by the United States Army during its encirclement of Paris in August 1944, and were later repatriated to Canada.

A wounded Athabaskan disembarks from T-24 at Brest with help from a German sailor.

On Sunday, 30 April, at 1000, Stoker McNeil was buried by the German authorities at Landeda. Father Saliou, rector of the parish of Landeda, had heard the evening before that the Germans were planning to bury him and appeared before the Commanding Officer to request permission to recite the last prayers of the church for the fallen sailor. The concerned priest was told that he would not be allowed to perform these last rites. Father Saliou was shocked by the officer's attitude and protested strongly, but the will of the conqueror prevailed and the sad priest was shown to the door.

Nevertheless, Father Saliou celebrated Mass on 1 May for the repose of Stoker McNeil's soul. It was attended by a large number of people from the district, including the family of a Dr. Mignard, who freely offered to care for the grave. The Germans had put a wooden cross on McNeil's grave with the following inscription:

JOHN MCNEIL
COGRE BUITON OSLAND
Kanada

John came from New Victoria, Cape Breton Island, Nova Scotia, and the Germans had used their own particular method of translation. The youthful stoker had just celebrated his twentieth birthday.

During the following days, scores of dead Athabaskans were washed up on the rocky coast of Finistere. The largest group, fifty-nine Athabaskans, was found on the Brittany shore near Plouescat. The body of Lieutenant-Commander Stubbs was among them. Other bodies were scattered for miles east and west of the disaster scene. Under the watchful eyes of the enemy, their remains were lovingly taken up by the French fisherfolk and tenderly prepared for burial. *Les Canadiens* were immediately recognized by these hardy people of the sea, who did all in their power, under trying circumstances, to provide decent Christian burials for the sailors. The Breton citizens adopted the Canadians as brothers-in-arms and insisted, at great personal risk to themselves, that they should be accorded all honours and the last rites of their church.

French citizens of Plougasnou walk behind the hearse carrying the body of an unidentified Athabaskan, proceeding to the cemetery.

In most cases the enemy co-operated and provided military funerals complete with guards of honour and three-salvo salutes. Local parish priests were called upon to recite prayers and invoke blessings for the dead. At Ile de Batz the local *Kommandant* ordered that no flowers were to be placed on the graves of the three Athabaskans buried there, but on the following morning their plots were piled high with freshly-cut flowers. Under the cover of the night, a thousand people from all over the island had gathered together to provide a cascade of colour for the seamen's graves—a beautiful gesture of their respect for *les Canadiens* liberators.

According to the French citizens who took up the Athabaskans from the sea, their bodies were in good condition and bore few marks of their recent torment. Positive identification was not always possible because dog-tags, in many instances, were missing. And so, in a matter of a few days, they were buried along the coast of Brittany at Brest, Brignogan-Plages, Cleden-Cap-Sizun, Ile de Batz, Landeda, Plouescat, Plougasnou, Pornic, and Sibiril. Ninety-one Athabaskans were laid to rest in the soil of France.

The remaining Athabaskans were detained in Germany for a year to suffer prisoner-of-war indignities at the hands of the enemy. They were interrogated continually in an effort to pry technical data from their memories, and when the prisoners didn't co-operate they were placed in solitary confinement for weeks at a time. And after this humiliation, they finally passed through the interrogation section to the misery of routine camp life, where they continued to feel the barbs of the enemy's anger. Mental abuse, daily harassment, threats, and the use of vicious guard dogs were commonplace.

The occasional Red Cross food parcel was gratefully received, encouraging the prisoners and supplementing their meagre diet. Insufficient prison food of minimal nutritional value sapped their strength to the point where each man lost an average 45 to 50 pounds of body weight during confinement. This, and the mental torture, would adversely affect many men for the rest of their lives. Nevertheless, the Athabaskans appreciated that they were far more fortunate than those Canadians who were prisoners of the Japanese, and this knowledge no doubt hardened their resolve to survive. They bore their individual burdens well, and it is to their honour that they carried on, all eventually to return safely to Canada.

A few Athabaskan prisoners of war at Milag und Marlag Nord, Westertimke.

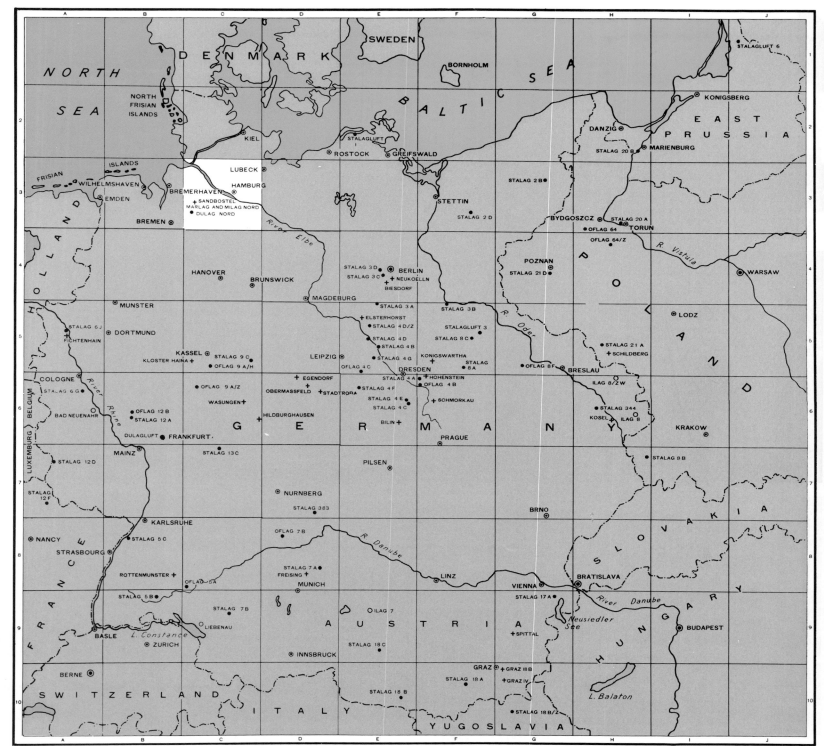

*Athabaskan Prisoners
Marlag und Milag Nord*

*Prisoner of War map
prepared by Department
of National Defence
April 15, 1944*

NORTH SEA

DENMARK

SWEDEN

BORNHOLM

BALTIC SEA

EAST PRUSSIA

KONIGSBERG

NORTH FRISIAN ISLANDS

KIEL

DANZIG

STALAG 20 B ⊙ MARIENBURG

FRISIAN ISLANDS

WILHELMSHAVEN

LUBECK

HAMBURG

STALAGLUFT 1

ROSTOCK

GREIFSWALD

STALAG 2 B

EMDEN

BREMERHAVEN

+ SANDBOSTEL
  MARLAG AND MILAG NORD
● DULAG NORD

STETTIN

BYDGOSZCZ ⊙ STALAG 20 A
                TORUN

BREMEN

River Elbe

⊕ OFLAG 64
OFLAG 64/Z

HOLLAND

HANOVER

BRUNSWICK

MAGDEBURG

STALAG 3 D ⊙⊙ BERLIN
STALAG 3 C ● + NEUKOELLN
              BIESDORF

POZNAN
STALAG 21 D

WARSAW

P O L A N D

MUNSTER

STALAG 3 A

STALAG 3 B

R. Oder

LODZ

STALAG 6 J
FICHTENHAIN +

DORTMUND

+ ELSTERHORST
+ STALAG 4 D/Z

STALAGLUFT 3

STALAG 8 C

STALAG 21 A
+ SCHILDBERG

KASSEL ⊙ STALAG 9 C
KLOSTER HAINA +   ● OFLAG 9 A/H

LEIPZIG

STALAG 4 D
● STALAG 4 B

STALAG 4 G

KONIGSWARTHA
+

STALAG 8 A

OFLAG 8 F ● BRESLAU

COLOGNE

River Rhine

OFLAG 4 C

DRESDEN
STALAG 4 A + ● HOHENSTEIN

ILAG 8/Z W

STALAG 6 G

+ EGENDORF
+
OBERMASSFELD + STADTRODA ● STALAG 4 F

● OFLAG 4 B

STALAG 344

BELGIUM

● OFLAG 9 A/Z

WASUNGEN +

STALAG 4 E
STALAG 4 C

+ SCHMORKAU

KOSEL + ILAG 8

BAD NEUENAHR

● OFLAG 12 B
● STALAG 12 A

+ HILDBURGHAUSEN

BILIN +

KRAKOW

LUXEMBURG

DULAGLUFT

FRANKFURT

G E R M A N Y

PRAGUE

STALAG 12 D

MAINZ

STALAG 13 C

PILSEN

STALAG 8 B

STALAG 12 F

NURNBERG

STALAG 383

BRNO

S L O V A K I A

KARLSRUHE

NANCY ⊙   ● STALAG 5 C

OFLAG 7 B

R. Danube

STRASBOURG

F R A N C E

ROTTENMUNSTER +
              OFLAG 6 A

STALAG 7 A
FREISING +
MUNICH

LINZ

BRATISLAVA

VIENNA ⊙

River Danube

STALAG 5 B

STALAG 17 A ●

H U N G A R Y

STALAG 7 B

ILAG 7

A U S T R I A

Neusiedler See

BUDAPEST

BASLE

L. Constance

LIEBENAU

ZURICH

STALAG 18 C

+ SPITTAL

BERNE ⊙

INNSBRUCK

GRAZ + GRAZ III B

S W I T Z E R L A N D

STALAG 18 A

+ GRAZ IV

L. Balaton

I T A L Y

STALAG 18 B

Y U G O S L A V I A

● STALAG 18 B/Z

DANGER!
WARNING WIRE!
There will be shooting without challenge.

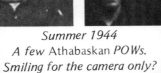

Summer 1944
A few Athabaskan POWs.
Smiling for the camera only?

Boundary fence around camp.

Main Square of Marlag und Milag Nord,
Westertimke. Here roll call took place three times
a day. In the centre is a loudspeaker, installed so
the prisoners could listen to Lord Haw-Haw's
English broadcasts on the German radio.

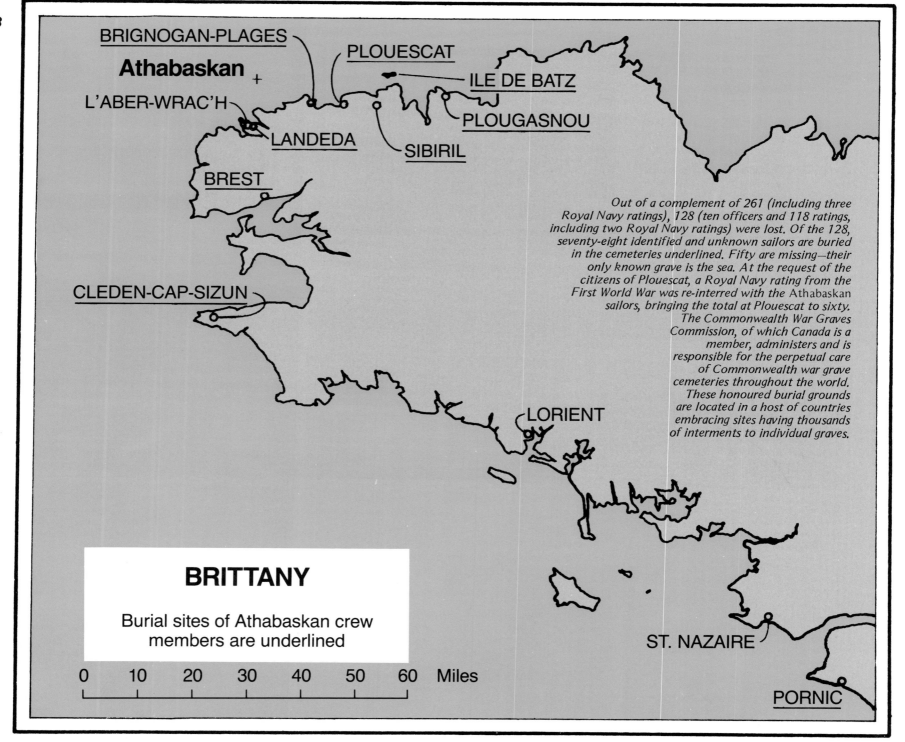

148

BRIGNOGAN-PLAGES

Athabaskan +

PLOUESCAT

ILE DE BATZ

L'ABER-WRAC'H

LANDEDA

PLOUGASNOU

SIBIRIL

BREST

CLEDEN-CAP-SIZUN

Out of a complement of 261 (including three Royal Navy ratings), 128 (ten officers and 118 ratings, including two Royal Navy ratings) were lost. Of the 128, seventy-eight identified and unknown sailors are buried in the cemeteries underlined. Fifty are missing—their only known grave is the sea. At the request of the citizens of Plouescat, a Royal Navy rating from the First World War was re-interred with the Athabaskan *sailors, bringing the total at Plouescat to sixty. The Commonwealth War Graves Commission, of which Canada is a member, administers and is responsible for the perpetual care of Commonwealth war grave cemeteries throughout the world. These honoured burial grounds are located in a host of countries embracing sites having thousands of interments to individual graves.*

LORIENT

BRITTANY

Burial sites of Athabaskan crew members are underlined

0   10   20   30   40   50   60   Miles

ST. NAZAIRE

PORNIC

In 1947 a former Athabaskan *officer, Lieutenant-Commander Dunn Lantier, was completing the Royal Navy Staff College course at Greenwich, England. It had always bothered him that no one had apparently troubled to find the graves of the Athabaskans who had been washed ashore. So, on his own, he travelled to Paris to call on the Canadian Ambassador, Georges Vanier, to seek help. He chanced to run into Madame Vanier and was invited to lunch with them. During the course of conversation Lantier brought up the subject of* Athabaskan, *and the Ambassador put him in touch with the Army attache, who in turn advised him to go to St. Malo where he could contact representatives of the British War Graves Commission. Eventually Lantier was directed to Plouescat, where volunteers were assisting the Commission in excavating graves to identify the bodies. The Commission had already been able to make several identifications, including Lieutenant-Commander John Stubbs, and in due course, with the help of dental records, dog-tags, etc., forty-two out of ninety-one bodies were identified at the nine cemeteries where Athabaskans are buried.*

Brest (Kerfautras) Lambezellec

Kerfautras Communal Cemetery is in Lambezellec, just over one mile (two kilometres) north-east of the Naval Arsenal and the centre of Brest. The main entrance is in the Chemin du Ronde opposite Rue Massillon, and there is another entrance in Rue Jean Jaures, which is off Rue Anatole France. There are British war graves of both world wars in this burial ground, in the various military plots which lie near the Rue Jean Jaures entrance. They are the graves of soldiers and sailors of different nationalities, but chiefly Franch, some of which ante-date the First World War.

These burials number thirty-three, but there are eighty-one burials of the Second World War, mostly in Plots 40, 46, and 47. Able Seaman Charles L. Pothier is buried in Plot 46, Row 5, Grave 15. The graves of six Canadian airmen are situated nearby.

Brignogan-Plages Communal Cemetery

Brignogan-Plages is a large village and commune some forty-six miles (seventy-four kilometres) north/north-west of Quimper and about twenty miles (thirty-three kilometres) north-east of Brest. The cemetery is west of the village, just off the main road from

Lesneven. In the southern corner are the graves of two airmen of the Royal Air Force, one of whom is not identified, and nine sailors of the Royal Canadian Navy, eight of whom are not identified. Able Seaman Marshall L. Gibbons is buried in Grave 10.

Cleden Cap Sizun Communal Cemetery

Cleden Cap Sizun is a village and commune about twenty-five miles (forty-one kilometres) west/north-west of Quimper and seven miles (twelve kilometres) west of the small town of Pont-Croix. The village is situated at the junction of the secondary road from Pont-Croix and a by-road to Plogoff. The cemetery is west of the village on the road to Plogoff. On the far left of the entrance, near the wall, is the grave of an unidentified sailor belonging to the Royal Canadian Navy.

Ile de Batz Communal Cemetery

Ile de Batz is a small island and commune two and one-half miles (four kilometres) off the coast at Roscoff. It is best reached from Morlaix, where there is a branch rail line to Roscoff. There is a good train service to Roscoff, but the ferry to the island is timed to suit the tides. The cemetery is on the right-hand side of the road from the landing stage, about fifteen minutes walk. Near the far corner left (north) of the entrance, at the end of the path, are the graves of three sailors of the Royal Canadian Navy, one of whom is unidentified. Able Seaman Robert J. Henry is buried in Grave 2 and Able Seaman Robert L. Yeadon is buried in Grave 3.

Landeda Communal Cemetery

Landeda is a village and commune about fourteen miles (twenty-three kilometres) north/north-west of Brest and two miles (four kilometres) north-west of the small town of Lannilis, whence a taxi is the only means of transport. The cemetery is on the northern side of the village, and south-east of the Calvary, in Plot 12, Row 3, Grave 18, Stoker John J. McNeil is buried.

Plouescat Communal Cemetery

Plouescat is a village and commune twenty-five miles (forty kilometres) north-east of Brest and about seventeen miles (twenty-eight kilometres) north-west of Morlaix, on the main coast road of this part of Northern Brittany. There are good bus services to and from Brest, St. Pol-de-Leon, and Morlaix. The small cemetery is south of the village some 400 yards from the church, at the end of Rue du Calvaire. Near the west wall are the graves of fifty-nine sailors of the Royal Canadian Navy, twenty-five of whom are unidentified. The graves are in a small plot of mown grass defined by a curb, with continuous flower borders along the lines of headstones. The Cross of Sacrifice, on a podium, stands on a lawn at the left of the graves. There is one First World War grave of a British Mercantile Marine seaman in the cemetery which, at the request of the local authorities, has been moved into the Athabaskan plot. See Appendix II for a list of the identified sailors.

Plougasnou Communal Cemetery

Plougasnou is a village and commune about nine miles (fourteen kilometres) north/north-east of Morlaix, on the main road to the coast. There is a railway station in the village on a branch line from Morlaix and the service is reasonably frequent. The cemetery is west of the village church. South/South-east of the monument, opposite the entrance toward the rear of the cemetery, are the graves of six airmen of the Royal Air Force and two sailors of the Royal Canadian Navy, one of whom is unidentified. Six of the graves are right of the path and two are on the left. In Plot 2, Row A, Grave 2, Able Seaman Paul H.A. Chamberland is buried.

Pornic War Cemetery

Pornic is a small seaside resort and fishing port on the north side of Brogneuf Bay about twenty-seven miles (forty-three kilometres) west/south-west of Nantes and twelve miles (twenty kilometres) south/south-east of St. Nazaire via the ferry across the River Loire. It can be easily reached by rail or bus. The cemetery is on the north-eastern outskirts of the town, 800 yards east of the church, on the south side of the V.O. 2 road to Chauve. It lies opposite to the south-eastern corner of Pornic Communal Cemetery. Many of those buried here were washed ashore after the sinking by the enemy of the troopship *Lancastria* in the Bay of Biscay on 17 June 1940. A total of 395 Allied servicemen are buried here, including thirteen sailors of the Royal Canadian Navy, eleven of whom are unidentified. Able Seaman Gordon F. Corkum is buried in Plot 2, Row AA, Collective Grave 7-16, and Able Seaman John A. Wood is buried in Plot 2, Row AA, Grave 17.

Sibiril Communal Cemetery

Sibiril is a village and commune about twelve miles (twenty kilometres) north-west of Morlaix and six miles (ten kilometres) south-west of Roscoff. It is best reached via Roscoff. There is a branch line from Roscoff and the trains are reasonably frequent. The cemetery is about twenty yards from the church. In the north-eastern corner are the graves of an airman of the Royal Air Force and two unidentified sailors of the Royal Canadian Navy.

Of the thirty-seven Athabaskans whose bodies were never found, doubtless some of them went down with their ship—at their particular action stations there could have been little hope of survival. Others probably escaped the trap of a sinking ship only to succumb to the cold Channel waters and drift quietly on the tide out to sea. The sea is their final resting place, and she will hold them in her embrace for eternity. It is not an impossible hope that some may have had the good fortune to drift ashore, find protectors, and disappear into anonymity. *Athabaskan's* dead represent a human sacrifice, part of the price that had to be paid for the sake of peace and freedom. But in a broader sense, their story is a reminder of man's inhumanity to man.

The Athabaskans have not been forgotten. During the post-war years relatives and friends visited Finistere to pay homage to the Canadian sailors. Faithful *Iroquois, Haida,* and *Huron,* on various European tours, paused over *Athabaskan's* position in the Channel to offer their respects to a brave sister. Other Canadian warships and their companies over the years have remembered the gallant sacrifice of their countrymen—the RCN could never forget its dead.

On 30 May 1954, the tenth anniversary of the sinking, three officers from HMCS *Quebec* travelled to Plouescat to honour the fallen Athabaskans on behalf of the RCN, and were warmly received by the French authorities. Members of the France-Canada Association visited Plouescat in early May 1964, twenty years after *Athabaskan's* final patrol. And thirty years after the sinking, a group of survivors, next-of-kin, and friends gathered in a pilgrimage overseas to honour the Athabaskans who did not return. At Plymouth they assembled with their British friends in a memorable service in front of the National Naval War Memorial. Then, beginning on 29 April 1974, *Athabaskan III* took them on a never-to-be-forgotten voyage from Plymouth to Brest, stopping en route over the position in the Channel where *Athabaskan* lies for an impressive memorial service at sea. In France the Canadian pilgrims were welcomed like brothers and sisters by the French people, and all joined together in solemn reverence at each of the different grave sites. *Les Canadiens* survivors were treated like liberators everywhere they went, and affectionate hugs and kisses became the pattern of the journey. In one town, Pors Guen, a street was named "Rue de l'Athabaskan" after the ship and her company.

But it was at Plouescat that emotions reached their highest pitch. The whole town turned out to witness the Canadian and French veterans march side by side into the communal cemetery and form up around the graves of the dead Athabaskans. Under threatening skies, the dedicated congregation added their silent prayers and tears to a simple but moving service of remembrance.

It is a matter of proud history for Canada that the Athabaskans' war effort was successful. They were pathfinders who cleared the way for the Allied invasion armies who landed on the Normandy beaches and breached the walls of Fortress Europe. No more could be asked of these brave young Canadians, for they had sacrificed their lives to ensure the survival of others.

Mrs. C. Bieber, the mother of Stoker Petty Officer Edgar Bieber, who was lost at sea, places a wreath at the cemetery at Plouescat.

Still stands thine ancient sacrifice,
A humble and a contrite heart:
Lord God of hosts, be with us yet,
Lest we forget, lest we forget.

Rudyard Kipling

In memory of those lost, Bay of Biscay, August 27th, 1943

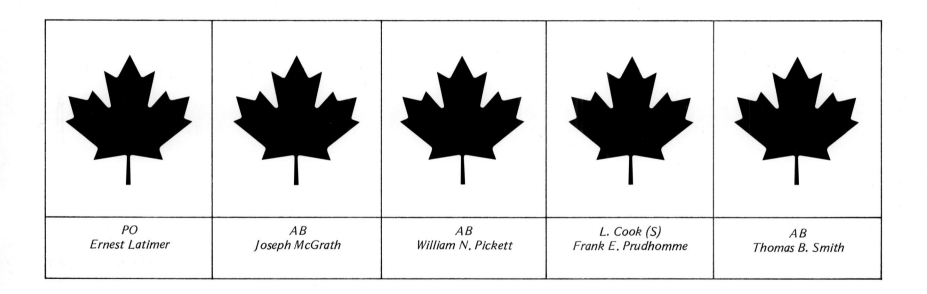

PO	AB	AB	L. Cook (S)	AB
Ernest Latimer	Joseph McGrath	William N. Pickett	Frank E. Prudhomme	Thomas B. Smith

A Hunt class escort destroyer
in the wake of Athabaskan, *out of Plymouth, 1943.*

In memory of those lost, English Channel, April 29th, 1944

Fix your eyes on the greatness of your country
as you have it before you day by day,
fall in love with her, and when you feel her great,
remember that her greatness was won by men with courage,
with knowledge of their duty, and with a sense of honor in action,
who, even if they failed in some venture,
would not think of depriving the country of their powers
but laid them at her feet as their fairest offering.

Pericles to the Athenians, in Thucydides: The Peloponnesian War, Book II, Chapter 43.

The beach at Pors Guen, Finistere
painted by Celia Pine, wife of Athabaskan Sam Pine.

AB John C. Adams	AB John Agnew	AB Albert E. Allison	Tel. Irvin V. Amiro	Sub. Lieut. (E) Robert I.L. Annett	AB George A. Armstrong
AB Percy G. Ashton	AB Arthur E. Barrett	Sto. (1) Donald A. Bell	OS Alfred G. Berkeley	CPO Laurent J.L. Bertrand	AB Anthony D. Bianco
Sto. PO Edgar E. Bieber	AB Harry C. Blinch	Pay. Lieut. Thomas L. Brandson	ERA (2) Victor H. Brighten	LS William O. Burrow	AB Paul H.A. Chamberland

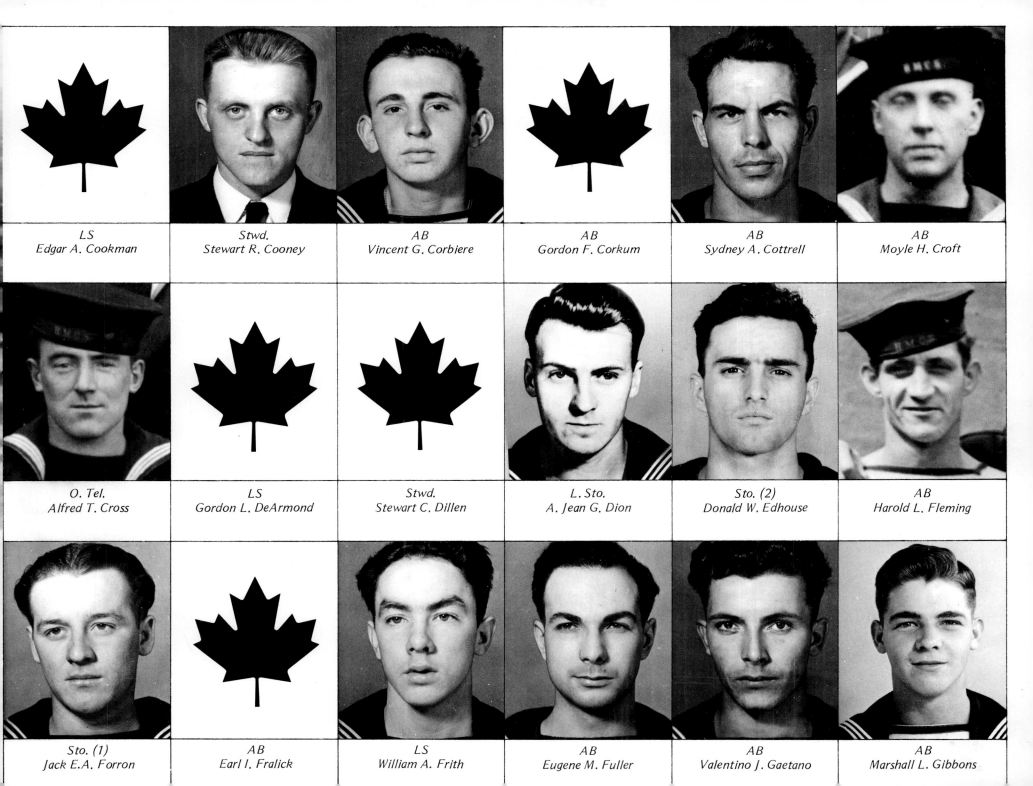

LS *Edgar A. Cookman*	*Stwd.* *Stewart R. Cooney*	*AB* *Vincent G. Corbiere*	*AB* *Gordon F. Corkum*	*AB* *Sydney A. Cottrell*	*AB* *Moyle H. Croft*
O. Tel. *Alfred T. Cross*	*LS* *Gordon L. DeArmond*	*Stwd.* *Stewart C. Dillen*	*L. Sto.* *A. Jean G. Dion*	*Sto. (2)* *Donald W. Edhouse*	*AB* *Harold L. Fleming*
Sto. (1) *Jack E.A. Forron*	*AB* *Earl I. Fralick*	*LS* *William A. Frith*	*AB* *Eugene M. Fuller*	*AB* *Valentino J. Gaetano*	*AB* *Marshall L. Gibbons*

CYS Thomas H. Goldsmith	AB Lloyd M. Gordon	Sto. (1) Robert J. Goulet	LSA Roy J. Grainger	AB Carlton G. Guest	OS Christopher Hayes
Sto. (1) John T. Heatherington	AB Robert J. Henry	Wrtr. (SP) P. Heston	L. Wrtr. George D. Houison	Sto. (1) Michael P. Hurley	AB Leonard C. Irvine
Lieut. (E) Theodore D. Izard	LS Edmund A. Jarvis	AB Elswood S. Johnson	L. Sto. Richard R. Johnson	AB Lawrence R. Johnston	Stwd. Lionel D. Kelly

LS John R. Kobes	LS Andre Lamoureux	Lieut. Ralph M. Lawrence
Sto. (1) Eric E. Lea	AB Louis Ledoux	Sto. (2) Stanely S. Lewandowski
Sto. PO Mekkel G. Lind	ERA (3) Walter M. Love	Sto. (2) Donald O. Lucas
PO Cook (O) Gerald W. MacAvoy	AB Ashley K. MacDonald	AB Alexander MacKenzie
L. Sto. John W. Maguire	Lieut. (SP) John D. Mahoney	Cook (O) John L. Manson
AB George H. Matthews	AB John L. McBride	Sto. (1) Thomas G. McCarroll

AB
William D. McCrindle

L. Sto.
William McGregor

AB
Daniel H. McLean

Sto. (2)
John J. McNeil

AB
Richard G. Meadwell

AB
Eric J. Mengoni

El. Art. (3)
Donald I. Metcalfe

AB
Victor Millar

C. ERA
Ernest G. Mills

ERA (4)
Leonard K. Mumford

Sub. Lieut.
Robert A. Nash

L. Sto.
Joseph R. Nicholas

AB
Joseph E.V. Ouellette

AB
Hubert J. Peart

AB
John D. Phillips

AB
Brenton J. Pike

AB
Charles L. Pothier

PO
John E. Rennie

AB
Joseph A.L. Riendeau

ERA (4)
John C. Roberts

AB
Raymond L. Roberts

AB
Eric Robertshaw

AB
Ian A. Robertson

Sto. (1)
William Robertson

Sto. (1)
Leo A. Roger

AB
Raymond B. Rolls

Rad. Mech. PO
Norman Rutherford

AB
Norman V. Ryan

AB
Joseph L.M. St. Laurent

AB
Francis L. Sampson

AB
Earl H. Sanderson

AB
Jean G.L. Senecal

Stwd.
Albert V. Sherlock

Gun.
George D. Sigston

AB
John C. Singleton

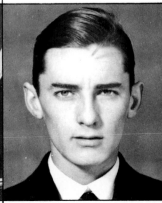

SBA
Francis G. Skyvington

AB Samuel W. Sommerfeld	Coder Paul E. Soucisse	Sto. (1) Elmer H. Stevenson	AB John L. Stewart	Sgm. William G. Stewart	Lieut. (E) Ernest O. Stockman
Lieut.-Com. John H. Stubbs	AB John W. Sutherland	CPO Charles C. Sweet	Sto. (1) Harry Thompson	Or. Art. (4) Allister R. Tupper	L. Stwd. James A. Vair
Sy PO Joseph V.W. Veinotte	AB Maurice Waitson	AB Peter W. Wallace	Lieut. (SB) Leslie Ward	Tel. Reginald J. Watson	ERA (4) Kenneth W. Williams

AB
John A. Wood

AB
Robert L. Yeadon

With willing hands they paid the price
Unconscious of the cost
But we must gauge the sacrifice
By all that they have lost
The joys of young adventurous ways
Of keen and undimmed sight
The carefree tramp through sunlit days
The dreamless sleep of night

Anonymous

*Monument erected in Plouescat, Finistere, France
in memory of the men of Athabaskan. Wreaths are laid
at its base at every French national or patriotic celebration.
Though it is now nearly forty years after the disaster,
it happens that an anonymous hand still places,
at the base of the cross, a little bouquet of wild flowers.*

164

Canada's fifteenth Governor-General, the late Lord Tweedsmuir, had a fond and lasting affection for all her people and endeared himself to them wherever he went. During his tenure in office, Lord and Lady Tweedsmuir travelled extensively throughout the country, sharing their company, observations, and native truths. Canada is a richer nation indeed for having had him as the Queen's representative. He carried out his duties with quiet dignity, and left behind a rich legacy of literature for everyone to enjoy. On 18 February 1938 Lord Tweedsmuir gave a speech at the Boy Scouts' Association Dinner, a speech which dwelt on the qualities of leadership. His message was primarily addressed to the Boy Scouts and their Leaders, but, in essence, he was also summing up the rugged spirit of the Athabaskans and their fellow Tribalists:

"Now with any purpose in life there must be two main duties. The first is to preserve what is worth preserving, and the other is to hand on something new to your successors. I was once the Warden of an ancient Border castle which stands in a narrow pass, through which flows the River Tweed. I have often thought that that old keep typified some of the greatest duties of human life. In the first place it defended the pass and the neighbourhood; in the second place, in the old days of English invasion the beacon on the roof passed on the warning light from the Border to the capital city. These two duties are before every man, and they were never more vital in the world than today. We have to hold the pass and defend our liberties and our heritage of civilization. But we have also to hand on the light. We have received from our forefathers a mighty bequest. We must hand that on to our successors not only undiminished, but increased, for the only way in which we can pay our debts to the past is by putting the future in debt to ourselves."

C-8507/Public Archives of Canada

Epilogue

FROM A HISTORICAL VIEWPOINT the loss of *Athabaskan* with almost half her ship's company is but a minor incident in the total war effort; an event which barely caught the headlines. It was only another destroyer action, and she was one of the inevitable sacrifices that had to be made in the long, hard struggle for victory. *Athabaskan* is scarcely mentioned in Captain S.W. Roskill's voluminous official British history, *The War at Sea,* and is not recorded at all in Winston Churchill's famous work *The Second World War,* despite the fact that the action took place on Britain's doorstep. Thus does *Athabaskan's* sacrifice become a matter of perspective, almost lost on the world stage as other pressing news and happenings crowded in and cried for their share of attention.

For Canada, it was a serious loss, one which caused grief and anxiety in many homes across the nation. *Athabaskan* was the sixteenth warship of the RCN to be lost in the grim war at sea, and others were to share the same fate. It is unfortunate, especially in view of the close wartime relationship between the RCN and RN, that there are still unanswered questions concerning the loss of *Athabaskan,* questions whose answers might indicate that some of the deaths of her company in the cold waters of the English Channel and the incarceration of others in prison camps were unnecessary.

On 1 May 1944 the Commander-in-Chief, Plymouth HQ, Admiral Sir Ralph Leatham, issued a memorandum calling for a Board of Inquiry to be assembled on Wednesday, 3 May 1944 for the purpose of investigating the circumstances surrounding the loss of HMCS *Athabaskan.* The Board of Inquiry consisted of four RN officers, all from Plymouth Command, who were given instructions to make a full and careful investigation into the sinking and to offer suitable recommendations which might prevent similar occurences in the future. Appropriate witnesses were to be called upon to testify.

The Board assembled at the appointed place at 0930 and immediately proceeded to examine reports and to question a few of those *Athabaskan* survivors who were fit and able to attend. After some discussion and consideration, the Board unanimously agreed that *Athabaskan* had been sunk by enemy action, the specific cause being either a torpedo or the explosion of the after 4-inch magazine.

The Board eventually recessed for lunch and gathered again at 1330 to prepare its report and have it typed, signed, and sent off to HQ promptly. One gets the impression from the records that the Board was primarily interested in the whereabouts of the confidential books—the fate of *Athabaskan's* company and other considerations did not seem to concern them. The hastily formed board then made an equally speedy exit, leaving a report that is open to criticism on a number of counts. For example, why was Commander De Wolf not requested to appear before the Board? His close personal relationship with the Commanding Officer of *Athabaskan* and the loss of one of the ships under his command in the recent action would normally require him to be one of the first persons to be summoned. If this capable and experienced officer had been given the opportunity to answer questions and to amplify his written report, he could have been of immeasurable assistance to the Board. Nevertheless, it chose to ignore him.

Why was the Commander of Motor Torpedo Boat *677* not called to appear? This officer had been ordered to reverse course and to rescue the remaining Athabaskans still struggling in the water. Why was the order cancelled and the MTB obliged to return to Plymouth empty-handed and frustrated? Strangely enough, his official report did not come to light until three weeks after the Board met! Why was Commander De Wolf not notified about the cancelled order when he made for Plymouth? If he had been made aware of this signal, he might well have turned around in mid-Channel and gone back to save his floundering countrymen (although he might have also been influenced by Lieutenant-Commander Stubbs's final shout to *Haida* to "get the Hell out" of the dangerous area).

One might also query the absence of adequate support for *Haida* and *Athabaskan* during the night's operation. Another sub-division of two destroyers as part of the strike force could easily have taken care of the escaping *T-24* while *Haida* was disposing of *T-27*. Captain R.S. Roskill states in his history that resources were so great at the time that invasion preparations caused no appreciable decrease in offensive minelaying.* And with Devonport Harbour crowded with warships at that particular time, it seems incongruous that the two Canadian Tribals were left to operate in enemy waters on their own.

All of this raises the question of what transpired at the meeting between Lieutenant-Commander Stubbs and Captain (D) prior to sailing. It is difficult to understand why, in the Board of Inquiry's report, Commander De Wolf and his men were not cited for rescuing forty-two Athabaskans, although the report hastens to mention the gallant act of Leading Seaman W.A. McClure (but not his shipmates Able Seaman Jack Hannam and Stoker William Cummings) in rescuing six Athabaskans in *Haida's* cutter. The Board also chose to ignore the German Radio announcement that eighty-five Athabaskans were safe and secure in German hands. Finally, the report failed to mention anything about the new Canadian life-jackets that had been issued to the Athabaskans shortly before they sailed on their fateful patrol. Every man who lived through that perilous night was convinced it was a major factor in his survival.

In fairness to the Board, it attached no blame to the officers and men for the loss of their ship—a finding that could not have been difficult to determine. Overshadowing this conclusion was a statement censuring one of *Athabaskan's* officers who was reported to have been in charge of confidential books for not destroying them, despite the fact that the young man was blown off his ship, being badly injured and burned in the process.[†] He was unable to be present at the Inquiry to defend himself, nor was he represented by a Canadian peer.

Unhappily, these questions and observations have remained unanswered. In retrospect, it is a sad reflection on four professional naval officers that they appeared to be so indifferent to the fate of *Athabaskan* and, in particular, of her company.

On 1 June 1944, almost a month after the Board of Inquiry had filed its report, Admiral Sir Ralph Leatham forwarded his own report with enclosures to the Secretary of the Admiralty. It was a three-page document describing the events leading to the sinking of *Athabaskan*. The report, eloquently outlining a number of points in naval language and terminology, might appear quite impressive to the layman, though perhaps not quite clear. A closer look at the details reveals a number of questionable statements:

*Captain R.S. Roskill, *The War at Sea*, V 3, Part 1, p. 289.

†The accused officer, Lieutenant John W. Scott, spent several years in and out of hospital after the war undergoing skin grafts and special treatments.

12. As soon as it was known at Area Combined Headquarters, Plymouth that Athabaskan had been hit, a signal was made to Offa and Orwell, who were on patrol off the Start Area covering Exercise Tiger, to proceed at full speed on a course 210°; their distance from the scene of action was, however, too great to allow their arrival before daylight, and, when it later became known that Athabaskan had sunk and that Haida was proceeding home, they were ordered to rendezvous with her in mid-Channel and return.

13. At 0448, orders were sent to the two M.T.B.'s with the mine-laying force to proceed to rescue survivors; but again, their distance from the scene of action was too great to permit them to arrive before first light, and as adequate fighter protection could not be supplied owing to other heavy commitments of aircraft, these orders were subsequently cancelled, as these craft could not be left unsupported off the enemy coast in daylight.

The RN had apparently turned and run away from a threat—a threat which did not actually exist. The struggling Athabaskans had been told by the Commanding Officer of Haida before he left that help was on the way, and this cheering news had sustained the wretched sailors for a time. But neither the MTBs nor the destroyers ever arrived, and many of the Canadians lost heart and succumbed to fatigue and exhaustion.

The Admiral's excuse implying the threat of an enemy air attack is completely unacceptable, because every senior officer in Britain at this critical time knew that the Luftwaffe was extremely weak. Any likelihood of it making an appearance on the scene was exceedingly remote, for the Germans would probably not hazard precious aircraft for such an insignificant affair. The enemy air force had been under steady pressure for months as the Allies prepared for D-Day, and was reduced to a state of near impotence. There was no reason why the RN ships should not have been allowed to complete their rescue mission—particularly the MTBs. These fast, highly manoeuverable, and relatively small warships could have been at the scene of the sinking within an hour, still hidden by a cover of darkness.* With their low freeboards, it would not have been a difficult job for the MTB crew to haul the Canadians aboard.

In paragraph fourteen, the Admiral admonished Commander De Wolf for not pursuing T-24 eastward, yet in the next breath

*Sunrise was at 0711 British Double Time, so there would have been ample time for the MTBs to complete their mission.

admitted that his action in going after T-27 was the proper one! If Haida and Athabaskan had had any support, the fight would probably have ended with two enemy ships destroyed.

The Commander-in-Chief agreed with the findings of the Board of Inquiry and accepted its report without question. He arbitrarily dismissed the MTB Commander's report about seeing an explosion at thirty miles. It will be recalled that this officer was also not called to appear before the Board of Inquiry. Neither the Commanding Officer of Haida nor his men were commended in the Admiral's report for their rescue of forty-two Athabaskans, although Leading Seaman William A. McClure was recommended for an award.

Probably the most puzzling element of the whole investigation of Athabaskan's sinking was that no RCN officer was appointed a member of the Board or invited as an observer. (It must also be said that the RCN itself appeared inexplicably indifferent to the circumstances surrounding the loss of one of its major warships.) The men on the Canadian Tribals had already become accustomed to being treated as chattels by the RN. Indeed, it is said that Lieutenant-Commander Stubbs, when at one time he considered that the Canadian Tribals were doing far more than their share of night patrols, signalled Captain (D), 'Has Britain signed a separate peace treaty with Germany?' This could hardly have endeared the intrepid Stubbs to his superiors, but it certainly reflected Canadian feelings. The RN's attitude during the investigation was typical of that experienced by Canadians in all three services during wartime days in Britain.

As a climax to the Athabaskan affair, a copy of the Commander-in-Chief's report to the Admiralty was sent to Naval Service Headquarters in Ottawa, but without any enclosures whatsoever. These enclosures consisted of all documents pertaining to the Board of Inquiry (including its report), and as late as December 1952, more than eight years later, naval authorities in Ottawa were still trying to secure copies of these documents from the Admiralty for their inspection and records.

In strange and vivid contrast to the RN's indifference was the rescue of eighty-seven Athabaskans (two of whom died on passage) by Kapitanleutnant Wilhelm Meentzen of T-24. This officer and his men, who but a few short hours before had been fighting the

Canadian Tribals, organized a rescue and in broad daylight steamed out into the Channel to pick up the exhausted survivors. Realizing that *Luftwaffe* air support was out of the question and that there was a danger of enemy air attack, he nevertheless pressed on with his damaged ship and tired men to rescue the Canadian sailors. He was under no obligation to make such a decision and could have stayed comfortably in harbour, but his strong sense of compassion and the code of the sea impelled him to venture out. There can be little doubt of the fate of those eighty-seven Athabaskans if Meentzen had not rescued them.

The RAF's role in the *Athabaskan* affair was negligible. Its "other commitments" excuse for not responding to the emergency emphasized once again the melancholy state of co-operation between the RN and the RAF which had prevailed on so many occasions before. With the thousands of available aircraft in Britain prior to D-Day, it seems incredible that a few could not have been spared to assist in a life-and-death struggle taking place only minutes away from England's shores. When some RAF planes finally managed to get airborne, they were just in time to sight *T-24* on her way to Brest. Fortunately, they knew that *Athabaskan* had been sunk and that many of the survivors were on board the German vessel.

It must be mentioned that the *Luftwaffe* did eventually make an appearance. Late in the afternoon of the 29th, more than twelve hours after the sinking, two aircraft appeared out of the clouds to buzz *Haida's* cutter as it slowly chugged northward to safety. After circling the lonely craft a couple of times, the pilots flew off to the south—they were all that the *Luftwaffe* could muster!

In reviewing all the evidence available bearing on the sinking of *Athabaskan*, it is impossible to avoid the conclusion that it was the Royal Navy's unjustifiable decision to call off rescue attempts in the face of a non-existent threat that was solely responsible for the deaths and captivity of so many of her company. The incident highlights the painful necessity for Canada to maintain an unceasing vigilance over her armed forces when they are operating under the command of another power.

During *Athabaskan's* career her men displayed many acts of kindness and bravery, too numerous to record here. Some which are representative should be cited on behalf of all, and it would be appropriate, even at this late hour, for the Canadian government to recognize and commend them. Able Seaman Eric J. Mengoni was a tower of strength when he assisted the two doctors during the Bay of Biscay action and conducted himself like a hero in the dark hours after the sinking. Able Seaman C. Owen Deal was safe on the deck of *Haida*, but elected to go to the assistance of a comrade in the water. In so doing he bought himself a one-way ticket for a year's duration in prison camp.

Some sort of formula should also be found to honour an RN officer, and also a former enemy. Surgeon-Lieutenant Drew of HMS *Egret* was extremely helpful in caring for *Athabaskan's* casualties during the Bay of Biscay action, and especially should be commended for his assistance in the operation to save the life of Telegraphist Charles Kent. *Kapitanleutnant* Meentzen and his men were responsible for saving eighty-seven Athabaskans after the battle while under extreme duress—their courage must not be forgotten.

These men are typical of those who go down to the sea in ships and who served and died in the war, upholding the finest traditions of their respective services and the unwritten code of the sea.

Before he was listed "Missing Presumed Dead", Lieutenant-Commander Stubbs was awarded the Distinguished Service Cross. In what must rank as one of the shortest citations in military history, his commendation read, 'For Good Service in Action with Enemy Destroyers.' Notwithstanding, the award was well deserved, and if the gallant Captain had survived he would have accepted it humbly on behalf of his ship's company.

*   *   *   *   *

After the war the second and then the third HMCS *Athabaskan* continued to uphold the proud name, and the original GO7 *Athabaskan* was all but forgotten—save by the men who had served on her, and who, when they met by chance, had plenty to talk about . . .

Herman C. Sulkers, a former Athabaskan, was on a business trip to Edmonton on a hot, sticky day in August 1964 when he decided to stop at Red Deer for a cold beer. As he sat quietly quenching his thirst, his eyes wandered to a corner of the room where another solitary figure sat in silence. The pair glanced at one another without recognition and returned to their glasses. But they looked up again and suddenly there was a spark of curiosity and interest. Herman approached the stranger, introduced himself, and discovered that he was speaking to Russell E. Phillips, one-time Athabaskan and fellow prisoner of war.

After twenty years the two comrades had met, quite by accident, in a pub in an Albertan city thousands of miles from where they had last parted company. It was a joyful reunion for the two veterans as they sat in animated conversation, swapping stories about wartime experiences and the whereabouts of former shipmates. The chance meeting was significant because it marked the beginning of a peacetime association which would grow and develop into a loyal, concerned group of veterans. Sulkers and Phillips arranged to meet again after that first joyful meeting, bringing other one-time Athabaskans into the fold, including Dr. James G. Fyfe, William B. Bint, Donald W. Newman, Robert D. Osborne, and Charles Kent. After two or three subsequent meetings, the enthusiastic group, through the facilities of the mass media, was able to contact and communicate with approximately seventy-five former shipmates. Plans were discussed for a general reunion to be held in Edmonton the following year. The Athabaskan Association was on its way, steaming at speed.

The first official gathering was a great success, because it brought many men together from all over the country for a taste of renewed fellowship and also gave them an opportunity to plot the Association's future course. It was at that first meeting that the members decided to name their group the GO7 Athabaskan Association, to distinguish and relate it to the first of name ship.

Succeeding reunions, both well-attended, took place in Toronto and Halifax. At the latter city, the members decided to celebrate the thirtieth anniversary of Athabaskan's sinking in 1974 with a commemorative pilgrimage to Europe, including a general meeting to be held in Brest. It proved to be a memorable personal experience which those who attended would always remember. Forty-six survivors with their next-of-kin and friends made the historic journey to pay homage to their ship and their comrades who died. The veterans met again in 1976 in Vancouver, in 1978 in Winnipeg, in 1980 in Ottawa, and last year, 1982, they met in Hamilton.

Athabaskan's sister ship, Haida, is now in glowing retirement, moored at Ontario Place, Toronto, as a permanent naval museum.

She was rescued from oblivion by the stalwart efforts of Neil Bruce, an airline pilot whose brother served in Haida, and his associates. Here she rests as a living symbol, the only ship of a class of twenty-seven British, Canadian, and Australian Tribals whose splendid records in peace and war have never been equalled.

Although Athabaskan now lies forty fathoms deep in the English Channel, there are those who will never feel that she was really lost. Her spirit lives on, perhaps dwelling with her sister Haida in Toronto, but also in the hearts of all those who served on her. This spirit carries a message of service and sacrifice which should never die, one which should be heard by Canada and the whole world, and which is perhaps epitomized by these words of John the Baptist recorded in St. Luke, 3:11:

'The man with two shirts must share with him who has none; and anyone who has food must do the same.'

Cdr. De Wolf and Admiral Leatham meet upon the return of Haida *to Plymouth on the morning of* Athabaskan's *loss.*

MYSTERY OF THE E-BOATS

During *Athabaskan's* last battle both her radar and that of *Haida* registered two fast-moving blips. The most logical explanation is that they were two of the German Motor Torpedo Boats known to the Allies as E-Boats. Their presence is unconfirmed by German records, but there seems to be no other explanation for the radar signals—unless Royal Navy Motor Torpedo Boats had strayed into the area. There were two of these boats with the minelaying force, the two which were first ordered to rescue the Athabaskans before that order was cancelled. Neither Allied nor German records show the presence of any boats on the scene, but something caused those radar blips. The truth remains a mystery.

The drawings depict S-8, an early version of the E-Boat with torpedo tubes on the fo'c's'le deck. Few of this type remained in service in 1944.

The S-8 was supplemented and then replaced with a more heavily-armed version, which had a raised and streamlined fo'c's'le deck enclosing the torpedo tubes. A typical example was S-39, shown in the photo below.

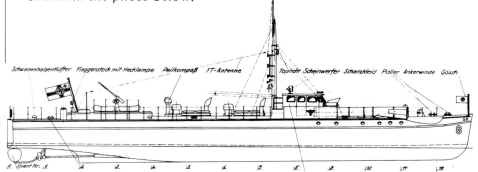

Len Burrow

Emile Beaudoin

Their Story Must Be Told

THIS STORY ABOUT HMCS *Athabaskan* was originally inspired by the message in Ernest Raymond's book *Tell England*, which describes a generation of British and Allied soldiers who served and died at Gallipoli. The plot of that narrative focuses on the lives of some English schoolboy soldiers, and its essence holds a deep and significant meaning for Canada, too. *Tell England* is a story in a generation, a generation that saw many of the Athabaskans' fathers, relatives, and friends place their lives on the line in the First World War for the cause of peace and freedom. Some were able to return to their homeland, but others stayed behind to be buried in some foreign soil.

In the final pages of Raymond's book, Padre Monty and Rupert are departing Gallipoli at the close of that ill-fated campaign. As they steam away leaving the shadows of Hunter Western Hill and Achi Baba behind, with all their painful memories, Padre Monty implores Rupert to write a book. "Tell 'em, Rupert, about the dead schoolboys of your generation."

A generation later, thousands of Allied sailors', soldiers', and airmen's lives were to be sacrificed for the same cause in the conflagration of the Second World War. Many of them, too, were schoolboys about to step over the threshold of life to manhood. In a sense, they were very natural and ordinary young men, fresh in the springtime of life, eager for adventure, and filled with a healthy zest for living. Like their forefathers, they faced the war with strong hearts and a determined will to get the job done. Some would live to fight another day, but many of their comrades would find eternal rest in some foreign field. Their's was the supreme sacrifice.

It was against this background of sacrifice in two world wars that the idea for *Athabaskan's* story matured. It came about when author Len Burrow and his wife Jessica sat down on the rocky French seashore of the English Channel on a sunny day in April 1973. They had just completed the personal pilgrimage part of an European tour which had taken them through Germany, Holland, Belgium, and France. And now, as they munched on cheese and a stick of French bread, with a bottle of wine, they discussed the many moving aspects of the past few days. Numerous battle sites, and their adjacent, reproachful war cemeteries, of both world wars had been visited. It had been a memorable journey, because both of these pilgrims had more than a passing interest in the historic panorama. Both had had fathers who had faithfully served as soldiers in the First World War and each had lost a younger brother in the Second World War. Consequently, a generation after the second conflict, the weary travellers had returned to pay homage to Canada's dead.

At the Canadian War Cemetery near Calais, they had paused to pay their respects to Trooper Joseph H. "Buddy" Rogers of the 1st Hussars, Canadian Second Corps of the Canadian Second

Division, who was killed during the fighting in September 1944 around Boulogne and Calais as the Canadian Army swept north-east toward Belgium. At his grave there had been a compelling desire to dig down deep into the French soil to embrace the nineteen year old schoolboy. Some tears were shed as the visitors placed a Canadian dime beside his stone marker in a symbolic gesture of devotion. Finally they had saluted and waved goodbye to the brave young man and his 800 comrades, including some Polish and Czech soldiers and a lone girl of the RAF (WAAF) by the name of Margaret Campbell.

At Dieppe they had stopped to salute the fallen soldiers of the Canadian Second Division and to gaze and ponder at the scene of this abortive European landing. There wasn't time to analyse the pros and cons of this famous assault on enemy-held territory, but it must have been a massacre. The Canadian couple had continued on their journey through Rouen, Chartres, Le Mans, Rennes, and Morlaix, finally arriving at the town of Plouescat where they had been welcomed by the Mayor and other officials. Flags of Canada and the Province of Quebec were presented and a special minute of the visit was officially recorded in the town's register. The party had then gone to the communal cemetery, where tribute was paid to the fifty-nine known and unknown members of *Athabaskan's* company who are buried there. And again, a Canadian dime was placed beside one of the stone markers inscribed to an unknown sailor. For conceivably, they thought, it could be the resting place of Leading Seaman William O. Burrow, whose whereabouts was unknown. This young sailor had been posted as missing, along with many of his shipmates, after the sinking of their ship, and not a single clue nor trace of him had surfaced in nearly thirty years. Official records list him as "Missing Presumed Dead".

So it was that during the precious moments of meditation beside the English Channel the idea for *Athabaskan's* story flourished. Now Canada could be told the story of *Athabaskan's* exploits and her gallant company. She was an unusual warship, because she had enjoyed a very brief but action-packed career, a career that her company of men would never forget. On her final patrol she had lost half her complement, about one-third were captured by the enemy, and the lucky remainder had been rescued by faithful

Haida and her cutter. *Athabaskan* was one of the very few, if not only, Canadian warship that never saw her native land. She had been built, launched, was in action, and perished in the European theatre of war. Furthermore, fascinating rumours and reports, which had been accumulating in the post-war years, were now begging for attention. At last the schoolboy sailors, like their counterparts at Gallipoli, could tell the world their story. They were synonymous in thought, word, and deed—only the element of time separated them.

But *Athabaskan's* story was almost scuttled before it began to take shape. How could a former member of the RCAF write a story about an RCN ship and endeavour to sustain a figment of naval credibility? Impossible. The two forces were miles apart in duties and tradition, and the unhappy relationship which often existed between them during wartime days could do little to foster an acceptable tale. Yes, there would have to be a strong naval link to begin the chain of events if a plausible account was to be made. Yet, in May of 1973 that first link was missing and the outlook for *Athabaskan's* story appeared bleak.

But wait! Hadn't the Secretary-General of Plouescat mentioned the name of a former company member who had passed through a year before on his way to a naval convention in Germany? His name was Beaudoin and he lived in Ste Foy, Quebec—perhaps this man could be of some help and assistance. Needless to say, the stranger was contacted the following summer, and he proved to be the missing first link in the long chain of events and activities which undergird this naval drama. The navy had arrived! Emile Arthur Beaudoin was born in Quebec City and had joined the RCNVR in 1940, graduating later as a telegraphist. He was aboard the *Levis* when she was torpedoed in the North Atlantic south of Iceland in 1941, so he was well aware of the perils of the deep. He was a member of *Athabaskan* when she made her last patrol; he was one of those rescued by the enemy and forced to spend a year as a POW. This pleasant, good-natured son of Quebec was a logical choice to begin the fascinating story and he gladly accepted the challenge.

His wartime experiences were manifold and provided a wealth of material to screen and use. His excellent spirit of co-operation made it possible for the navy and air force to work closely together on a significant combined operation. Thus English and French speaking Canada agreed to generate a determined and dedicated effort to make *Athabaskan's* story known.

The ground rules for the enterprise were to be simple and uncomplicated. First, the story had to be a faithful record and an inspiring remembrance of the ship and her company. It had to be told in simple language so that anyone, from six to sixty-six or older, could read and comprehend its true meaning and value. In this connection, naval jargon was to be avoided as much as possible so that the reader's interest would not be dulled by repetitious nomenclature. And finally, the navy's recognition of God the Creator was to be reflected throughout the story to add a spiritual quality that men who go down to the sea in ships, and others, would appreciate.

Athabaskan's story therefore demanded attention and immediate action. It is a true story and a Canadian one sprinkled with an international flavour, representing one small part of Canada's wartime history. As soon as the course had been charted, the authors never looked back. The spark of an idea which came to life in Plouescat developed and grew till it became like a beacon in the night, guiding the travellers on their way. They knew that the story was valid and would be successful because their enthusiastic spirits never faltered. Indeed, they grew from strength to strength, sustained too by the overwhelming offers of help from former Athabaskans and other interested people.

Essentially, *Athabaskan's* saga belongs to her fine company of men, because they are the people who lived and died with her, and consequently provided a virtual mountain of information to glean. The host of completed questionnaires, letters, photographs, diaries, and assorted paraphernalia that they submitted was impressive, and could fill two or three volumes. It proved later to be a sad and reluctant task for the authors to have to screen and condense the mass of data to economic and manageable size. Notwithstanding, the final excerpts were chosen so that they would be representative experiences of the company as a whole, and if the authors have erred in this respect, it has been a human failing. To a man the Athabaskans said, 'Yes—by all means use the material as you like.'

So it is to their everlasting credit that the enthusiastic response has yielded many individual human anecdotes that sparkle and reflect the active life of sailors at sea. Without their help, the result would have been little more than a manual of questionable importance.

In addition to the Athabaskans' efforts, countless relatives and friends around the world offered substantial aid in many ways. Their assistance is deeply appreciated, and several gems were drawn from this welcome reservoir. There is no doubt that they have added immensely to the fascinating plot. Throughout the thousands of miles covered by the authors in several countries, including most of the Canadian provinces, the name *Athabaskan* seemed to ring a bell of recognition wherever they went. It was like a password that opened a welcoming gate of friendship, thereby strengthening the lines of communication at home and abroad.

Therefore, may it be stated unequivocally that the characters and places mentioned are very real—that the schoolboys and men walked among us in another generation. They were as Canadian as the Maple Leaf, full of daring, adventure, and a keen relish for living. Later in the course of time, when the call for service arose, they volunteered like their forefathers without question. It has been a signal honour and rare privilege for the authors to have had the opportunity to present this naval adventure for the records. They sincerely hope that the Athabaskans' spirit of service and sacrifice will not be lost in the rush of modern life, but rather, that it will serve as an example and be of significant value somehow, in helping to strengthen and sustain the bonds of national loyalty, honour, and fellowship in our fair land. Essentially, the Athabaskans would prefer to have their country mature this way.

Len Burrow

Emile Beaudoin

COPY

FROM: The Commanding Officer, H.M.C.S. ATHABASKAN
DATE: 27th April, 1944.   FILE: K-18-2 (d).
TO: The Senior Officer, Force 26, H.M.S. BLACK PRINCE.
COPY: The Captain (D), Plymouth

REPORT ON ACTION WITH ENEMY DESTROYERS A.M. 26th APRIL, 1944

SUBMITTED:

The following report on action with enemy destroyers A.M. 26th April, 1944, in accordance with D.D.M. 0402.

1. *Nature of Action*

Encounter with three Elbing Class destroyers which developed into a long stern chase, gradually overtaking the enemy.

2. *Own Forces*

Force 26, H.M.S. BLACK PRINCE S.O., H.M.C. Ships HAIDA, ATHABASKAN, H.M.S. ASHANTI and H.M.C.S. HURON.

3. *Preliminary Movements*

(a) Force 26 carrying out operation "Tunnel" in accordance with Commander-in-Chief's 251235B (attached).

(b) Force 26 disposed as follows:

1st Sub Division—BLACK PRINCE
2nd Sub Division—HAIDA and ATHABASKAN stationed
                1½ miles on BLACK PRINCE's starboard bow.
3rd Sub Division—ASHANTI and HURON stationed
                1½ miles on BLACK PRINCE's port bow.

4. *Weather Conditions*

Moonset—0016/26 Wind—N.E. -2 Sea—10 Weather—b - 6

5. *Narrative of Events*

(a) When Force 26 altered course to 070 at 0130, several bright flashes were observed on the enemy coast bearing 210. These appeared at irregular intervals and were primarily taken for enemy gun fire from shore. The flashes appeared to indicate three-gun salvoes. However, there was no fall of shot near the ship, so the flashes remain unexplained.

(b) The first warning of the enemy was the signal timed 0202 from S.O. Force 26. Our own Radar 276 was discovered to be giving inaccurate bearings about ten minutes before, and the set was being lined up again. This was completed just after S.O. Force's signal had been received and three echoes were then distinguishable bearing 076 degrees, distance eight miles. The Plot gave enemy's course and speed as 070 degrees, eighteen knots. Enemy speed increased rapidly to twenty-eight knots.

(c) Speed was increased to twenty-eight knots at 0212 and to thirty-one knots shortly afterwards. ATHABASKAN was stationed astern of HAIDA and hauled out slightly on her starboard quarter to clear the range. Enemy course appeared to vary between 075 and 090. BLACK PRINCE opened fire with starshell, and fire was withheld until HAIDA'S first salvo at 0226. The forward group then opened fire at a range of 14,000 yards by 285 Radar, at the right hand destroyer. Blind firing by Radar was employed, as the enemy ships could not at first be distinguished in spite of BLACK PRINCE'S starshell. Enemy destroyers opened fire immediately afterwards, and their fire was apparently directed at the Third Sub Division on our port beam. Soon after the gun flashes were seen, the main armament went into Director control. The enemy could now be distinguished and a number of straddles were seen, though no direct hits were observed. A direct hit was observed later at 0232 but it is not known what ship was responsible. Constant fire with S.A.P. was kept up.

(d) At 0249 starshell illumination by BLACK PRINCE ceased and I was ordered by HAIDA to provide illumination. This was done at a range of 9,000 yards with 10,000 yard fuze settings. We seemed to be closing the range slowly. At 0305 the right gun of "B" jammed making it impossible to depress either of the guns below thirty degrees, and as a result some of the starshell burst short until the range was further reduced.

(e) Previous to this, at 0250, ASHANTI had reported that the enemy had fired torpedoes. As we were then end on to the Elbings, I took no evasive action.

(f) The enemy dropped smoke floats and were attempting to withdraw behind the screen and when it was no longer possible to see the destroyers, the main armament again resorted to blind firing.

(g) At 0258 one destroyer appeared by Radar to disengage to the South-Eastward and was very quickly lost in the land echoes. At 0314 a second disengaged to the southward; firing was kept up on this ship until she was lost in the land echoes.

(h) At 0322 the Second Sub Division executed a 3 Blue to bring "A" arcs to bear and to allow the firing of starshell from "X" gun. All of "B" gun's starshell had been expended. This manoeuvre brought us close to the Third Sub Division and I formed astern of HAIDA to keep clear. At this time, a destroyer well in to land to the southward began firing at us, some splashes being within two hundred yards. HAIDA altered five minutes later back to starboard to about 110 degrees, where one Elbing was slightly on fire. Target was shifted to this ship and two direct salvoes from HAIDA were observed to hit before she was clear of our line of fire. A further turn to starboard in line ahead was executed and I ordered all torpedoes to be fired at the enemy at a range of 3,000 yards. Unfortunately, I assumed that she was still under way steering about 110 degrees which could not have been the case, as there were no hits.

(i) Fire was again opened when HAIDA was clear, and many direct hits were observed. HAIDA altered 120 degrees to port and ATHABASKAN followed her in. We passed the Elbing at a range of 2,000 yards. It was hard to miss at this range and we pounded her heavily with main armament and close range weapons. Although by this time burning fiercely, the Elbing maintained a constant fire of close range weapons as we were circling her. HURON and ASHANTI joined and there was a certain amount of dangerous cross fire although this was unavoidable. Fighting lights had to be switched on on several occasions to avoid collision.

(j) Destroyers were formed up in line ahead at 0400. ASHANTI joined the line between HAIDA and ATHABASKAN and from this point I lost direct touch with HAIDA'S movements and remained astern of ASHANTI. We were still directly astern of ASHANTI when she collided with HURON after an "S" turn, although the details of how the accident occurred are not known to me.

(k) Enemy destroyer sank at 0420. Ships were again formed up

up and course set for Plymouth at twenty-five knots.

(l) Very slight damage was sustained by enemy close range weapon fire. One rating received minor shrapnel wounds and two others were scratched. The Sick Berth Attendant, who was sitting in the Sick Bay waiting for casualties, received a bullet through the seat of his trousers, with a resultant scar on his business end!

(m) The conduct of the Ship's company throughout the action was excellent and left nothing to be desired. Particular credit accrues to the gun's crew of "A" gun, who fired almost continuously for 1½ hours getting off 350 rounds.

6. *Gunnery and Torpedo*

(a) During the action, the right gun of "B" mounting recoiled and failed to run out. This was caused by the roller of the rolling lever (on the safety interlocking gear for the loading tray) hanging up on the tray bracket. This caused the gun to jam in the recoil position, thus putting the right gun permanently out of action. The mounting was, therefore, out of balance and neither gun could be depressed below 30 degrees of elevation.

(b) Ammunition expended: S.A.P.—562 H.E.D.A—50
Starshell 4"—16 4.7"—77 Close range—1000

(c) All torpedoes fired without mishap, but it is noted that there was no sound of their exploding when they hit the beach.

7. *Radar*

(1) 276 was most satisfactory for giving information to the Plot via the Chart House P.P.I.

(2) The 285 worked efficiently throughout the action. The position of the Cathode Ray Tube in the 285 office, which was fitted in this ship as an experiment, proved entirely satisfactory. It was possible to pick out own splashes around the target at 9,000 yards.

8. *Communications*

(1) No trouble experienced. It is felt that type 86 VHF R/T adds immeasurably to efficiency and speed of passing vital information.

(2) A record of some signals received on type 86 during the action was lost due to the failure of the light in the operators bay on the bridge, but this did not prevent the information from being passed to the Commanding Officer at once.

9. *Conclusions*

When actions of this type are fought, very close to the

enemy coast, great difficulty will always be experienced when the enemy runs in to the land for shelter, thereby rendering Radar useless. This is particularly the case on the stretch of coast in question, where many small islands give Radar echoes and it is not possible to plot them all to discover which one gives movement.

The enemy undoubtedly received warning of our presence at the same time that we received warning of his.

10. *Recommendations*

As an alternative, which might be worth a try, it is suggested that the direction of sweep of our forces should be reversed; that is, to overtake the enemy, as this has on one occasion enabled

Hunt Class destroyers to approach within 4,000 yards, possibly because enemy policy is not to sweep with Radar abaft the beam. Speed of sweep would necessarily have to be high. It is understood that this does away with the initial, always hoped for, chance of closing the range rapidly, but it may well be the only way to get in to decisive gun range before opening fire. A head on running action will result whichever method of approach is used.

[Sgd.] J.H. Stubbs

Lieutenant-Commander, R.C.N.
Commanding Officer.

APPENDIX II List of *Athabaskan's* Company Present on Her Last Patrol, 28/29 April 1944

Name	Number	Rank	Age	Domicile	Fate
1. ACORN, John J.	V-1589	L. Sto.	20	Cardigan, P.E.I.	POW
2. ADAMS, John C.	V-17001	AB	31	London, Ont.	MPD
3. AGNEW, John	V-1383	AB	22	Charlottetown, P.E.I.	MPD
4. AIKINS, James O.	V-64833	OS	19	Toronto, Ont.	Haida
5. ALLISON, Albert E.	V-8402	AB	30	Hamilton, Ont.	MPD
6. AMIRO, Irvin V.	V-26054	Tel.	21	Pubnico, N.S.	Plouescat
7. ANNETT, Robert I.L.	O-2450	Sub. Lieut. (E)	19	Consort, Alta.	Plouescat
8. ARMSTRONG, George A.	V-12833	AB	24	Fort Saskatchewan, Alta.	Plouescat
9. ASHTON, Percy G.	V-31508	AB	19	Toronto, Ont.	MPD
10. AUDET, Jean F.A.	V-35565	AB	21	Montreal, P.Q.	Haida (C)
11. BACKUS, Robert G.	V-12122	PO	32	Victoria, B.C.	Haida
12. BANDICK, Paul V.	V-53713	OS	22	Brandon, Man.	Haida
13. BARRETT, Arthur E.	V-12346	AB	26	Edmonton, Alta.	Plouescat
14. BARTON, John J.	V-32345	ERA (4)	24	Sudbury, Ont.	Haida
15. BEACH, Ernest R.	V-10831	AB	24	Balgonie, Sask.	POW
16. BEAUDOIN, Arthur E.	V-3690	L. Tel.	24	Quebec, P.Q.	POW
17. BELL, Donald A.	V-53224	Sto. (1)	20	London, Ont.	Plouescat
18. BELL, Joseph A.	4339	AB	21	Victoria, B.C.	POW
19. BENNETTS, Henry J.	3271	L. Tel.	24	Esquimalt, B.C.	Haida
20. BERKELEY, Alfred G.	V-54498	OS	19	Edmonton, Alta.	MPD
21. BERTRAND, Laurent J.L.	2408	CPO	33	Halifax, N.S.	Plouescat

22. BIANCO, Anthony D.	V-34263	AB	19	Peterborough, Ont.	MPD
23. BIEBER, Edgar E.	V-9844	Sto. PO	27	Winnipeg, Man.	MPD
24. BINT, Benjamin W.	V-11479	AB	21	Saskatoon, Sask.	POW
25. BLINCH, Harry C.	4265	AB	21	Abbotsford, B.C.	MPD
26. BOWER, Milton C.	A-4553	AB	26	Jordon Falls, N.S.	POW
27. BRANDSON, Thomas L.	O-8360	Pay. Lieut.	28	Winnipeg, Man.	MPD
28. BRIGHTEN, Victor H.	21930	ERA (2)	25	Verdun, P.Q.	MPD
29. BUCK, Stanley J.	V-27655	AB	21	Toronto, Ont.	Haida (C)
30. BURGESS, Arthur	V-31538	AB	22	Prince Albert, Sask.	POW
31. BURGESS, Charles T.	2438	CPO	31	Victoria, B.C.	Haida (C)
32. BURROW, William O.	V-7988	LS	22	Toronto, Ont.	MPD
33. BURROWS, Berchman R.	V-32266	LS	21	Ottawa, Ont.	POW
34. BUSHIE, Victor A.	V-22240	LS	24	Halifax, N.S.	Haida
35. CAMPBELL, George M.	V-56444	AB	32	New Waterford, N.S.	POW
36. CARR, John J.	V-9472	AB	28	Winnipeg, Man.	Haida
37. CASSWELL, George W.T.	V-7823	PO	24	Victoria, B.C.	Haida (C)
38. CATTANI, Robert F.P.	V-16567	LS	21	Port Arthur, Ont.	Haida
39. CHADSEY, Allen R.	4174	L. Sgm.	21	Vancouver, B.C.	Haida
40. CHAMBERLAND, Paul H.A.	V-3677	AB	22	Quebec, P.Q.	Plougasnou
41. CLARK, William	O-14130	Lieut.	29	Montreal, P.Q.	POW
42. CLARKE, Stanley J.	V-23104	AB	25	Verdun, P.Q.	POW
43. CONNOLLY, William E.	V-40271	Sgm.	23	Hamilton, Ont.	POW
44. COOKMAN, Edgar A.	3210	LS	23	Esquimalt, B.C.	MPD
45. COONEY, Stewart R.	V-35579	Stwd.	21	Belleville, Ont.	MPD
46. COOPER, Hector H.	40532	Sy CPO	26	Head of Jeddore, N.S.	POW
47. CORBIERE, Vincent G.	V-34003	AB	20	St. Catharines, Ont.	MPD
48. CORKUM, Gordon F.	A-1169	AB	24	Halifax, N.S.	Pornic
49. COTTRELL, Sydney A.	V-18362	AB	23	Trenton, Ont.	Plouescat
50. COWLEY, Arthur E.	V-41591	AB	37	Oshawa, Ont.	POW
51. CROFT, Moyle H.	A-4958	AB	31	Rose Bay, N.S.	MPD
52. CROSS, Alfred T.	V-25039	O. Tel.	26	Armdale, N.S.	MPD
53. CUMMINS, Ralph H.	V-11692	L. Sto.	22	Wild Rose, Sask.	POW
54. DALZELL, Robert G.	4141	AB	23	Prescott, Ont.	POW
55. DEAL, Cornelius O.	V-31445	AB	26	South Rawdon, N.S.	POW
56. DeARMOND, Gordon L.	V-11568	LS	22	Saskatoon, Sask.	MPD
57. DEMPSEY, Frank J.	V-59818	OS	20	Toronto, Ont.	POW
58. DEMPSEY, William B.	V-33968	Tel.	29	Winnipegosis, Man.	Haida
59. DICK, Stanley R.	V-7995	LS	22	Toronto, Ont.	POW

60. DILLEN, Stewart C.	V-34261	Stwd.	27	Brockville, Ont.	MPD
61. DION, Albert J.G.	V-3373	L. Sto.	24	Quebec, P.Q.	MPD
62. DOLAN, John J.	V-35529	Sto. (1)	21	Batley, Yorkshire	POW
63. DOWNEY, John	V-23421	Sgm.	23	Montreal, P.Q.	POW
64. DUNNELL, Stephen T.	V-30419	Or. Art. (2)	37	Victoria, B.C.	POW
65. EADY, Thomas G.	V-19177	Sgm.	24	Welland, Ont.	Haida (C)
66. EDHOUSE, Donald W.	V-58286	Sto. (2)	23	Toronto, Ont.	MPD
67. EDWARDS, John	V-12916	AB	24	Edmonton, Alta.	Haida
68. EDWARDS, Lloyd E.	V-16555	AB	20	Fort William, Ont.	POW
69. EVANS, James E.	2390	CPO	37	Halifax, N.S.	POW
70. FAIRCHILD, John W.	V-4709	AB	19	Quebec, P.Q.	POW
71. FILLATRE, Samuel M.	A-5043	AB	25	Purcell's Cove, N.S.	POW
72. FLEMING, Harold L.	V-12849	AB	28	Calgary, Alta.	MPD
73. FORRON, Jack E.A.	V-17506	Sto. (1)	20	London, Ont.	MPD
74. FRALICK, Earl I.	V-31885	AB	22	Port Dufferin, N.S.	MPD
75. FREES, William K.	A-2712	Sto. PO	27	Dalhousie Junction, N.B.	POW
76. FRITH, William A.	V-17806	LS	20	London, Ont.	Plouescat
77. FULLER, Eugene M.	V-8808	AB	24	Brantford, Ont.	Plouescat
78. FYFE, James G.	O-25690	Surg. Lieut.	30	Winnipeg, Man.	POW
79. GAETANO, Valentino J.	V-35858	AB	20	Sault Ste. Marie, Ont.	MPD
80. GALLANT, Paul G.	A-1889	AB	29	Tignish, P.E.I.	POW
81. GIBBONS, Marshall L.	V-51109	AB	19	London, Ont.	Brignogan-Plages
82. GOLDSMITH, Thomas H.	2980	CYS	27	Victoria, B.C.	Plouescat
83. GORDON, Lloyd M.	V-1267	AB	23	Clyde River, N.S.	MPD
84. GOULET, Antoine A.	V-42224	Sto. (1)	21	Ottawa, Ont.	POW
85. GOULET, Robert J.	V-42673	Sto. (1)	20	Ottawa, Ont.	MPD
86. GRACIE, Robert B.	V-36493	Sto. (1)	23	Toronto, Ont.	Haida
87. GRAINGER, Roy J.	V-17877	LSA	27	Port Hope, Ont.	MPD
88. GRENIER, Roger	V-33249	AB	20	Verdun, P.Q.	POW
89. GUEST, Carlton G.	V-17487	AB	20	London, Ont.	Plouescat
90. HAYES, Christopher	V-34725	OS	28	Toronto, Ont.	MPD
91. HAYES, William	V-8722	L. Coder	30	Hamilton, Ont.	Haida
92. HAYWARD, Robin B.	O-31940	Lieut.	23	Duncan, B.C.	POW
93. HEARL, John H.	V-69248	AB	22	New Westminster, B.C.	POW
94. HEATHERINGTON, John T.	V-31647	Sto. (1)	21	Regina, Sask.	MPD
95. HENRICKSON, Wilfred O.	V-16590	AB	20	Allanwater, Ont.	POW
96. HENRY, Robert J.	V-16777	AB	20	Fort William, Ont.	Ile de Batz
97. HESLER, Geoffrey	V-23323	Cook (S)	21	Montreal, P.Q.	POW

98.	HESTON, P.	C/MX 678680	Wrtr. (SP)	24	London, England	MPD
99.	HEWITT, Ted C.	V-17860	AB	22	Woodstock, Ont.	Haida
100.	HINDS, Edward	V-6477	ERA (4)	24	Timmins, Ont.	Haida
101.	HOLWELL, John B.	V-8875	AB	20	Hamilton, Ont.	POW
102.	HOPKINS, Robert W.	V-35886	Sto. (1)	19	Sherbrooke, P.Q.	POW
103.	HOUISON, George D.	V-23114	L. Wrtr.	24	Hamilton, Ont.	MPD
104.	HOWARD, George C.	V-1468	AB	25	Kensington, P.E.I.	POW
105.	HOWARD, William S.	V-40160	ERA (5)	20	Niagara Falls, Ont.	Haida
106.	HUBBARD, Frederick M.	V-44405	Sto. PO	30	St. Catharines, Ont.	POW
107.	HURLEY, Michael P.	V-36734	Sto. (1)	30	Toronto, Ont.	MPD
108.	HURWITZ, Harry	V-31067	AB	22	Montreal, P.Q.	POW
109.	IRVINE, Leonard C.	V-11886	AB	20	Saskatoon, Sask.	Plouescat
110.	IZARD, Theodore D.	O-35880	Lieut. (E)	26	Victoria, B.C.	MPD
111.	JAKO, Leonard W.	21818	L. Sto.	24	Vancouver, B.C.	Haida
112.	JARVIS, Edmund A.	3330	LS	23	Morrisburg, Ont.	MPD
113.	JOHNSON, Elswood S.	V-16839	AB	19	Edmonton, Alta.	MPD
114.	JOHNSON, Ira F.	2792	CPO	25	Saint John, N.B.	POW
115.	JOHNSON, Richard R.	V-5801	L. Sto.	23	Hamilton, Ont.	MPD
116.	JOHNSTON, Lawrence R.	V-51370	AB	19	Winnipeg, Man.	Plouescat
117.	KANE, John F.	V-8971	LS	24	Hamilton, Ont.	Haida
118.	KELLY, James A.	3670	PO	24	Calgary, Alta.	POW
119.	KELLY, Lionel D.	V-4445	Stwd.	24	Montreal, P.Q.	MPD
120.	KETTLES, Stuart A.	V-6748	L. Wrtr.	26	Ottawa, Ont.	POW
121.	KING, John A.C.	V-48770	AB	19	Saint John, N.B.	POW
122.	KNIGHT, Russell N.	3209	PO	24	Grand Prairie, Alta.	Haida
123.	KOBES, John R.	3074	LS	24	Victoria, B.C.	MPD
124.	LAIDLER, John	V-11667	AB	24	Saskatoon, Sask.	POW
125.	LAMBERT, William S.	V-5883	Tel.	24	Montreal, P.Q.	Haida
126.	LAMOUREUX, Andre	V-4348	LS	22	Montreal, P.Q.	POW
127.	LANTIER, Dunn	O-40520	Lieut.-Com.	27	Montreal, P.Q.	POW
128.	LAURIE, Douglas T.L.	21532	Sto. PO	25	Port Alberni, B.C.	POW
129.	LAURIN, Bernard	40748	L. Cook (S)	24	Perkinsfield, Ont.	Haida
130.	LAWRENCE, Ralph M.	O-40930	Lieut.	24	Glasgow, Scotland	MPD
131.	LEA, Eric E.	V-47397	Sto. (1)	21	Victoria, B.C.	MPD
132.	LEDOUX, Louis	V-4433	AB	21	Montreal, P.Q.	Plouescat
133.	LEGGETT, Reginald V.	V-33303	L. Sto.	26	Worthing, Sussex	POW
134.	LEGH, Norris J.	V-36139	L. Coder	25	New Westminster, B.C.	Haida
135.	L'ESPERANCE, Joseph W.	V-9580	LS	26	Winnipeg, Man.	POW

136. LEWANDOWSKI, Stanley S.	V-61813	Sto. (2)	19	Windsor, Ont.	MPD
137. LIND, Mekkel G.	V-13918	Sto. PO	28	Innisfail, Alta.	MPD
138. LIZNICK, Harry H.	V-33930	AB	20	Montrock, Ont.	POW
139. LOVE, Alexander W.R.	V-8620	C. Sto.	24	Welland, Ont.	Haida
140. LOVE, Walter M.	V-8030	ERA (3)	40	Dartmouth, N.S.	MPD
141. LUCAS, Donald O.	V-60018	Sto. (2)	19	Winnipeg, Man.	MPD
142. LYNCH, Donald A.	V-13359	PO Tel.	23	Calgary, Alta.	Haida
143. MacAVOY, Gerald W.	40500	PO Cook (O)	27	Halifax, N.S.	MPD
144. MacDONALD, Ashley K.	3625	AB	23	Ottawa, Ont.	MPD
145. MacDONALD, Hugh T.	V-58962	Sto. (2)	19	Toronto, Ont.	Haida
146. MacKENZIE, Alexander	V-19875	AB	22	Riverside, Ont.	MPD
147. MacNEILL, Glenn R.	V-49124	OS	20	Regina, Sask.	POW
148. MAGUIRE, John W.	40911	L. Sto.	25	Evansburg, Alta.	Plouescat
149. MAHONEY, John D.	O-45890	Lieut. (SP)	22	Toronto, Ont.	Plouescat
150. MANCOR, Claude A.	40464	Sto. PO	25	Irma, Alta.	Haida
151. MANSON, John L.	V-23559	Cook (O)	26	Montreal, P.Q.	Plouescat
152. MARTIN, James A.	V-44560	Tel.	19	Westmount, P.Q.	POW
153. MARTIN, William M.	V-45798	Tel.	23	Hamilton, Ont.	Haida
154. MATTHEWS, George H.	V-2809	AB	22	Red Head, N.B.	MPD
155. McBRIDE, John L.	V-45461	AB	19	Winnipeg, Man.	Plouescat
156. McCABE, Jesse A.	V-34420	AB	23	Prince George, B.C.	POW
157. McCARROLL, Thomas G.	V-39522	Sto. (1)	22	Hamilton, Ont.	MPD
158. McCLOY, Edward H.	V-18488	AB	23	Brockville, Ont.	POW
159. McCRINDLE, William D.	V-1854	AB	23	Nipawin, Sask.	MPD
160. McGREGOR, William	V-30291	L. Sto.	32	Victoria, B.C.	Plouescat
161. McKEEMAN, Lester B.	A-4311	AB	34	Gaspereaux, P.E.I.	POW
162. McLEAN, Daniel H.	V-14742	AB	23	Vancouver, B.C.	MPD
163. McNEIL, John J.	V-59518	Sto. (2)	20	New Victoria, N.S.	Landeda
164. MEADWELL, Richard G.	V-49203	AB	20	Sioux Lookout, Ont.	MPD
165. MELOCHE, Raymond	V-35940	AB	20	Montreal, P.Q.	POW
166. MENGONI, Eric J.	3980	AB	23	Dartmouth, N.S.	MPD
167. METCALFE, Donald I.	V-11603	El. Art. (3)	32	Vancouver, B.C.	MPD
168. MILLAR, Victor	V-27555	AB	28	Lakeview, Ont.	MPD
169. MILLER, Joseph R.P.	V-3922	OS	24	Quebec, P.Q.	Haida
170. MILLS, Ernest G.	21508	C. ERA	27	Saanich, B.C.	MPD
171. MITCHELL, William D.	A-3042	C. Sto.	42	Vancouver, B.C.	POW
172. MOAR, Raymond F.	V-34808	AB	27	Chatham, N.B.	POW
173. MUMFORD, Leonard K.	V-42353	ERA (4)	25	Hagersville, Ont.	MPD

174. MYETTE, Vincent L	A-5095	AB	25	Tracadie, N.S.	POW
175. NASH, Robert A.	O-54790	Sub. Lieut.	22	Seattle, Washington	Plouescat
176. NEAVES, Harry B.	40844	El. Art. (3)	28	Victoria, B.C.	Haida
177. NEWLOVE, Thomas G.	V-11936	Cook (S)	22	Star City, Sask.	Haida
178. NEWMAN, Donald W.	V-31264	AB	19	Calgary, Alta.	POW
179. NICHOLAS, Joseph R.	V-16615	L. Sto.	22	Fort William, Ont.	MPD
180. NORRIS, Guy J.	V-48316	Sgm.	24	Nelson, B.C.	Haida (C)
181. O'BRIEN, Earl	V-26333	Sto. PO	24	New Waterford, N.S.	Haida
182. OGILVIE, Robert B.	V-27800	SBPO	24	London, Ont.	POW
183. OSBORNE, Robert D.	V-11851	AB	20	Saskatoon, Sask.	POW
184. OUELLETTE, Joseph E.V.	V-50769	AB	20	Sabrevoix, P.Q.	MPD
185. PARSONS, George J.	V-18056	AB	26	Belleville, Ont.	Haida
186. PARSONS, Gordon J.	V-25782	L. Sto.	25	North Sydney, N.S.	POW
187. PEART, Hubert J.	A-927	AB	28	Glace Bay, N.S.	MPD
188. PHILLIPS, John D.	V-19152	AB	24	Windsor, Ont.	Plouescat
189. PHILLIPS, Russell E.	V-926	AB	22	Ocean Falls, B.C.	POW
190. PIKE, Brenton J.	V-36417	AB	22	Saint John, N.B.	Plouescat
191. POLSON, Edwin A.	V-33438	Sto. (1)	29	Ville La Salle, P.Q.	POW
192. POTHIER, Charles L.	V-4752	AB	19	Yarmouth, N.S.	Brest
193. QUIGLEY, George	V-7980	L. Tel.	24	Toronto, Ont.	Haida
194. RENNIE, John E.	3075	PO	23	Kelowna, B.C.	MPD
195. RICHARDSON, Alfred T.	A-5468	L. Cook (S)	25	West Dover, N.S.	Haida
196. RIENDEAU, Joseph A.L.	V-6869	AB	21	Ottawa, Ont.	Plouescat
197. ROBERTS, John C.	V-41049	ERA (4)	22	Stratford, Ont.	MPD
198. ROBERTS, Raymond L.	V-10880	AB	22	Moose Jaw, Sask.	Plouescat
199. ROBERTSHAW, Eric	V-8634	AB	21	Hamilton, Ont.	Plouescat
200. ROBERTSON, Ian A.	V-33909	AB	20	Saskatoon, Sask.	Plouescat
201. ROBERTSON, William	V-55418	Sto. (1)	37	Glasgow, Scotland	MPD
202. ROCK, J.M.G.	C/MX 677366	Wrtr. (SP)	24	London, England	Haida
203. ROGER, Leo A.	V-38436	Sto. (1)	22	Toronto, Ont.	Plouescat
204. ROLLS, Raymond B.	V-34863	AB	21	St. Stephen, N.B.	Plouescat
205. ROUSE, Edward A.	V-37897	Sto. (1)	21	Tillsonburg, Ont.	POW
206. RUTHERFORD, Norman	PMX-124283	Rad. Mech. PO	24	London, England	MPD
207. RYAN, Norman V.	V-52603	AB	19	Sault Ste. Marie, Ont.	MPD
208. ST. LAURENT, Joseph L.M.	V-37192	AB	20	Quebec, P.Q.	MPD
209. SAMPSON, Francis L.	V-174	AB	27	Halifax, N.S.	Plouescat
210. SANDERSON, Earl H.	V-34973	AB	24	Midgell, P.E.I.	MPD
211. SAUNDERS, Walter B.	V-2801	AB	22	Saint John, N.B.	POW

212. SAVAGE, Francis J.	4761	LS	23	Edmonton, Alta.	Haida
213. SCANLON, Delbert D.H.	V-7702	Sgm.	26	Toronto, Ont.	POW
214. SCOTT, John W.	O-65660	Lieut.	22	Halifax, N.S.	Haida
215. SCRATCH, Elmer W.	V-50726	AB	20	Blytheswood, Ont.	POW
216. SENECAL, Jean G.L.	V-15272	AB	20	St. Vincent de Paul, P.Q.	Plouescat
217. SHARP, Kenneth G.	4316	AB	24	Toronto, Ont.	Haida
218. SHEA, John T.	21801	C. ERA	24	Winnipeg, Man.	Haida
219. SHEPPARD, Walter R.	4420	Tel.	20	Vancouver, B.C.	POW
220. SHERLOCK, Albert V.	V-861	Stwd.	33	St. Lambert, P.Q.	MPD
221. SIGSTON, George D.	O-66930	Gun.	32	Dartmouth, N.S.	MPD
222. SIMALUK, Walter	V-10998	AB	24	Regina, Sask.	POW
223. SINGLETON, John C.	V-17334	AB	29	Delaware, Ont.	MPD
224. SKYVINGTON, Francis G.	V-46829	SBA	19	Toronto, Ont.	MPD
225. SMYTH, James W.	V-6532	AB	33	Ottawa, Ont.	POW
226. SOMMERFELD, Samuel W.	V-32952	AB	20	Saskatoon, Sask.	MPD
227. SOUCISSE, Paul E.	V-836	Coder	23	Montreal, P.Q.	MPD
228. STATZ, Clarence K.	V-46767	OS	22	Edmonton, Alta.	POW
229. STENNING, Raymond B.	40848	CPO Cook (S)	26	Victoria, B.C.	POW
230. STEVENSON, Elmer H.	V-53221	Sto. (1)	23	Havelock, Ont.	MPD
231. STEVENSON, Richard H.	O-69990	Lieut.	24	Montreal, P.Q.	POW
232. STEWART, John L.	V-1362	AB	32	Charlottetown, P.E.I.	MPD
233. STEWART, William G.	V-8866	Sgm.	22	Hamilton, Ont.	MPD
234. STOCKMAN, Ernest O.	O-70390	Lieut. (E)	35	Toronto, Ont.	MPD
235. STUBBS, John H.	O-70990	Lieut.-Com.	31	Victoria, B.C.	Plouescat
236. SULKERS, Herman C.	V-24660	AB	23	East Kildonan, Man.	POW
237. SUTHERLAND, John W.	V-12533	AB	21	Edmonton, Alta.	MPD
238. SUTHERLAND, William G.	V-36523	Sto. (1)	19	Winnipeg, Man.	POW
239. SWEENEY, Daniel T.	V-23913	AB	20	Montreal, P.Q.	POW
240. SWEET, Charles E.	2563	CPO	30	Victoria, B.C.	Plouescat
241. TAKALO, Ernest	V-33953	Sto. (1)	19	Port Arthur, Ont.	Haida
242. THERIAULT, Joseph C.M.	V-38688	Sto. (1)	21	Montreal, P.Q.	Haida
243. THOMPSON, Harry	V-38485	Sto. (1)	20	Montreal, P.Q.	MPD
244. THRASHER, Allen B.	3654	L. Sgm.	22	Toronto, Ont.	POW
245. TOURANGEAU, Joseph G.M.	V-3650	AB	22	Quebec, P.Q.	POW
246. TRICKETT, William D.	V-38773	AB	20	Kelwood, Man.	POW
247. TUPPER, Allister R.	V-40751	Or. Art. (4)	26	New Glasgow, N.S.	MPD
248. TYRIE, James	V-18295	Cook (S)	21	Kingston, Ont.	POW
249. VAIR, James A.	A-4980	L. Stwd.	30	St. Joseph's Island, Ont.	MPD

250. VEINOTTE, Joseph V.W.	V-25606	Sy PO	27	Marie Joseph, N.S.	MPD
251. WAITSON, Maurice	V-18646	AB	19	Napanee, Ont.	MPD
252. WALLACE, Peter W.	V-11722	AB	21	Saskatoon, Sask.	MPD
253. WARD, Leslie	O-76040	Lieut. (SB)	36	Ottawa, Ont.	MPD
254. WATSON, Reginald J.	V-35953	Tel.	23	New York, N.Y.	Plouescat
255. WEBSTER, Gerald W.	V-11468	LS	24	Saskatoon, Sask.	POW
256. WESTAWAY, Roy A.	V-34915	AB	19	Toronto, Ont.	POW
257. WILLIAMS, Kenneth W.	A-5402	ERA (4)	33	Peterborough, Ont.	Plouescat
258. WILLOCK, Samuel C.	V-52873	SA	37	Vancouver, B.C.	POW
259. WOOD, John A.	V-34862	AB	28	Hampstead, N.B.	Pornic
260. YEADON, Robert L.	V-272	AB	23	Halifax, N.S.	Ile de Batz
261. YOUNG, Charles	V-41759	Shipwrt. (4)	42	London, Ont.	Haida
262. GINGER (ship's cat)	GO7	Mascot	2	Newcastle, England	MPD

Legend for Column Six

Brest	Buried in Kerfautras Cemetery, Brest, Finistere, France	Landeda	Buried at Landeda, Finistere, France
Brignogan-Plages	Buried at Brignogan-Plages, Finistere, France	MPD	Missing Presumed Dead
Ile de Batz	Buried on Ile de Batz, Finistere, France	Plouescat	Buried at Plouescat, Finistere, France
Haida	Rescued by HMCS *Haida*	Plougasnou	Buried at Plougasnou, Finistere, France
Haida (C)	Rescued by *Haida's* cutter	Pornic	Buried at Pornic, Loire-Inferieure, France
		POW	Prisoner of War

See page 149 for directions to the individual cemetery sites. These include Sibiril where two unidentified Athabaskans are buried and Cleden Cap Sizun where one unidentified Athabaskan is buried.

APPENDIX III   List of *Athabaskan's* Company Who Served Prior to Her Final Patrol

Name	Number	Rank	Domicile	Name	Number	Rank	Domicile
ADAMS, S.	V-19451	L. Stk.	Ontario	BARKER, J.	KX 165728	Stk.	
ALFORD, W.C.	V-23389	L. Stk.	Montreal, Que.	BASKETT, H.	V-17947	Tel.	London, Ont.
ANDERSON, E.	3530	LS	Edmonton, Alta.	BATES, P.J.	40578	PO Wrtr	Windsor, Ont.
ANDERSON, H.F.	V-9893	AB	St. Vital, Man.	BAZINET, C.	V-10407	AB	Regina, Sask.
ANDREWS, C.	A-4785	AB		BEANLANDS, G.A.	21423	ERA (2)	Halifax, N.S.
ANSLOW, C.	2810	PO	Bickerton West, N.S.	BEAVER, K.	KX 154785	Stk.	
ARMSTRONG, J.S.	V-32303	SA	Ottawa, Ont.	BEDDOE, C.E.	V-6386	PO	Ottawa, Ont.
ARNOLD, W.S.	4217	AB	Victoria, B.C.	BEER, J.	V-1340	AB	Clyde River, P.E.I.
ARNOTT, A.B.	V-6726	AB	Ottawa, Ont.	BENNETT, G.	V-7383	Stk. PO	Toronto, Ont.
ATTWOOD, H.G.	V-7614	L. Tel.	Toronto, Ont.	BERRY, E.K.	V-22429	Stk.	Ontario

Name	Number	Rank	Domicile	Name	Number	Rank	Domicile
BERRY, W.	A-2083	Stk. PO	Petrolia, Ont.	COUSINS, H.	V-7709	Sgm.	Toronto, Ont.
BIBEAULT, C.R.	V-4497	Stk. (1)	Montreal, Que.	COX, A.	PJX 253699	LS	
BLAIN, J.	V-15267	AB	Montreal, Que.	CREWS, T.W.	A-4822	AB	Grand Banks, Nfld.
BLAIN, W.	31697	Stk. (1)		CRIPPS, W.	V-32040	Stk.	Ottawa, Ont.
BLISHEN, B.	40550	SBPO	Athenry, England	DADSON, H.W.	0-17670	Sub-Lieut.	Vancouver, B.C.
BOLDUC, M.	40584	Sy PO	Montreal, Que.	DALLIN, E.	21811	L. Stk.	
BONHOMME, G.	V-4343	OS	Montreal, Que.	DALY, F.	DKX 598294	Stk.	
BOWELL, N.C.	3588	AB	Vancouver, B.C.	DAVENPORT, J.R.	V-11861	AB	Vancouver, B.C.
BRADY, W.E.C.	V-32338	SA	Ottawa, Ont.	DAVEY, K.	V-9585	Sgm.	Winnipeg, Man.
BREBBER, G.	21720	L. Stk.		DAVIS, A.	V-31142	OS	Nova Scotia
BREBNER, J.A.	0-8460	Sub-Lieut.	Montreal, Que.	DAVIS, T.	DKX 178037	Stk. (2)	
BRICK, C.J.	V-32949	L. Stk.	Kindersley, Sask.	DECLE, D.	V-5593	LS	Montreal, Que.
BROOKER, P.	DKX 178025	Stk. (2)		DENTREMONT, P.J.	A-5181	AB	Lower West Pubnico, N.S.
BROWN, D.M.	0-?	Lieut.	Vancouver, B.C.	DERBY, J.	V-4823	Stk. PO	Montreal, Que.
BROWN, J.	V-42097	Cook (S)	Barnsley, England	DICK, J.	V-23988	L. Stk.	Montreal, Que.
BURKHOLDER, O.R.	V-27970	Tel.	Stayner, Ont.	DOCKER, T.	0-19940	Wt. Eng.	Halifax, N.S.
BURKMAR, G.P.	2350	L. Sgm.	Esquimalt, B.C.	DOCKSEY, D.C.	3745	AB	London, Ont.
BUSH, W.G.	V-17164	AB	Sarnia, Ont.	DODDS, J.R.	0-19980	Surg-Lieut.	Toronto, Ont.
CALDWELL, F.B.	0-11210	Lieut.	Ottawa, Ont.	DOYLE, J.	KX 121868	Stk.	
CALDWELL, J.B.	0-11220	Lieut. (E)	Victoria, B.C.	DRABBLE, D.	V-12371	Stk. (1)	Edmonton, Alta.
CALDWELL, M.W.	V-24934	AB	Shoal Lake, Man.	DRONE, W.	V-44404	Shipwrt (4)	
CALKINS, V.	V-16362	Stk. (1)	Thunder Bay, Ont.	DUKIN, C.	DMX 68391	L. Cook (S)	
CALVERLY, E.	2501	PO	Victoria, B.C.	DUNDEN, J.	V-38381	Cook (S)	
CANNON, J.	DKX 178033	Stk.		DYKES, J.G.	0-?	Lieut.	Toronto, Ont.
CANNON, M.	A-4414	L. Stk.		EASTWOOD, W.J.	0-21660	Lieut.	Ottawa, Ont.
CAPSON, J.S.	V-2527	AB	St. John, N.B.	ELLIS, C.	KX 146777	Stk.	
CHADWICK, R.G.	V-10458	Sgm.	Regina, Sask.	ELLIS, F.W.	A-2039	PO Stwd	
CHAPMAN, J.	V-18017	AB	Lyndhurst, Ont.	EVANS, L.M.	V-21506	Chief ERA	Vancouver, B.C.
CLARK, P.R.	V-26087	AB	Halifax, N.S.	FAULKNER, C.	3114	Stk. (1)	
CLAXTON, L.	V-17413	L. Tel.	London, Ont.	FEE, H.	V-40148	ERA (5)	Ontario
CLEARWATER, R.	3942	LS	Toronto, Ont.	FENNEL, W.	V-27390	Stk. (2)	Hamilton, Ont.
CLIFFORD, R.	21827	L. Stk.		FIGG, R.A.	3847	LS	Vancouver, B.C.
CLOUTHIER, J.	V-32156	OS	Ottawa, Ont.	FRAME, D.W.	V-4974	AB	Hamilton, Ont.
COCKBURN, M.	V-23019	LS	Montreal, Que.	FREISEN, R.W.	3682	LS	Medicine Hat, Alta.
COLVIN, S.	2299	CPO	Toronto, Ont.	GEORGE, J.A.	V-9714	L. Stwd	Winnipeg, Man.
COMNOR, J.	KX 106654	Stk.		GIBSON, E.	KX 78170	Stk. PO	
COOPER, G.E.	V-19741	Stk. PO	Windsor, Ont.	GLOECKLER, L.	40708	Stwd	Swift Current, Sask.
COOPER, J.	KX 146361	Stk.		GOOGAN, A.	KX 30409	Mechanic	
CORBY, G.	KX 95735	L. Stk.		GORDON, J.O.	V-8281	AB	Hamilton, Ont.
CORDALL, A.	KX 138070	Stk.		GOSNELL, H.	2665	LS	
COUGHLAN, F.	V-2252	LS	St. John, N.B.	GOULET, J.G.A.	V-6627	PO	Ottawa, Ont.
COULTER, B.W.	V-7827	AB	Toronto, Ont.	GREENHALG, J.	V-35670	Stk. (1)	Quebec

Name	Number	Rank	Domicile	Name	Number	Rank	Domicile
GUERTIN, J.T.	V-31857	OS	Nova Scotia	LAWSON, C.	A-3315	Stk. PO	Victoria, B.C.
GUNTER, J.	KX 95064	L. Stk.		LEIGHTON, S.	KX 76918	Stk.	
HAGGETT, T.	MX 53621	Cook		LIGGAT, A.B.	V-37475	Stk. (1)	Kimberley, B.C.
HAMLETT, W.	KX 163442	Stk.		LIVERSIDGE, R.A.	2601	PO	Halifax, N.S.
HANDY, H.A.	V-26959	Stk. (1)	Toronto, Ont.	LOVE, J.	KX 135016	Stk.	
HANN, P.M.	40551	L. Stwd	Halifax, N.S.	LOWE, C.D.	V-17674	AB	Mimico, Ont.
HARBOUR, F.R.	V-4150	LS	Montreal, Que.	LOWTHER, W.H.	V-8813	Stk. (1)	St. Catharines, Ont.
HAROLD, C.W.	V-9948	AB	Brandon, Man.	MACGREGOR, K.	A-5423	AB	Red Bank, N.S.
HAWES, C.	V-19630	AB	Windsor, Ont.	MACKENNA, J.	KX597970	Stk.	
HEARN, J.H.	V-39837	ERA	Halifax, N.S.	MACKENZIE, C.	V-1705	OS	Prince Edward Island
HERRING, R.	V-1557	AB	Murray Harbour, P.E.I.	MADDEN, D.	KX 525986	Stk.	
HINGSTON, F.	D 307084	Chief Mech.		MAGGS, J.	M 20707	ERA	
HOPKINS, W.	KX 153590	Stk.		MANCOR, B.H.	3233	PO	Nanaimo, B.C.
HOWELL, C.	V-22248	AB	Ontario	MANUEL, A.	21973	Stk. (1)	
HOYLE, T.P.	V-17213	AB	London, Ont.	MARSHE, W.	V-26150	Stk. (1)	New Waterford, N.S.
HUNT, S.	K-60596	L. Stk.		MARTIN, H.H.	V-12714	Stk.	Red Deer, Alta.
JACKSON, A.	V-8520	L. Coder	Hamilton, Ont.	MARTIN, W.	A-2243	AB	
JACKSON, E.R.	V-17904	Stk. (2)	London, Ont.	MASLOVE, N.P.	V-33677	Stwd	Saskatchewan
JAMES, A.	KX 597948	Stk.		MASTBOOM, J.	A-2815	PO Stwd	
JARVIS, D.	KX 165761	Stk.		MAYMAN, C.	2442	AB	
JENNINGS, M.A.	4095	LS	Napanee, Ont.	MAZERALL, G.	A-946	PO Stwd	
JEWETT, G.	2227	PO	Esquimalt, B.C.	MCCAW, R.A.	V-17419	L. Stk.	London, Ont.
JOHNSON, C.	V-2401	L. Stk.	New Brunswick	MCCLELLAND, J.H.C.	0-48000	Surg. Lt-Cdr	Ottawa, Ont.
JOHNSON, L.	V-23858	AB	Montreal, Que.	MCCORMICK, R.J.	V-19188	AB	WIndsor, Ont.
JOHNSTON, C.	KX 134508	Stk.		MCDONALD, G.F.	A-4685	Stk. (1)	
JOLLICLIFFE, T.	KX 115716	Stk.		MCDONALD, R.	V-362	AB	Nova Scotia
JONES, E.	KX 178054	Stk.		MCDOUGALL, W.	V-36934	Stwd	Shawbridge, Que.
JONES, F.E.	A-2736	L. Stwd	Montreal, Que.	MCGRATH, D.	V-5602	Sgm.	Montreal, Que.
JONES, W.	V-31862	OS	Nova Scotia	MCGRATH, J.	V-11616	AB	Saskatoon, Sask.
JORDAN, A.	KX 162301	Stk.		MCKINNON, A.A.	A-4902	L. Stk.	Halifax, N.S.
KEAN, E.	KX 111355	Stk.		MILES, G.H.	V-5504	AB	Verdun, Que.
KENNEDY, G.S.	21770	Stk. (1)		MILES, G.R., OBE	0-51550	Cdr	Ottawa, Ont.
KENT, B.A.	A-4880	AB	Halifax, N.S.	MILES, H.F.	21820	L. Stk.	
KENT, C.	3688	Tel.	Calgary, Alta.	MILNE, A.	V-33170	Stk. (1)	Montreal, Que.
KING, W.	KX 93598	L. Stk.		MILOT, G.J.	V-4135	AB	Montreal, Que.
KINISKY, F.	V-12548	Tel.	Alberta	MOORE, R.F.	V-30868	OS	Arcala, Illinois, USA
KIRBY, W.	JX 557472	OS		MORRIS, J.	V-3771	AB	Quebec
KIRKBY, A.	A-4079	AB		MOSES, S.G.	V-16903	Stk. (2)	Carlisle, Ont.
KIRKENDALE, G.	40445	Chief EA	Victoria, B.C.	MUNCER, E.	PMX 101537		
KIRKPATRICK, J.	V-13662	L. Stwd	Alberta	MURRAY, F.	KX 118187	Stk.	
LATIMER, E.	2418	PO		MYLREA, R.P.	2815	PO	Vancouver, B.C.
LAUDER, G.A.	3115	LS	Halifax, N.S.	NELSON, D.H.	40631	OA	Victoria, B.C.

Name	Number	Rank	Domicile	Name	Number	Rank	Domicile
NORWOOD, W.	KX 104669	Stk.		SAINT PIERRE, F.	3244	LS	Victoria, B.C.
O'CONNELL, J.B.	3862	Tel.	Ottawa, Ont.	SALISBURY, W.C.	V-7581	LS	Toronto, Ont.
O'NEILL, D.	A-2770	AB		SANDERS, R.	V-27480	AB	Toronto, Ont.
O'ROURKE, W.A.	40375	Sy. CPO		SANDERS, S.	A-5291	AB	
PAGE, V.H.	V-9975	AB	Winnipeg, Man.	SCOTT, A.	KX 133993	Stk.	
PAGE, W.	V-23154	AB	Verdun, Que.	SEALEY, E.	KX 597867	Stk.	
PALLIN, H.	3748	AB	Red Deer, Alta.	SENIOR, J.A.	21198	Chief Stk.	Halifax, N.S.
PARKER, G.	KX 130794	Stk.		SEYMOUR, W.	V-12334	Tel.	Edmonton, Alta.
PARKER, R.	V-31867	OS	Nova Scotia	SILLARS, W.	KX 158110	Stk.	
PARKES, R.	KX 139454	Stk.		SMITH, A.J.	21841	Stk. (1)	
PARSONS, T.	JX 570507	OS		SMITH, G.	V-3312	AB	Kamloops, B.C.
PATTON, H.R.	0-58000	Sub-Lieut.	Montreal, Que.	SMITH, G.W.	3618	Sgm.	Sault Ste. Marie, Ont.
PEARCE, C.	2959	AB	Halifax, N.S.	SMITH, J.	KX 107746	Stk.	
PENNELL, F.W.	A-2254	PO Cook		SMITH, J.N.	3831	LS	
PENNY, E.V.	2659	L. Tel.	Hanna, Alta.	SMITH, O.W.	V-37393	AB	
PERCIVAL, E.C.	4090	LS	Victoria, B.C.	SMITH, T.B.	3722	AB	New Westminster, B.C.
PERIN, H.W.	V-19749	AB	Windsor, Ont.	STAPLES, W.	DKX 178070	Stk. (2)	
PETERSEN, G.	A-4147	Stk. (1)		STARK, H.	A-4447	Stk. (1)	
PFRIMMER, E.	V-24313	AB	Winnipeg, Man.	STARR, C.L.	V-40835	LSA	Prince Rupert, B.C.
PICKETT, W.N.	V-2987	AB	Lower Bars, N.B.	STRACHAN, L.G.	3206	PO	Vancouver, B.C.
PINE, S.J.	V-8923	L. Stk.	Welland, Ont.	STRACHAN, W.	KX 102994	L. Stk.	
POPE, G.	A-2188	Stk. PO		SWAFFER, D.	3944	AB	Dartmouth, N.S.
POTTER, W.H.	V-6463	AB	Ottawa, Ont.	SYGROVE, J.	V-26316	L. Stwd	Nova Scotia
POTTIE, S.D.	V-324	Stk. (1)	Nova Scotia	SYLVESTER, R.	3560	LS	
POWELL, N.C.	3888	AB		TATE, W.		Stk.	
PRIEST, G.	KX 76481	Stk.		TAYLOR, J.	KX 99498	Stk.	
PRIMEAU, G.	V-4217	AB	Montreal, Que.	TAYLOR, M.O.	2493	PO Tel.	British Columbia
PRUDHOMME, F.E.	40702	L. Cook (S)	Halifax, N.S.	TEMPLETON, J.	V-8930	AB	Toronto, Ont.
RAFUSE, C.E.	V-31865	AB	Halifax, N.S.	THISBY, G.	KX 135243	Stk.	
RAMSEY, A.	NX 65692	Cook (S)		THOMAS, J.	V-2354	LS	New Brunswick
RENAUD, L.	V-4323	AB	Montreal, Que.	THOUIN, J.	V-4417	Stk. (1)	Montreal, Que.
REYNOLDS, F.	DJ 25460	PO		TURNER, R.E.	V-6132	CPO	Victoria, B.C.
RIGBY, J.	KX 123843	Stk.		ULLATHORNE, T.	KX 157137	Stk.	
ROACH, F.A.C.	V-1913	SA	Prince Edward Island	VERDEN, P.	V-24184	AB	Winnipeg, Man.
ROACH, J.	DMX 509558	ERA (5)		VIRGINT, S.	V-7391	LS	Toronto, Ont.
RODIN, P.	3805	AB	Vanderhoof, B.C.	WALKER, E.	KX 165789	Stk. (2)	
ROSE, W.S.	V-19038	AB	Windsor, Ont.	WALLACE, W.B.	0-75800	Surg-Lieut.	Toronto, Ont.
ROSS, C.	21827	L. Stk.	Ontario	WALLEN, S.		EA	
ROSS, J.D.	0-63620	Lieut.	Edmonton, Alta.	WALLER, C.	V-18245	AB	Kingston, Ont.
ROWBOTTOM, H.	KX 146868	Stk.		WENDON, F.W.	2329	PO	Big Bras d'Or, N.S.
RUSSELL, R.	KX 524794	Stk.		WHITE, J.	KX 102707	Stk.	
SABEAN, C.	3856	Tel.	Granville Ferry, N.S.	WHITSON, J.A.	A-4165	L. Stk.	

Name	Number	Rank	Domicile	Name	Number	Rank	Domicile
WIGGINS, D.H.	2770	LS	Montreal, Que.	WOODBRIDGE, J.	KX 83362		
WILKINSON, M.	KX 59807	Stk.		WOODS, L.	KX 80126	Stk. PO	
WILLETS, F.	V-33365	Shipwrt (4)	Halesowen, England	WOOLLEY, P.A.	V-38278	Stk. (1)	Lethbridge, Alta.
WILLIAMS, A.	KX 77174	Mechanic		WOOLSEY, L.R.	V-10860	Tel.	Toronto, Ont,
WILSON, E.	V-37006	Stk.		YOUNG, T.M.	V-24746	Sgm.	Vancouver, B.C.
WILSON, R.V.	V-11282	LS	New Westminister, B.C.	YOURKE, J.	3024	PO	
WISEMAN, W.	KX 82916	Stk. PO					

APPENDIX IV

Geographic Features in Canada Named for *Athabaskan* Casualties

As a permanent tribute to some of the fallen Athabaskans, no less than thirty-five Canadian
geographical features have been named by the Department of Energy, Mines & Resources in their honour.
Names have been picked at random for this significant program, regardless of rank or background. Their names are marked forever
upon the land they came from, and, in the broadest point of view, it is an honour to be shared by all the Athabaskans.

Casualty Name	Feature	Location	Map Reference	Date of Approval
Anthony D. Bianco	Bianco Lake	52° 54' — 89° 59'	*Wunnummin L. 53-A (1964) Edition 1 MCE	7-4-60
Stewart R. Cooney	Cooney Lake	49° 54' — 89° 26'	*Gull Bay 52 H/14 (1970) Edition 1 MCE	5-5-60
Vincent G. Corbiere	Corbiere Lake	52° 57' — 89° 44'	*Wunnummin L. 53-A (1964) Edition 1 MCE	7-4-60
Stewart C. Dillen	Dillen Lake	52° 12' — 89° 56'	*Wunnummin L. 53-A (1964) Edition 1 MCE	28-10-59
Donald W. Edhouse	Edhouse Lake	52° 52' — 87° 42'	*Lansdowne House 43-D (1966) Edition 1 ASE	4-8-60
Jack E.A. Forron	Forron Lake	52° 10' — 89° 07'	*Wunnummin L. 53-A (1964) Edition 1 MCE	7-4-60
William A. Frith	Frith Lake	49° 52' — 88° 41'	*Kelvin Island 52 H/15 (1967) Edition 1 MCE	5-5-60
Valentino J. Gaetano	Gaetano Lake	46° 51' — 82° 18'	*Whiskey Lake 41 J/8 (1960) Edition 2 (1:50,000)	15-1-59
Marshall L. Gibbons	Gibbons Lake	52° 38' — 88° 04'	*Wunnummin L. 53-A (1964) Edition 1 MCE	7-4-60
Richard G. Meadwell	Meadwell Lake	50° 50' — 91° 09'	*Sioux Lookout 52-J (1965) Edition 2 ASE	26-6-64
Joseph A.L. Riendeau	Riendeau Lake	52° 21' — 88° 09'	*Wunnummin L. 53-A (1964) Edition 1 MCE	7-4-60
Eric Robertshaw	Robertshaw Lake	52° 27' — 87° 24'	*Lansdowne House 43-D (1966) Edition 1 ASE	4-8-60
Ernest O. Stockman	Stockman Lake	52° 56' — 87° 06'	*Lansdowne House 43-D (1966) Edition 1 ASE	4-8-60
James A. Vair	Vair Lake	45° 17' — 79° 59'	*Seguin Falls 31 E/5 (1973) Edition 3 MCE	6-11-58
Maurice Waitson	Waitson Lake	52° 03' — 88° 57'	*Wunnummin L. 53-A (1964) Edition 1 MCE	7-4-60

ONTARIO

	Casualty Name	Feature	Location	Map Reference	Date of Approval
MANITOBA	Edgar E. Bieber	Bieber River	56° 49' – 96° 13'	Split Lake 64-A (1963) Edition 2 ASE	8-1-63
	Thomas L. Brandson	Brandson Lake	59° 52' – 101° 51'	Kasmere Lake 64-N (1963) Edition 1 ASE	26-4-72
	Donald O. Lucas	Lucas Lake	56° 49' – 100° 16'	*Barrington Lake 64 C/16 (1972) Edition 2 ASE	4-7-57
SASKATCHEWAN	Gordon L. DeArmond	DeArmond Lake	56° 01' – 104° 27'	Upper Foster Lake 74-A (1964) Edition 4 MCE	2-8-56
	John T. Heatherington	Heatherington Lake	59° 25' – 108° 48'	*Crackingstone 74 N/7 (1962) Edition 2 MCE	17-1-52
	Leonard C. Irvine	Irvine Island	56° 59' – 103° 42'	Wathaman Lake 64 D/13 (1962) Edition 1 ASE	19-8-63
	William D. McCrindle	McCrindle Lake	56° 26' – 102° 50'	Reindeer Lake South 64-D (1965) Edition 3 MCE	5-6-58
	Joseph McGrath	McGrath Lake	59° 52' – 108° 09'	*Ena Lake 74 N/16E (1962) Edition 1 ASE	17-1-52
	Raymond L. Roberts	Roberts Lake	56° 56' – 103° 33'	Wathaman Lake 64 D/13 (1962) Edition 1 ASE	19-8-63
	Ian A. Robertson	Robertson Islands	56° 50' – 103° 38'	Wathaman Lake 64 D/13 (1962) Edition 1 ASE	19-8-63
	Samuel W. Sommerfeld	Sommerfeld Lake	56° 21' – 105° 27'	Upper Foster Lake 74-A (1964) Edition 4 MCE	4-8-60
	Peter W. Wallace	Wallace Bay	56° 52' – 103° 44'	Wathaman Lake 64 D/13 (1962) Edition 1 ASE	19-8-63
BRITISH COLUMBIA	Harry C. Blinch	Blinch Lake	49° 26' – 122° 11'	*Stave Lake 92 G/8E (1961) Edition 1 ASE	4-7-57
	Thomas B. Smith	Smith Peak	50° 05' – 115° 09'	*Mount Peck 82 J/3E (1966) Edition 1 ASE	2-9-64
	John H. Stubbs	Mount Stubbs	50° 10' – 117° 14'	*Rosebery 82 K/3 (1962) Edition 1 ASE	2-3-61
IN PROVINCE OTHER THAN DOMICILE	Donald I. Metcalfe	Metcalfe Lake, Sask.	56° 48' – 103° 58'	Wathaman Lake 64 D/13 (1962) Edition 1 ASE	19-8-63
	Robert A. Nash	Nash Lake, Alta.	59° 16' – 113° 26'	*Peace Point 84-P (1967) Edition 3 MCE	3-11-49
	William D. Robertson	Robertson Narrows, Sask.	56° 49' – 103° 43'	Wathaman Lake 64 D/13 (1962) Edition 1 ASE	19-8-63
	Charles E. Sweet	Sweet Lake, Man.	55° 02' – 99° 49'	Nelson House 63-O (1965) Edition 2 ASE	19-5-70
	John E. Rennie	Rennie Point, Ont.	45° 08' – 80° 07'	*Sans Souci 41 H/1 (1974) Edition 3 MCE	5-5-60

Indicates feature is named on the map mentioned.

AFTER. Toward the stern of the ship.

ASDIC. An apparatus which sends a beam of supersonic impulses through the water. Upon contact with objects of certain densities an echo or "ping" is returned. Asdic is an acronym derived from Anti-Submarine Detection Committee, a group formed to study methods of locating submarines under water.

BOATSWAIN. Senior rating in charge of upper deck.

BOATSWAIN'S CALL. Shrill whistle carried by boatswain's mate, who pipes the boatswain's message.

BUFFER. Chief Boatswain's Mate, the senior chief or petty officer of the Seaman Branch in Royal and Royal Canadian Navy ships.

BULL-RING. Large eye at the stem of a destroyer for mooring.

Athabaskan's *bull-ring*.

BUZZ. Rumour.

CAPTAIN (D). Service abbreviation for Captain (Destroyers), the senior officer in command of a flotilla.

CARLEY FLOAT. Lifesaving device with slat floor suspended inside a floating tube. Paddles are provided. The twenty-foot long, five-foot wide float will support twelve people inside and eight clinging to the life-line attached to the outer edge.

CLEAR LOWER DECK. An order mustering the entire ship's company.

CORK NET. Net made of cordage woven through rings of cork to support a number of people in the water. A nine by twenty foot net will support twenty-two people.

DOCKYARD MATEYS. Dockyard workmen, who assisted in ship construction and repairs.

DOGWATCH. Halfing, or "dogging", of a regular four-hour watch, usually being the 1600 to 1800 and 1800 to 2000 watches.

E-BOAT. Small, highly manoeuvrable German motor torpedo boats, called *Schnellboot* (literally, fast boat) by the Germans.

ENGINE-ROOM ARTIFICER. Naval mechanic with specialized technical duties, including the maintenance and repair of the engine-room equipment.

GEORDIE. A Tynesider.

HEAVING LINES. Light lines thrown from ship to shore when coming alongside.

KY or KI. Cocoa.

KISBIE BUOY. A circular float made of buoyant material such as cork or balsa wood and covered with painted canvas, with a life-line attached.

LIBERTY BOAT. A boat for transporting sailors on leave from ship to shore.

NAUTICAL MILE. The nautical or sea mile is equal to 6080 feet, or about 2000 yards.

NUMBER ONES. The ceremonial blue or white dress of a ship's company.

POM POM. Single or multi-barrelled automatic gun firing a two-pound shell.

RATING. Any non-commissioned sailor.

SCRAMBLE NET. Weighted nets made of cordage used to allow people floating in the water alongside a rescuing ship to climb up her side. When unfurled they hang about a foot clear of the ship.

SPONSON. Projection from the side of a warship to enable a gun to be trained forward and aft.

U-BOAT. Short for *Unterseeischeboot*, a type of German submarine primarily used to attack surface vessels with torpedoes.

WATERTIGHT BULKHEAD. Tightly-fitted upright partition separating compartments on a ship.

WATERTIGHT HATCH. Opening with lid in a ship's deck to allow access to the compartments below.

ACKNOWLEDGMENTS

MUCH OF THE HUMAN interest material for this book was contributed by Athabaskans; their responses are acknowledged with thanks and appreciation. When the call went out for research information, they replied with a host of valuable data including diaries, letters, maps, clippings, photographs, drawings, and personal reports. For reasons of space and economy it was not possible to include everything they contributed. To those who read the manuscript and offered positive criticisms, we are abundantly grateful. The time, talents, and resources of a number of individuals and organizations also played an important role in helping to prepare the story, and their names are mentioned with appreciation.

Yvette Beaudoin
John Norman Stuart Buchan
Alice F. Burrow
Jessica E. Burrow
Philip Chaplin
Mary M. Coomber
Vice-Admiral H.G. de Wolf (retired)
Mr. C.E. Drew
Heather Ebbs
Patricia Giddy
Jorg Ernst Grote
Jean Helies
Mary A. Hughes
Mrs. W.G. Hunt
John W. Irwin
Pamela Izard
Eric A. Johnson
Kapitanleutnant Wilhelm Kampmann (retired)
Edna M. King
Abbe Paul le Pape
Ruth Lewis
David J. Lyon

Margery Makovski
Joseph May
Sarah Miles
Vello Muikma
H.A. Nightingale
J.W. O'Brien
Joseph Oulben
Jack Owen
Gerard Patenaude
George T. Phillips
Joan Phillips
Frederick C. Polischuk
Mrs. D.S. Ramsay
Allan Rayburn
Peter Robertson
Captain S.W. Roskill (retired)
Anne B. Rumbelow
J.M. Ruttan
Edward A. Stewart
Mr. and Mrs. G.T. Stewart
Lieutenant Commander Frank Stockwell
Lady Susan Tweedsmuir

Carl Vincent
Arthur Walton
Karl Heinz Woll
Major J.A. Young
Canada Post
Canadian Forces Photographic Unit
Canadian War Museum
Charles Hill & Sons Limited
Commonwealth War Graves Commission
Department of National Defence
Department of Veterans' Affairs
Edward A. Stewart Limited
Geographical Names of Canada Secretariat
HMCS Haida Association
Ian Allan Limited
Imperial War Museum
Maritime Photo Library
Musson Book Company
National Maritime Museum
National Museums of Canada
National Museum of Man
Public Archives of Canada
Vickers Limited

And finally, to the host of individuals who offered moral support during the years of preparation, we extend our heartfelt thanks. This record and memorial to a splendid ship and her fine company of men has reflected their faith in us, thereby making it possible to complete an inspiring labour of love.

The Authors

Tribals astern.

Athabaskan during Spitsbergen operation.

Two Canadian WRENs come aboard in Plymouth.

Captain's cutter coming alongside.

Athabaskan *turning sharply to starboard.*

The last known photograph of HMCS Athabaskan.

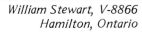
William Stewart, V-8866
Hamilton, Ontario

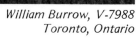
William Burrow, V-7988
Toronto, Ontario

BROTHERHOOD

In 1940 I was eleven years old, the kid brother who watched his three older brothers join the Navy and live that grand adventure that would so mark the later lives of those who survived.

Oldest Brother Bill became a signalman and joined *Athabaskan* at commissioning. He was lost in that final action. Brother Jim served on the corvette *Eyebright*, making those North Atlantic 'derry runs, later serving on the destroyer *Qu'Appelle* as an oerlikon gunner (missing a reunion with Bill when *Qu'Appelle* entered Plymouth harbour on the day of *Athabaskan's* loss). Then Dave, like so many, lied about his age, and became a signalman serving on the corvettes *Stellarton* and *Humberstone*.

The home front was a neighbourhood that emptied, never to be the same again, losing its own at Dieppe and when the destroyer *St. Croix* was torpedoed. Highs and lows of arrivals and departures, tears, leaves that flew too fast, uniforms that fit too tight or not tight enough, kitbags that had a smell of their own. To me, how lucky they were; to them, how lucky I was! The letters, sometimes censored and looking like lace, and filled with lies like "alls well", "don't worry", "hope to be home for Christmas", sustained the family. Then Mother as she opened those telegrams, quietly praying, relieved to find it was a request for money or a homecoming! Finally, while the family was seated at Sunday morning breakfast, came the shock of Earl Cameron's announcement of the sinking of *Athabaskan*. How to me the lines, "they also serve who stand and wait" ring true.

Perhaps we loved our brothers but didn't really know how much until they were taken, so young, from us. *Unlucky Lady* will serve as a tribute to the sacrifice of those brothers, who were such good friends given us by nature, and to that legion which kept the home fires burning.

Ed. Stewart
Graphic Designer

Ed Stewart in his studio with Len Burrow during the production of Unlucky Lady.

INDEX

Edward Stewart wishes to personally thank the illustrators:

Harold Beament (Assiniboine's Battle with U-210 & Athabaskan's Last Fight)
George Hopp (Maps)
Zig Kucharski (Photo-mechanical)
Robert Meecham (Athabaskan Sinking)
Celia Pine (Beach at Pors Guen)
Graham Wragg (end papers—Athabaskan at Speed)